Pelican Books
The Idea of Law

Dennis Lloyd was born in 1915 and
educated at University College, London, and
Gonville and Caius College, Cambridge. He
was called to the Bar in 1936 and has been
in practice at the Common Law Bar since
1937, with the exception of the war years
when he served with the Army in Italy and
the Middle East. He received a Doctor of
Laws degree from Cambridge in 1956 and has
been Quain Professor of Jurisprudence at
University College, London, since the same
year. From 1962 to 1964 he was Dean of the
Faculty of Laws at the University of London.
He is the author of a number of books on
such subjects as public policy, unincorporated
associations, jurisprudence, and landlord and
tenant, and has contributed many articles to
legal periodicals.

Dennis Lloyd was created a life peer in 1965
with the title of Lord Lloyd of Hampstead.
He was elected a Fellow of University
College, London, in 1963 and serves as a
member of the Lord Chancellor's Law Reform
Committee. He was a member of the Joint
Select Committee on Theatre Censorship
which reported in 1967, and he is Chairman
of the committee to advise on the need for a
National Film School. Lord Lloyd is married
and has two daughters.

Dennis Lloyd

The Idea of Law

Penguin Books

Penguin Books Ltd, Harmondsworth,
Middlesex, England
Penguin Books Inc.,
7110 Ambassador Road, Baltimore,
Maryland 21207, U.S.A.
Penguin Books Australia Ltd,
Ringwood, Victoria, Australia

First published 1964
Published in Penguin Books 1964
Reprinted 1968
Reprinted with revisions 1970

Made and printed in Great Britain by
Cox & Wyman Ltd, London, Reading
and Fakenham
Set in Monotype Baskerville

Contents

Preface

Law is one of the institutions which are central to the social nature of man and without which he would be a very different creature. A glance at the table of contents of this book should be enough to indicate to the reader the great areas of thought and action in which the law has played and continues to play a major role in human affairs. Leading philosophers, from Plato to Marx, may have urged that law is an evil thing of which mankind would do well to rid itself. Yet, for all the philosophic doubts, experience has shown that law is one of the great civilizing forces in human society, and that the growth of civilization has generally been linked with the gradual development of a system of legal rules, together with machinery for their regular and effective enforcement.

Laws do not, however, exist in a vacuum, but are found side by side with moral codes of greater or less complexity or definiteness. The relationship of law to moral rules and standards is obviously one of great and abiding importance in every human society, and certainly not least in our own, as can be instanced from many current controversial issues. To mention but a few of these, there is the liability of adult males to prosecution for homosexuality even when carried out in private and by consent; the burning question of capital punishment, and the whole philosophy underlying the purposes for which punishment is inflicted by the criminal law; legal problems where the sanctity of human life is concerned, as in the case of euthanasia, suicide, and abortion; whether divorce should be grounded on the notion of guilt or depend upon the breakdown of the marriage; all such problems serve to indicate the stresses and tensions which arise between the moral ideas current in a given community and the rules which seek to lay down precise legal rights and duties.

Moreover, the belief in a Moral Law has had a tremendous impact upon man's thought about the actual law which prevails in his own particular society. The notion that behind and above all the individual systems of law which operate in different societies, there exists a higher law by which mere man-made law can be judged, and on occasions found wanting, has produced significant consequences at many crucial stages of human history. For the conclusion has been drawn that not only does such a higher law override and nullify the actual rules of a particular society which are shown to violate it, but that it follows from this conclusion that the individual citizen may be relieved from his duty to comply with the actual law, and even possess a lawful basis for revolt against the legitimate authority of the state. Nor must it be thought that this sort of argument has ceased to be canvassed at the present day or that it lacks practical implications. Those who argue, for instance, that there are certain basic human rights which are guaranteed by Moral Law or Natural Law may and do urge that segregation laws which discriminate against sections of a community, on grounds of race or religion, are so contrary to fundamental morality that they are not entitled to be treated as valid laws at all and that refusal to adhere to these is both legally and morally justified. An attempt is made in this book to explore these fundamental issues which are the concern of every citizen in the modern world.

Perhaps the most vital issue in the modern state is what we mean by the freedom of the citizen, and what measures must be accepted in order to preserve this freedom. The relation of law to liberty is obviously a very close one, since law may be used either as an instrument of tyranny, as has frequently occurred in many ages and societies, or it may be used as a means of giving effect to those basic freedoms which in a democratic society are regarded as an essential part of the good life. In such a society it is not enough that the law should merely confer security upon the citizen in his person and property. On the contrary he must be free to express his opinions without restraint and to associate with his fellow citizens; he must be free to come and go as he pleases and to seek employment of such kind as he will; he must be entitled to enjoy the benefits of what has come to be known as the Rule of Law; and he must be relieved of basic insecurities due to want and misfortune. All such questions raise legal problems of great complexity within the framework of the modern welfare state, and an attempt is made in this book to discuss some of the more pressing of these issues.

In modern times the functioning of the law has been closely associated with the idea of a sovereign power located in each particular state and possessing authority to make or unmake laws as it pleases. This theory has had important consequences both in regard to national legal systems, and also in the international sphere. If a state is sovereign, how, for instance, can it be argued that such a sovereign state is itself subject to an overriding system of international law? And suppose such a state binds itself by international treaty to accept the legal authority of some overriding international organ, as, for instance, has occurred in the case of the Common Market Treaty. When the notion of the United Kingdom joining the Common Market was being ventilated recently, serious questions were raised at the time as to the effects of such a course upon the ultimate sovereignty of our own Parliament. This is only another illustration of the ways in which a philosophy of law may bestride great questions of state policy.

In our own day the social sciences, although even now perhaps only in their infancy, have carved out an important place for themselves in many spheres of human thought and activity. Their impact upon legal thinking and practice has already proved to be considerable, and the legal sociologist is presented with an immense field for research, much of which remains virtually unexplored. Still, there have been important attempts to link legal thinking with developments occurring in such fields of study as anthropology, psychology, sociology, and criminology. The lawyer, as a practical man of the world, has tended, especially in common-law countries, to be somewhat impatient of theory and to adopt the attitude that his task is to solve practical problems, and that for this purpose he is better equipped by virtue of his legal experience than those who, however well versed in other disciplines, lack his grasp of legal essentials. In the last resort, however, the claims of the social sciences to be heard, even in the arcana of the law itself, must depend both on the light they can be shown to shed upon legal institutions, and the assistance they can render in the solution of the actual legal problems of our day and age.

The role of the judiciary in a modern legal system is of immense social significance, and an attempt is therefore made in this work to indicate the nature of the judicial process, and the vital contribution that it has to make to the effective functioning of the law. Closely linked with these questions are the very character and structure of legal reasoning. Law is in a constant process of flux and development, and though much of this development is due to the enactments of the legislature, the judges and the courts have an essential role to play in developing the law and adapting it to the needs of their society. Not only the general way in which this result is achieved is discussed in these pages, but also a considerable number of detailed illustrations are given, to enable the reader to see what is involved in the process of applying and interpreting legal rules and principles in the context of a modern legal system.

In conclusion, the book provides a brief review of some of the more urgent problems which the Idea of Law will be called upon to tackle in the more immediate future. The need is emphasized for a creative approach to the Idea of Law in our own age, if law is to come within measurable distance of performing the social functions which it should subserve. It is surely the task of all those concerned with the exposition of the law, or with its application in practice, to make continual efforts to refurbish the image of the law, so that it may remain in touch with the social realities of our times.

Finally I should like to express my gratitude to I. H. Jacob, Esq., Master of the Supreme Court, without whose encouragement this work would never have been undertaken; he has been good enough to read the whole book both in typescript and in proof, and has made many valuable suggestions. Needless to say, he is not responsible for any errors or opinions it contains.

DENNIS LLOYD

April 1964

Is Law Necessary?

Que veux-tu, mon pauvre ami, la loi est nécessaire, étant nécessaire et indispensable, elle est bonne, et tout ce qui est bon est agréable. (Ionesco, *Victimes du Devoir*.)

The highest perfection of society is found in the union of order and anarchy. (Proudhon.)

It may seem strange that at the very outset of our inquiry into the Idea of Law the question should be raised whether law is really necessary at all. In fact, however, this is a question of primary significance which we ought not and indeed cannot take for granted. For it arises out of an uneasy and perplexing doubt not only whether law may be 'expendable' as being unnecessary to the creation of a just society, but also whether law may not perhaps be something positively evil in itself, and therefore a dangerous impediment to the fulfilment of man's social nature. Fantastic though this viewpoint may seem to the members of a well-ordered democratic society – whatever its particular shortcomings or imperfections may be – it is useful to remember that in many less well-regulated societies the operation of law may appear in a more unfavourable guise. Moreover, the feeling that law inherently is or should be necessary for man in a properly ordered society receives little encouragement from the long succession of leading Western philosophers from Plato to Karl Marx who, in one way or another, have lent their support to the rejection of law. Hostility towards law has also played an important part in many of the great religious systems of East and West, and was a crucial element in the ideology of the Christian Church in its formative period. And, apart from Marxists, there are still to be found other serious supporters of a doctrine of anarchism as an answer to man's besetting personal and social problems. Every age – and certainly our own is no exception – produces individuals or groups who feel a general restlessness against all authority and who respond to this feeling by giving vent to various acts or demonstrations against the forces of law and order. No doubt such people are often sincerely motivated by the vague notion that in some mysterious way their demonstrations will lead to a better and happier life for mankind, but such sporadic outbursts have generally had little influence on the main currents of human thought and feeling.[1] We must therefore look deeper than the external manifestations of social restiveness in trying to explore the ideological foundations of dissatisfaction with the very idea of law in order to find out what it is that has urged so many, in civilizations geographically and culturally so far apart, and throughout human history, either to reject law altogether or to regard it at best as a necessary evil suited only to an utterly imperfect state of human society.

Later in this book the role of law as a social phenomenon will engage our attention as well as its function as part of the cement of social control and its relation to a conception of a just society. We shall not here anticipate the discussions of these matters but will concentrate on the lines of thought which have led, on the one hand, to the total rejection of the need for law at all, or, on the other, to the notion that law is an evil thing only to be tolerated as a temporary expedient while man remains unwilling or unable to achieve a just society.

THE NATURE OF MAN

When we talk of some idea or concept as being 'ideological' in character, we mean that it forms part of our outlook upon the world, upon the relation of man to the world and to society in all its manifestations. The idea of law certainly partakes of this ideological character so that our view of it will inevitably be coloured by our general thinking about man's place in the world, the view we may adopt of the nature of man, or of the 'human condition', as some modern writers prefer to call it, and the aims or purposes which man may be called upon or required to fulfil. When we assert that law either is, or is not necessary to man, we are clearly not just trying to state a simple physical fact, such as that man cannot live without food and drink – we are engaged in a process of evaluation. What we are really saying is that man's nature is such that he can only attain a truly human condition given the existence or non-existence of law. Such a statement contains implicit within it an assumption as to man's goal or purposes, as to what is good for man, and what he needs for the attainment of those objectives.

It is no doubt because of man's perennial and intense preoccupation with such issues that thinkers of all ages and societies have been drawn into the interminable dispute as to the ethical quality or potentiality of man's nature. This dispute may indeed be thought by many today to be not only interminable but also senseless, but whether this is so or not, the position taken up has formed the major premiss in leading to the deduction whether, or to what extent, law is necessary for man, and so its importance for this purpose remains undeniable. For those who see in man either the incarnation of evil or at best an amalgam of good and bad impulses constantly in conflict, the bad tending repeatedly to prevail over the good, it seems evident that here are dark and dangerous forces implanted in man's very nature which need to be sternly curbed and which, if not curbed, will lead to the total destruction of that social order in whose absence man's state would be no higher than that of the animals. Law then, in this view, is the indispensable restraint upon the forces of evil, and anarchy or the absence of law the supreme horror to be warded off. On the other hand, those who view man's nature as inherently good seek to find the sources of the ills of man's present condition in situations external to man himself and hence look for some fundamental defect in man's social environment as the true cause of the evils which afflict him. And as the most conspicuous features of this environment are of course the government of the reigning powers and the legal system through which they exert their political authority, it is hardly surprising that criticisms centre upon these as the true source of human tribulations.

In an age of social reform, such as the last hundred years in the West, it might seem that such critics would have better directed their shafts to the reform of the existing law rather than to its total elimination, but on the other hand it must be borne in mind that in many societies the evils of the legal régime must have seemed to the religious or philosophically minded to be inescapable, and that to replace one régime based on legal repression by another could only result in a comparable series of afflictions and oppressions. The only course, therefore, was to condemn legal restraint root and branch.

THE LAW AND THE FORCES OF EVIL

Two very different starting-points were taken by those who looked upon law as a means of attaining social harmony by the curbing of the evil passions of man. On the one hand, some postulated that man's nature was intrinsically evil and that no social progress could be attained without the restraints of penal laws. On the other hand were those who held that man was originally created good by nature but that due to sin, corruption, or some other internal weakness, such as avarice, man's original and true nature had become distorted and thus required for its control the rigours of a punitive system of law. Those who favoured this more optimistic assessment of human failings tended to look backwards to an earlier Golden Age of primeval innocence when men lived simple, happy, and well-ordered lives without the need for any external system of legal rules or coercion to restrain their impulses, which were wholly unselfish and directed to the common good of mankind. Such was the idyllic primitive scene as depicted by many writers from Seneca to Rousseau and even in our own day, and this roseate view of man's remote past has often served as a pattern for a movement towards a return to nature, in the sense of man's primitive, unspoiled nature, and therefore opened up a future prospect of a happier society in which uncorrupted natural impulse will replace a coercive régime of law.

Examples of both these ideological views of man's nature and destiny can be drawn from very widely scattered sources. Only a few need be mentioned here. In ancient China of the third century B.C. we find, for instance, the important school of so-called 'Legists', who argued that man's nature was initially evil and that the good ways in which men often acted were due to the influence of the social environment, particularly the teaching of rituals and the restraints of penal laws. 'A single law, enforced by severe penalties, is worth more for the maintenance of order than all the words of all the sages,' was one of their governing maxims.[2] About the same period the *shastra* writers in India were asserting that men are by nature passionate and covetous and that if left to themselves the world would resemble a 'devil's workshop', where the 'logic of the fish' would reign, that is, the big ones would eat up all the little ones.[3] Comparable views are not difficult to locate among some of the seminal writers of modern Western Europe. Thus for Bodin the original state of man was one of disorder, force, and violence, and Hobbes's description of the life of primitive man as a state of perpetual warfare, where individual existence was 'brutish, nasty, and short' has become classical. For Hume, too, without law, government, and coercion, human society could not exist and so in this sense law was a natural necessity for man. Machiavelli based his celebrated advice to princes to disregard their pledges when these conflicted with their own interests on the argument that men 'are naturally bad and will not observe their faith towards you, so you must, in the same way, not observe yours to them'.[4]

The hypothesis of a primitive Golden Age has in one form or another also played an important role in the history of Western ideology. Two of the best-known statements of this hypothesis in classical antiquity are to be found in the pages of Ovid and of Seneca. Ovid, in the first book of his *Metamorphoses* refers to it in these terms:

> The Golden Age was first; when Man yet new,
> No rule but uncorrupted reason knew;
> And with a native bent, did Good pursue.

> Unforc'd by punishment, unaw'd by fear,
> His words were simple, and his soul sincere:
> Needless was written Law, where none opprest;
> The Law of Man was written in his breast;
> No suppliant crowds before the Judge appeared:
> No Court erected yet, nor cause was hear'd;
> But all was safe, for Conscience was their guard.[5]

Seneca's celebrated account, as befitted a philosopher, was more circumstantial:

> In this primitive state men lived together in peace and happiness, having all things in common; there was no private property. We may infer that there could have been no slavery, and there was no coercive government. Order there was of the best kind for men followed nature without fail and the best and wisest men were their rulers. They guided and directed men for their good, and were gladly obeyed as they commanded wisely and justly. . . . As time passed, the primitive innocence disappeared; men became avaricious and dissatisfied with the common enjoyment of the good things of the world, and desired to hold them in their private possession. Avarice rent the first happy society asunder . . . and the kingship of the wise gave place to tyranny, so that men had to create laws which should control their rulers.[6]

Although Seneca asserts that this primitive innocence was rather the result of ignorance than of virtue, he attributes the later social evils and the necessity for the introduction of a régime of law to the corruption of human nature from its initial state of innocence, and this corruption he explains as due specifically to the development of the vice of avarice. This idea of vice and corruption as the reason for the establishment of coercive institutions became a key feature of Western thought for many centuries, adapted as it was by the early Church Fathers to the Judaeo-Christian version of the Fall of Man. The Biblical account of paradise was equated with Seneca's primitive state of innocence, and the necessity for human law and all its familiar institutions, such as the coercive state, private property, and slavery, was derived from man's sinful nature, which resulted from the Fall. Law was a natural necessity after the Fall to mitigate the evil effects of sin. Even the family was treated as a consequence of the Fall, for it represented the coercive domination of the male as against the freedom and equality of the primitive paradise. Slavery, too, was regarded as one of the inevitable consequences of the Fall, for man, though in his uncorrupt state free and equal, as a result of sin was made a fit subject for enslavement, and thus in a corrupt age slavery was a legitimate institution.

This theory of law and government attained its classic restatement in the writings of Augustine. State-law and coercion were not in themselves sinful but were part of the divine order as a means of restraining human vices due to sin. Hence all the established legal institutions and the state powers were legitimate and coercion could properly be used to enforce them. Augustine saw the future hope for mankind, not in the sphere of social reform by promoting a juster social régime on earth, but rather by the attainment of a commonwealth of God's elect, a mystical society, which would ultimately, in God's good time, replace the existing régime dominated by man's sinful nature.

Augustine's assertion that law was a natural necessity to curb man's sinful nature held the field for many centuries. Augustine wrote at a time when the great system of the Roman Empire was on the point of disintegration and there seemed but little prospect of a rise of an orderly, let alone a just, society by mere human dispensation. But gradually life became more settled and provided scope for social and economic advancement. Moreover, by the thirteenth century, some of the more scientific and philosophic reflections of classical antiquity upon man's social condition, especially those of Aristotle, had filtered through to Western Europe. The time was ripe for a change of emphasis. Man's nature might be corrupt and sinful but he still possessed a natural virtue which was capable of development. Leaning heavily upon Aristotle's conception of the natural development of the state from man's social impulses, Aquinas held that the state was not a necessary evil but was a natural foundation in the development of human welfare. Aquinas, as a pillar of orthodoxy of the medieval Catholic Church, strove to reconcile this position with the established theology of his day. Nevertheless, he also provided an important basis for the later secular view of law as at least potentially a beneficent force, not merely for restraining the evil impulses of man but also for setting him upon the path of social harmony and welfare. In this way law came to be envisaged not as a purely negative force, for the restraint of evil, but as a positive instrument for realizing those goals towards which man's good or social impulses tend to direct him.

IS MAN NATURALLY GOOD? THE ANARCHIST'S VIEWPOINT

We have seen how the attempt to regard law as a natural necessity directed to restraining, in the only way possible, the evil instincts of man gave way to a new view of law as a means of rationalizing and directing the social side of man's nature. Yet in all ages there have been thinkers who have utterly rejected this approach to the coercive forces of law and order. For such thinkers man's nature is and remains basically good, but it is the social environment which is responsible for the evils of man's condition,[7] and above all the existence of a régime of law imposed by force from above.

A mood of wistful primitivism, a nostalgia for a primeval Golden Age, has coloured a good deal of what may be termed anarchist thought from ancient to modern times. Plato, for instance, showed strong leanings towards primitivism as is illustrated by his assertion that 'the men of early times were better than we are and nearer to the Gods'.[8] Yet this approach tends to be an altogether more sophisticated one, concentrating far less on a mythical past than on man's potentiality in the future for an ideally just society. Moreover, such a society is not to be one with an ideally conceived legal régime but, on the contrary, one free from all legal rules in which rational harmony will prevail as a result of the good sense and social impulses of its members.

An idealist picture of a state without law, whose inner harmony derives from human reason carried to its highest potential of development by a succession of philosopher-kings chosen for their wisdom and knowledge, is presented by Plato in his *Republic*. Plato pins his faith upon a system of education which will not only produce adequate rulers but will also serve to condition the rest of the population to the appropriate state of obedience. Modern experience certainly supports Plato in his belief that education or 'brain-washing' may condition people to subservience but remains divided on the notion that any system of education can provide a royal road to wisdom, or that there is any foolproof manner of selecting or training persons who are naturally pre-ordained for rulership.

It may be said that Plato's leanings were not so much towards anarchism as towards what we should today term 'totalitarianism', as his proposals for an inflexible and rigorously enforced legal system in his late dialogue, *The Laws*, sufficiently demonstrate. Again, though there was unquestionably an anarchic flavour about certain aspects of primitive Christianity this was manifested in a contempt for, rather than a rejection of, human law, and indeed the injunction to render unto Caesar what was Caesar's became accepted as conferring a divine legitimacy on the established powers. At the same time the cult of non-violence appeared to many opponents of the early Christians as a threat to state authority and has afforded a base for the anarchistic doctrines of some influential modern writers, such as Bakunin and Tolstoy.

The modern period from the seventeenth century has been marked by the rise of science and technology and with this has developed the ideology of human progress, a world-view which rejects the belief in a primitive paradise and looks forward to an ever brighter future for mankind. For long this doctrine was wedded to the notion that the social evolution of man could be left to the free play of economic forces which, if not interfered with, could be assumed to work towards ultimate social harmony. This was the theory of *laissez faire*, which, though applied by Adam Smith especially to economic affairs, carried with it the broader doctrine that all government and law were in principle evil in so far as they constricted or distorted the natural development of the economy and of society. Far from being anarchist, however, this theory strongly favoured the use of coercive law for the protection of private property, which it regarded as an indispensable feature of a free market.

The nineteenth century represented perhaps the heyday of the more sophisticated anarchist writers, though Godwin's celebrated contribution, *Political Justice*, first appeared in 1793. Godwin argued that the evils of society arose not from man's corrupt or sinful nature but from the detrimental effects of oppressive human institutions. Man is inherently capable of unlimited progress and only coercive institutions and ignorance stand in the way. With touching faith in human reason and perfectibility Godwin held that voluntary cooperation and education would enable all law to be abolished. Such moral and social norms as were required for maintaining social order and progress would be made effective in that their violation would incur the moral censure of the free individuals of which society would consist. This type of philosophic anarchism was further expounded by the leaders of the Russian school of anarchists, Bakunin and Kropotkin, for whom the state, law, coercion, and private property were the enemies of human happiness and welfare. These writers stressed the beneficent role of cooperation in human history and believed that in the inevitable course of evolution the principle of mutual aid would replace the miseries of the coercive community. Tolstoy, on the other hand, propounded a form of anarchy based on his conception of the simple Christian God-inspired life led by the early Christian communities. Many of his enthusiastic supporters attempted to set up 'Tolstoy colonies' on these lines in various parts of the world, but the results were hardly inspiring. In his very sympathetic *Life of Tolstoy*, Aylmer Maude relates some of the strange and comic ways in which these societies speedily collapsed. In one such colony, for instance, a boy stole a waistcoat from a fellow-colonist. This youth had previously been indoctrinated by his companions in the view that private property is wrongful, and that the police and the law-courts are part of an immoral régime of coercion. When the return of the waistcoat was demanded, the youth proved to have learned his lessons only too well. If property is wrong, he inquired, why was it more wrong for a boy to have it than a man? He wanted the waistcoat as much as the man did. He was quite willing to discuss the subject but he would not alter his opinion that he was going to keep the waistcoat and that it would be very wrong to take it from him.[9]

Another such colony came to a rather drastic end. The property of the colony was bought in the name of a member who held it for the use of his fellow-members. One day an eccentric individual appeared on the scene and after some discussion with the colonists suddenly rose and made the following announcement. 'Gentlemen! I have to inform you that from today your colony will have neither house nor land. You are astonished? Then I will speak more plainly. Your farmhouse, with its outbuildings, gardens, and fields, now belongs to me. I allow you three days to go!' The colonists were thunderstruck but none of them resisted and they all cleared out of the place. Two days later the legal owner presented the property to the local Commune.[10]

A cynic might well chuckle at this vindication of his disbelief in the natural goodness of man, but the outcome of these naïve anarchist exercises undoubtedly points to the fundamental dilemma which must face those who believe that human society can function without the external cement of coercive law. As Maude remarks: 'Remove the law, and induce men to believe that no fixed code or seat of judgment should exist, and the only people who will be able to get on at all decently will be those who, like the Russian pre-revolutionary peasantry, follow a traditional way of life. . .[11] The root evil of Tolstoyism is that it disdains and condemns the result of the experience gained by our forefathers, who devised a system which, in spite of the many defects that still hamper it, made it possible for men to cooperate practically and to carry on their diverse occupations with a minimum of friction.'[12]

Perhaps the most remarkable of the theses of the modern anarchists, and certainly the most influential, is that of Karl Marx. Marx envisaged the overthrow of the capitalist society by a violent revolution of the oppressed proletariat. Law was nothing but a coercive system devised to maintain the privileges of the property-owning class; by the revolution a classless society would be brought into being, and law and the state would 'wither away' as being no longer needed to support an oppressive régime. The Marxist looks forward rather than backward to a Golden Age when social harmony will be attuned to the natural goodness of man unimpeded by such environmental snares as the institution of private property. Such a social paradise cannot, however, arise overnight and therefore we have the paradox that during an interim period – likely to be of indefinite duration – there is need for a vast increase of state activity supported by all the apparatus of legal coercion so abhorrent to the anarchist. More will be said of the Marxist theory of law later on in this work,[13] but it seems incontestable that the introduction of Marxist socialism has so far entailed more and more law and legal repression rather than its abolition.

INNATE GOODNESS AND THE PRICE OF CIVILIZATION

Despite these discouraging experiences there still remain distinguished exponents of the view that man at the primitive level is innately good and that it is the social and political organization of civilized life which has introduced the seeds of violence and disorder and which in their turn have led to systems of legal coercion. One of the main theses of Elliot Smith's[14] book on *Human History*, first published in 1930, is the innate goodness and peacefulness of mankind. 'The evidence is so definite and abundant that it becomes a problem of psychological interest to discuss why men persist in denying the fact of Man's innate peacefulness. Each of us knows from his own experience that his fellows are, on the whole, kindly and well-intentioned. Most of the friction and

discord of our lives are obviously the result of such exaspera-
tions and conflicts as civilization itself creates. Envy, malice,
and all uncharitableness usually have for the object of their
expression some artificial aim, from the pursuit of which
Primitive Man is exempt.'[15]

Few will deny that numerous ills from which we suffer
are the direct result of the stresses, tensions, and conflicts
characteristic of a civilized and therefore complex mode of
existence. All the same Elliot Smith's contrast between
natural and civilized man seems one-sided and oversimpli-
fied. Readers of Mary Shelley's *Frankenstein* will recall how
Frankenstein creates a monster in human form, which,
though possessed of human feelings, eventually turns upon
and slays its creator. The romance seems symbolic of the
duality of human nature. Man may well possess innate
tendencies towards what we call 'goodness', namely, those
relationships which arise out of sympathy and cooperation,
for without these all social life – the distinctive character of
man – would be impossible. But there is also a dynamic side
to human nature, which may be directed to either creative
or destructive ends.

The well-meaning philosophic anarchist, even when he is
most concerned to give scope to man's creative impulses, is
apt to gloss over or ignore the darker side of the nature of
man. Sir Herbert Read, for instance, argues that human
groups have always spontaneously associated themselves into
groups for mutual aid and to satisfy their needs, and so can
be relied upon voluntarily to organize a social economy
which will ensure the satisfaction of their needs.[16] The
anarchist, he tells us conceives society as a balance or
harmony of groups. The only difficulty is their harmonious
interrelation. But is not the promotion of such harmony a
function which must be conferred on some state organization? Sir Herbert Read's answer is two-fold. In the first
place, he believes that this function would largely disappear
with the elimination of economic motivation from society.
Crime, for example, is largely a reaction to the institution of
private property. And secondly, matters such as infant

education and public morality are matters of common sense, to be solved by reference to the innate good will of the community. With the universal decentralization of authority and the simplification of life, including the disappearance of 'inhuman entities' like the modern city, any disputes can be resolved on a local basis. 'Local associations may form their courts and these courts are sufficient to administer a common law based on common sense.' It will be noted that Read differs from some anarchists in recognizing the need for some kind of general law and insists only on rejecting all the coercive apparatus of centralized control. 'Anarchism,' he explains, 'means literally a society without an *arkhos*, that is to say without a ruler. It does not mean a society without law and therefore it does not mean a society without order. The anarchist accepts the social contract, but he interprets that contract in a particular way, which he believes to be the way most justified by reason.'[17]

The recognition that even in the simplest form of society some system of rules is necessary seems almost inevitable. In any society, whether primitive or complex, it will be necessary to have rules which lay down the conditions under which men and women may mate and live together; rules governing family relationships; conditions under which economic and food-gathering or hunting activities are to be organized; and the exclusion of acts which are regarded as inimical to the welfare of the family, or of larger groups such as the tribe or the whole community. Moreover, in a complex civilized community, even if simplified to the degree dear to the heart of an anarchist like Read, there will have still to be a large apparatus of rules governing family, social, and economic life. The idea that human society, on whatever level, could ever conceivably exist on the basis that each man should simply do whatever he thinks right in the particular circumstances is too fanciful to deserve serious consideration. Such a society would not be merely, as Read puts it, 'a society without order', but the very negation of society itself.

At this point then, the discussion can move over from the

necessity of law in human society to the closely related question: whether the idea of law can be divorced from a régime of coercion. This is the issue which will engage our attention in the ensuing chapter.

In the pantheon of ancient Mesopotamia two deities were singled out for special reverence. These were Anu, the god of the sky, and Enlil, the god of the storm. The universe was regarded as a state in which the gods ruled, but a crucial distinction emerged between the role of the two principal deities in the hierarchy. On the one hand the sky god issued decrees which commanded obedience by the very fact of having emanated from the supreme divinity. Obedience was thus an ineluctable necessity, a categorical imperative which admitted of no questioning. Anu was the very symbol of authority in the cosmic order. Yet even so these ancient worshippers of divine authority, absolute and unqualified as it might be, recognized that there was no guarantee of automatic compliance with the orders from on high. Thus provision must be made for chastening the recalcitrant, whether gods or mortals. Hence the power of the storm was invoked, the power of compulsion, the god of coercion, who executes the sentences of the gods and leads them in war.[1]

If we penetrate below the surface we may find in mythology much that is fundamental in human attitudes and purposes. The myths of Anu and Enlil reveal the deeply felt human need for order and the concomitant belief that such order, whether on a cosmic or a terrestrial level, demands the combination of two essential elements, authority and coercion. Without the recognition of some authority whose decrees and sentences determine the structure of order in the world there can be no organized society and therefore the authority of divine rule makes possible the functioning of the universe as a social whole. But without the element of force to ensure obedience to the divine decree the universe could never attain the role of statehood. So on the broad canvas of the whole universe the ancient Mesopotamians saw reflected the essential preconditions of their own human society and sought to provide a cosmological foundation for the linking of legitimate authority with force here on earth.

The idea that even the gods themselves need to invoke force to impose their authority is a familiar enough phenomenon in the earlier and less sophisticated stages of religion. Zeus, as readers of Homer will recollect, is not sparing of his thunderbolts against either his fellow Olympians or lowly mortals who disregard his injunctions or otherwise incur his displeasure. But we have chosen here to emphasize this feature of human thought in the less familiar guise of early Mesopotamian mythology because it seems to bring out, with exceptional clarity, the two elements of authority and force without which no order, divine or human, can survive. It is now necessary to say something more of each of these conceptions in the context of legal theory.

AUTHORITY

There is much more involved in the idea of law than simple obedience, but the factor of obedience is nevertheless a crucial one. We must, however, distinguish the kind of obedience which is characteristic of legal relationships. The victims of a bank robbery may respond speedily enough to the commands of gangsters armed with revolvers but such compliance has little connexion with the obedience of a vassal to his feudal overlord, of a citizen to the directions of a police officer, or of an unsuccessful litigant to the order of the court which tried his case. This contrast is not just between willing and unwilling compliance, for the vassal, the citizen, and the defeated litigant may all be as reluctant to yield to the superior authority, either in the particular instance or even more generally, as are the bank officials to hand over the valuables to their assailants. The distinction must therefore be looked for in some deeper kind of motivation.

What is entailed in the notion of authority is that some person is *entitled* to require the obedience of others regardless of whether those other persons are prepared to find the particular order or rule enjoined upon them as acceptable or desirable or not. Of course the person so entitled to obedience need not be a simple individual human being, as in the case of an absolute monarch, but may in some orders of society be conceived as a supernatural entity or as some collective human organization, such as the Queen in Parliament in England, or Congress in the United States. However, for the convenience of the present discussion we will confine ourselves to the case of the single individual who is entitled to obedience.

It is obvious when we consider the instances given above that the vassal regards his overlord as entitled to his obedience, and the same assumption can also be made regarding the citizen and the police officer, and the litigant and the judge. In other words there is something which we may call a peculiar aura or mystique investing the lord, the policeman, or the judge which arouses a certain response on the part of the other party, namely that he feels that superior party (for so we may call him for this purpose) can legitimately give orders which he, the inferior party, feels in some sense obliged, willingly or unwillingly, to obey. This feeling of legitimate subordination is clearly one of great significance in law and calls for further explanation.

Why should one person in some curious way feel himself bound to acknowledge the authority of another person and so constrained to obey the orders of that person? Or, to put it another way, what is the source of the obligation which is apparently imposed or assumed to be imposed on the subject party (the obligee)?

One preliminary answer which may be suggested is that fundamentally the obligation is a moral one, in the sense that what the obligee really feels is that he is under a moral duty to obey the behests of the lord, the policeman, or the judge as the case may be. The concept of morality and its relation to law involve many difficulties which will call for consideration at a later stage. What needs to be pointed out here is that clearly there is a very definite connexion between the idea of legitimate authority, which has to be obeyed because of its very legitimacy, and moral obligation, which imposes a rule which calls for voluntary adherence by virtue of its intrinsic rightness. Both are treated as binding because of something in them which without any force or physical necessity seems to require obedience. Hence the feeling that there is a moral duty to obey the law because the law represents legitimate authority.

There are however considerable dangers in seeking to carry this argument too far, as it may lead to the erroneous belief that legitimacy and morality can in some way be equated. In some societies indeed this conclusion has been fully drawn, and the divine right of kings has been held to entail the necessary corollary that the king can do no wrong. When we come to examine later, and in detail, the relation of law to morality we shall see that there are compelling reasons for rejecting this monolithic view and for acknowledging that the two spheres of lawful authority and morality, while closely interconnected, are none the less separable and distinguishable. All we are emphasizing here, therefore, is that the notion of authority which is acknowledged as legitimate derives much of its strength from its link with moral obligation. So much is this so that in rebellions against established authority the rebels have usually sought to reinforce their case by proving that the authority is in fact illegitimate for some reason, so divesting the rulers of either legal or moral claim to obedience. Such arguments were particularly common and effective in the sixteenth and seventeenth centuries, when government was regarded as established by a social contract and where a fundamental breach of that contract by the ruler, as in the case of James the Second, could be represented as releasing his subjects from their obligations to yield to his authority.

Charisma

The most illuminating analysis into the ways in which authority establishes itself in human society has come from the leading German sociologist, Max Weber, who died in 1920. Authority, or legitimate domination, as Weber describes it, may take one of three forms, namely, charismatic, traditional, or legal.[2] The word 'charismatic' is formed from the Greek word *charisma*, meaning 'grace', and is used by Weber to refer to that peculiar form of personal ascendancy which an individual may acquire in a particular society, and which confers an indisputable aura of legitimacy over all his acts. Such a position is frequently associated with a military conqueror, of whom Alexander the Great, Julius Caesar, and Napoleon may be regarded as the prototypes. In our own day we have seen enough of this form of charismatic rule in the shape of dictators such as Hitler, Mussolini, and Stalin to have little doubt both as to its reality and as to the character which it is likely to take in the modern technological age. No more striking illustration can be given of the hypnotic effect that this charismatic feature possessed by certain individuals can exert, not only on their immediate followers but on whole nations, than the extraordinary tale revealed in Professor Trevor-Roper's account of the last days of Adolf Hitler, virtually impotent in the depths of his bunker and yet still giving insane orders which none dared to question let alone disobey.[3]

Traditional Domination

In a sense the idea of personal charisma is really the key to understanding the conception of legitimacy because it emphasizes in an extreme form the psychological forces which underlie this conception. The important point, however, is that while charisma may create authority by the sheer personal ascendancy of a new leader, and though there may be a natural tendency for this to be extinguished on his death, it by no means follows that such charisma will attach to his person alone. As Weber points out, authority derived in the first instance from the personality of the leader may pass, if in an attenuated form, to his successors. This phenomenon is to be observed in the case of new monarchies where the descendants of the charismatic founder of the dynasty derive their legitimate authority from their descent, even though they may lack all or most of the qualities of their ancestor. The same situation may be observed in spheres other than the political. Founders of religions generally possess a charismatic quality which causes their words to be treated as authoritative and on their death their disciples may be able to retain and even enlarge the scope of this authority, though partaking of very little of the personal charisma which enabled their founder to dominate his followers. If this situation continues for any length of time the original charisma will become 'institutionalized', that is to say, it will become embodied in certain permanent institutions which will be formed largely by traditional usages.

A clear instance of this kind of institutionalization is an established monarchy in a feudal order of society. The charisma still exists but it attaches not so much to the individual king as to the kingship itself, or the 'Crown', as we still say in English constitutional practice. Rule still remains personal in the sense that the king retains a large field of arbitrary power which he may exercise legitimately, but at the same time the institutional character of the kingship has created a mass of traditional customs which are regarded as binding, thus restricting the freedom of action of the actual incumbent of the kingly office. This conception was given its most well-known expression by the medieval jurist Bracton in his dictum that 'the king ought to be under God and the Law'.

Legal Domination

Such a form of domination, which Weber describes as 'traditional', and which is a complex of personal and institutional elements, may gradually merge into the more developed form which Weber calls 'legal' domination. This terminology is misleading in that it suggests that law in the strict sense only arises in the latter type of authority. This is not so, and the implication is not intended by Weber himself. Even under a reign of a purely charismatic kind there is no reason why there should not be rules which we could reasonably regard as legal though they may depend wholly on the will of the charismatic leader. In this connexion it may be recalled that the codification of Roman Law by Justinian, which has been of such vast influence in the development of modern European law, occurred under a régime of which the basic constitutional maxim was that 'what the Emperor willed was law'. A traditional system of domination will not lack legal rules either, though those rules may be customary rather than legislative. What Weber desires to emphasize by applying the word 'legal' specifically only to the third type of domination is that under this system legitimate domination has become impersonal and legalistic, so that the institutional character of authority has largely if not wholly displaced the personal one. For instance, the modern democratic state has largely abandoned charismatic authority in favour of an institutionalized legislature, bureaucracy, and judiciary which operate impersonally under a legal order to which is attached a monopoly of the legitimate use of force.

In such a state of affairs legal domination can dispense with personal charisma but it still rests on a belief in its legitimacy. For without such a belief, so widely disseminated as to be largely unchallenged or unchallengeable, the automatic and impersonal operation of legal authority would cease to function and would be replaced by anarchy and disorder.

It will be appreciated that this belief in legitimacy, which is as fundamental to the working of the modern state as it was to the empire of Charlemagne, is not really a logical one in the sense that it can be justified in logical terms. This may be sufficiently demonstrated by bearing in mind that the belief in the legitimacy of legal domination involves a circular argument: laws, we are told, are legitimate if they are enacted; and an enactment is legitimate if it conforms to those rules which prescribe the procedures to be followed. We need not perhaps go so far as Weber when he says that this circularity is intentional in order to allow for a belief in legitimacy divorced from any particular ideals or value judgments.[4] What seems more pertinent is the fact that human society rests on beliefs which may be rational or irrational but which need to be understood clearly in their functioning. Much thought has been given by modern jurists to whether some ultimate formula can be devised or demonstrated as the logical or necessary foundation of legal domination in a given society, or indeed on the international level, and we shall consider this fundamental problem in its due place. For the present it is enough to say that authority, both in its broadest and in its specifically legal context, rests on a firm belief in its legitimacy.

Lest it be thought that Weber's analysis is too neat to be applicable to the historical situation of any actual societies, it should be emphasized that Weber himself was not here engaged in historical evaluation but rather in establishing what he called 'ideal types' representing, so to speak, the full development of possibilities inherent in certain kinds of social organizations. Such types are not 'ideal' in any moral or Platonic sense but are simplifications which provide an analytical structure within which sociological research may be conducted. The analysis is therefore typological, not developmental, for, in Weber's view sociology is only concerned with general tendencies; how, for instance, Western society has developed historically is a task not for the sociologist but for the historian. Weber fully acknowledges that his ideal types do not occur in history as such but always in combinations of varying degrees of complexity.[5] Thus, to take one instance, the German Nazi state combined to a remarkable degree features of personal charisma with those features of modern bureaucracy which are associated with legal domination. Such an analysis does however contribute to an understanding of the various strands which go to form the legal structure of any society and of the general nature of that authority which must inevitably form one of its principal pillars.

FORCE

We have now discussed in general terms the element of legitimate authority, which is so essential to the functioning of law in any community – the role of Anu in the Mesopotamian legend. We have still to say something of his counterpart, force, symbolized in that legend by Enlil, the storm god.

And first, we may bring out the relation of force to authority by drawing attention to societies where fully effective 'domination' occurs but without any belief, on the part of the subjects at any rate, in its legitimacy. This does not necessarily apply to all societies composed to a large extent of subject or slave populations as, for instance, ancient Sparta and its helots or the Roman Empire with its enormous slave population. For even in such a society, despite all the miseries that it entailed, the legitimacy of the authority wielded by the state may still have been widely believed in by the populace as a whole.

Societies may, however, exist which, without being in a state of anarchic disruption, still lack, so far as the bulk of their population is concerned, a belief in the legitimacy of the authority that controls them. For instance, during the occupation by Nazi forces of many European countries during the Second World War, it is clear that the Nazis possessed the power to enforce their will on the population even when the occupied peoples entirely rejected the legitimacy of the domination of their Nazi oppressors. It is true that this was a temporary situation and that given victory the Nazis might eventually have induced a belief in the legitimacy of their rule as did the Norman conquerors of Anglo-Saxon England. It is indeed questionable how far domination may be maintained by sheer brute force and fear alone without the element of legitimacy; that, in certain circumstances and for limited periods, it may be achieved is beyond question.

Does this therefore imply that in the last resort law can be explained in terms of force alone and that, as Thrasymachus argued in Plato's *Republic* concerning justice, it is simply 'the rule of the stronger'? Is it true that law is nothing more than those rules which coercion can impose?

There are many objections to such a view but perhaps the most cogent is that to rest such a view upon the case of the Nazi occupation forces is to try and force law into the pattern of a marginal and altogether exceptional situation rather than comprehend it in its typical and characteristic pattern. Indeed some have argued that rules enforced under the conditions of the Nazi occupation, lacking as they did any foundation of morality or legitimacy, were not entitled to rank as laws at all, but were more equivalent to rules imposed by gangsters or terrorist organizations such as the Mafia in Sicily. But be this as it may – and we shall return later to this form of argument – it is enough at this stage to point out that the fact that, in exceptional periods of war or revolution, a society can temporarily be dominated by sheer force or terror is not a reason, certainly not a compelling reason, for treating law as in the last analysis nothing but force incarnate.

Yet, on the other hand, is law really conceivable, or at least possible in any practical sense, when it is not ultimately backed by effective force? Certainly the force of law is and seems always to have been linked with rules which are capable of being enforced by coercion; the hangman, the gaoler, the bailiff, and the policeman are all part of the seemingly familiar apparatus of a legal system. This popular view is well embodied in the dictum of an English judge that the best test of whether a person alleged to be insane was legally responsible for his act was whether he would have done what he did if a policeman had been standing at his elbow.

One argument against the essentially coercive character of law deserves consideration here: it is affirmed by people of undoubted sincerity that any force or violence is wrong in itself and that law which rests ultimately on violence must therefore offend the principles of true morality. Such people are apt to assert that force is the very negation or breakdown of law and that recourse to violence therefore lies outside the law itself as an extraneous element which is invoked when the rule of law has broken down. It is evident, however, that this sort of approach, however well-meaning, involves confusions which, far from contributing to our understanding of the functioning of law, merely serve to blur important distinctions without which the operation of law in human society can hardly be grasped.

In the first place what some of the proponents of this viewpoint may be urging is that the only law which they recognize as being *really* law at all is the moral law, and that for them such moral law is one which eschews all coercion and appeals only to the conscience of humanity. Such an approach may be merely a semantic one in the sense that all this may come down to a refusal to accept any definition of law other than one which extends only to the moral law, understood as a rule based not on force but on conscience, or whatever else is appealed to as the mainspring of morality. More fundamental is the view that no system of rules is entitled to qualify as law unless it coincides with, or can at least be subsumed under, the rule of morality. Those who wish to argue that force is the antithesis of law still need to go a step further than this and establish that the rule of morality excludes coercion. The fact remains that this type of argument is clearly directed to establishing a particular kind of relationship between law and morality, and the question of the role of force in a legal system thus becomes a subsidiary issue in that main question. Subsidiary, that is, not in the sense of being relatively unimportant, but technically subsidiary. For what has first to be shown is that law necessarily entails a certain relation to morality, and only if this hurdle can be overcome will the further question arise as to what is the content of morality as affecting law, and whether that content extends to the use or non-use of violence. This aspect can thus be reserved until the later discussion of the relation of law to morals, when it will be seen that very great difficulties lie in the path of those who seek to establish a necessary link between these two and that even if it can be established, perhaps even greater difficulties confront any attempt to establish a necessary content of morality, whether as to a rule of non-violence or anything else.

Not all the opposition to the coercive approach to law comes from the moralist. Another relevant attitude is to assert that any emphasis on coercion in the operation of law is entirely to misunderstand its functioning. For, it is argued, people obey the law not because they are constrained to do so by force but because they consent or at least acquiesce in its operation and it is this consent rather than any threat of force which causes the legal system to work. Such a view was in the past particularly associated with the idea of society and its law being based on a social contract underlying the consent of free men in a state of nature who thereby agreed to submit to law and government. In this form the 'consent' was very largely, if not entirely, a legal fiction and at the present day, since the fiction of a social contract has been abandoned, it has been replaced in democratic societies by the idea that universal suffrage and majority rule is the means by which the individual can, from time to time, manifest his adhesion to the operative system of government. Leaving aside the question whether this latter position in its way does not involve as much fiction as the older social con- tract theory, it will be seen that what this mode of thought is seeking to achieve is not to eliminate force in the legal process, but rather to move the emphasis from coercive sub- ordination to voluntary consent or acquiescence. More par- ticularly, what is aimed at is a demonstration that law, far from depending upon the successful and regular applications of force to subjects who defy or disregard its dictates, in the last analysis exists in its own right regardless of whether force can or cannot be brought to bear upon offenders against its rules. Thus the existence of legal coercion is relegated to a mere matter of incidental procedure, not in any way essential to its existence.

Force in International Law

In the modern world this viewpoint is regarded as of par- ticular significance in the international rather than in the purely national sphere. In the latter sphere few would deny the actual role of coercion in the legal process, though even here (as we shall see later) it is said that undue emphasis on force involves imposing the pattern of criminal law on the whole of national law and thus distorts its true nature. In the realm of international relations, however, there has developed in modern times a system of rules, admittedly not always clearly ascertained, which all civilized countries acknowledge to be binding upon them and which are not enforceable by coercion since there are no regular international forces empowered to perform the role of the policeman and bailiff in a system of national law. These rules are nevertheless treated as a system of international *law* and much of the foregoing argument is directed towards justifying this treatment notwithstanding the absence of any regular system of international coercion. It is indeed somewhat ironic that the occasional and very tentative efforts at international coercive enforcement, which represent the first gropings towards making international law truly effective, have been greeted in some quarters as a repudiation of law in favour of force by the United Nations. This criticism has, for instance, been made of the employment of international forces by the United Nations to deal with the recent crises of Suez and of the Belgian Congo.

It will be seen that the anti-coercionists are really seeking to describe the legal process exclusively in terms of authority to the neglect, if not the rejection, of the element of force, while the coercive view of law aims at putting force in the forefront to the neglect of authority. In fact both these elements need to be taken into account if we are to obtain a comprehensive conception of law, though this does not imply that we must tie ourselves to a semantic position where nothing can be treated as law which does not possess these two elements to the fullest degree. Law, like morality, is a highly flexible conception and there are, as we shall see, many marginal situations where it may be fully justifiable and desirable to employ the conceptual apparatus of law even though some features of law viewed, in Weber's terminology, as an 'ideal type', are absent, or at least present in only an attenuated form. Thus for instance we may have good reason to regard coercion as a feature of law as an 'ideal type' while still recognizing, for other reasons, that international law is properly so-called despite the small measure of organized coercion which that system has so far attained. Again, we shall see that in less developed societies coercion tends to take the form not of the centralized forces of the state but rather of each man helping himself with the aid of his kinsfolk to enforce his rights. From the point of view of the moralist the blood-feud may well seem the antithesis of law, while to the jurist there may yet be decisive reasons for classifying this seemingly anarchic process within the terminology of law, however remote it may appear from the 'ideal type' of law which is the theoretical subject-matter of legal science.

The legal theorist, like those engaged in other social studies, is concerned to expound the general structure of his field of inquiry; for this purpose he needs a conceptual apparatus which will provide him with a limiting scheme within which he can expound and correlate the various phenomena which he encounters in human societies. It is this sort of categorization which Weber described as an 'ideal type'. This is no more than 'a unified *analytical* construct. In its conceptual purity, this mental construct cannot be found empirically anywhere in reality. It is a *Utopia*. . . . It has the significance of a purely *limiting* concept with which the real situation or action is *compared*.'[6]

That legal science needs to be viewed as a continuing process is sufficiently illustrated by considering the place of coercion in international law. For just as there are infinite gradations of force, from the blood-feud to proceedings for contempt for failing to comply with an injunction issued by a modern court, so in the international system there is likely to develop a wide range of differing processes in which some form of coercion may be operated. Yet coercion between nations can never be identical with the pattern which emerges in state law where coercion is applied to individuals. The very nature of the problem is different where whole nations have to be coerced into conformity, for the ultimate use of force could here entail destruction of life and property on a vast scale. It is true that even on the level of national law, the law is obliged in modern conditions to apply legal coercion to whole groups as well as to individuals – where, for example, criminal proceedings are taken against huge corporations owning property as great as that of some independent countries. The fact remains that national law can always in the last resort enforce its decrees against individuals – for instance, the directors or officers of the corporation – and can sequestrate the corporate property in much the same way as that of individuals. That comparable processes, though differing in character and extent, may gradually be evolved in international spheres seems reasonably probable, though the evolution may be long and difficult and not always in one direction. It will be the task of legal science to accommodate these re-formulations, and it can better achieve this not by insisting on a definition of law, which does or does not stipulate the need for coercion, but rather by continually re-assessing the forms of coercion and the role that coercive processes play in legal relations. Such a study, taking account of evolving human relationships, may call for continual re-assessment of the models or concepts in the light of which human law is analysed and classified. In other words modern legal theory calls for a dynamic rather than a static approach.

Can We Dispense with Force?

The question remains as to what justification there may be at the present day for insisting on the inclusion of the element of coercion in our model of the law. In the international sphere coercion, as we have seen, plays a small part, and even in national law it is generally recognized that people usually obey the law because it is the law, and not just because they are afraid of being punished if they disobey. Why then all this emphasis on force, which seems to many to be a feature of tyranny rather than law, and which may be regarded as liable to undermine the moral authority of the law itself? Here it is important to bear in mind that while our model, or 'ideal' pattern of law, may not exactly correspond to the law actually found in any given society, it must nevertheless be constructed out of elements which do correspond to human experience, for otherwise the model would be as useless as it would be irrelevant. What then does experience show? Surely that at all levels of society human law has depended for its ultimate efficacy on the degree to which it is backed by organized coercion. Primitive society may seem to repudiate this, but this belief, once firmly held, is now, as we shall see later in our study of customary law, generally rejected by modern anthropology, which has carefully explained and elucidated the role of sanctions in many primitive communities of the past and the present. Again, when we compare the relative anarchy of a feudal society, dependent for its law enforcement largely on kinship groups supplemented by the strong arm of feudal barons, with the centralized machinery of a modern state, we can see how much the authority of the law gains by the availability of machinery of regular enforcement.

But the explanation of the role of coercion in human law lies perhaps at a deeper level. Psycho-analysis has taught us of the unconscious factors in man's psychological make-up. Among these unconscious factors are to be reckoned, not only forces which make for social cooperation and which exemplify Aristotle's famous dictum that man is a political animal, but also powerful aggressive drives which require to be effectively repressed in order to subject man to the needs of social discipline. Hence the need, as Freud himself fully recognized, for coercion. Freud believed that these aggressive urges could be repressed and sublimated but not eliminated, so that civilization would always involve a struggle between the social impulses and the basic drives towards aggression. Referring to the possibility of eliminating the latter altogether, Freud wrote: 'That would be the Golden Age, but it is questionable if such a state of affairs can ever be realized. It seems more probable that every culture must be built up on coercion and instinctual renunciation.'[7] And later he writes as follows: 'Men are not gentle, friendly creatures . . . who simply defend themselves if they are attacked . . . ; a powerful measure of desire for aggression has to be reckoned with as part of their instinctual endowment.'[8] Moreover the very process of repressing the antisocial urges itself sets up frustrations which are an important causal factor in many of the familiar *malaises* of a developed civilization. A recent commentator referring to the role of ethical rules in human society summarizes Freud's attitude in these words: 'These ethical precepts had been indispensable – without them civilization could never have been built – but at the same time they had grievously thwarted man's deepest urges. It was for this reason that Freud insisted so strongly on the necessary connexion between civilized society and coercive social order.'[9] It may be added that recent history has so emphasized the existence and the power of those aggressive urges as well as the fundamental frustrations which beset our civilization that Freud's diagnosis, gloomy though it may be, cannot be brushed aside, though it cannot be said to be established in a fully scientific sense.[10]

It is true that it is always open to us to hope that human nature may change and that a new and more harmonious social order may eventually prove practicable. 'Even if de Maistre were right and the structure of civil society had always been founded on the hangman, it was always possible to reply that it need not be so, that it would not always be so.'[11] Things being as they are, and from what we know of human history, a model of law as an operative factor of social control which ignored or discounted the element of coercion would have but little relevance to present-day society. Of course if we believe that a new order of society will ultimately dawn which will banish the need for repression then our model may call for radical revision. For the present, however, a strong measure of scepticism seems justified.

RULES ABOUT FORCE

An important section of our 'model' legal system will thus

comprise rules governing the use of violence as a mode of enforcing other sections of the system, in which are laid down rules governing the conduct of those subject to that system. This section may be said to contain the rules about force and may vary from a primitive order, where they may contain little more than rules for regulating a blood-feud; an international order, where they may contain no more than rather rudimentary provisions empowering some body such as the United Nations to raise an international force *ad hoc* to try and control a situation which involves a threat to peace, as for instance the recent disorders in the Congo; to a highly developed state system with all its regulated apparatus of courts, officials, policemen, bailiffs, and so on.

It has been a characteristic of developed state law that as the use of force has become more closely regulated and more efficiently brought to bear upon the recalcitrant it has been pushed further and further into the background. And so the bureaucratized state tends to resemble, in this respect, the order from which it theoretically differs most, namely the charismatic personal rule, where the element of authority overshadows the need for force. This in time leads to the view, which we have already discussed, that force never was or at least has ceased to be an essential feature of law. This has been described, by a modern jurist, as 'a fatal illusion', in a passage which deserves citation here:

Actual violence is, however, kept very much in the background. The more this is done, the smoother and more undisturbed is the working of the legal machinery. In this respect many modern states have been successful to an extent which is something of a miracle, considering the nature of man. Under suitable conditions the use of violence in the proper sense is so much reduced that it passes almost unnoticed.

Such a state of things is apt to create the belief that violence is alien to the law or of secondary importance. This is, however, a fatal illusion. One essential condition for reducing the application of violence to this extent is that there is to hand an organized force of overwhelming strength in comparison to that of any possible opponents. This is generally the aim in every state organized on modern lines. Resistance is therefore known to be useless. Those who are engaged in applying force in criminal and civil matters of the ordinary kind are few in number, it is true, but they are thoroughly organized and they are in each case concerned with only a single individual, or a few individuals.[12]

Two final points need to be made before leaving the subject of this chapter. The first is that, in the case of a developed legal system, what we have designated rules about the use of force may be properly broadened to cover all the procedural apparatus of the law. For the rules which govern the ultimate use of violence in the state, such as imprisonment or the infliction of the death penalty, represent purely the final stage – and one which in many cases, and in civil matters in practically all cases, is hardly ever reached – of a long procedural process whereby proceedings are instituted, regulated, and adjudicated upon, and orders are made in respect of which the forces of the state may be brought to bear upon designated individuals.[13] Such procedures are not necessarily judicial or purely judicial, for under state law coercion may result from the executive or administrative process, for instance, in England when the Home Secretary orders an illegal immigrant to be detained and deported. The rules about force may thus be regarded as forming merely a chapter, though a very vital chapter, in the larger book of rules setting out the procedural apparatus through which primary rights and duties are translated into effective action. This is not to say that legal systems in fact are to be found with their rules neatly categorized in this way, but such distinctions are of value for the purpose of forming an effective view of that 'ideal type' of law to which actual systems correspond, to a greater or less degree.

The second point is that the importance of the element of coercion in law has sometimes been misunderstood or stretched so as to imply that no rule whose breach cannot entail the application of state force (or a 'sanction', to use the word generally employed by lawyers) can be regarded as a rule of law. This is a view particularly associated with the so-called 'command theory of law', expounded by the jurist John Austin, which has had much influence in common-law countries, and especially in England. That theory can be left to be dealt with in its proper place; here it suffices to observe that though coercion may be an indispensable part of an effective system of law, there seems to be no reason why we should insist that this necessarily entails annexing penal consequences to every individual rule comprised in a legal system. On the contrary, the increasing tendency of modern systems, as we shall see, is to define important duties to which no sanctions are annexed; it would be strange if we were forced to treat these obligations as non-legal.

We have seen in the foregoing chapter that much of the aura of legitimacy which surrounds the authority of the law is associated with a belief in a moral obligation to obey the law, but at the same time the warning was added that the relation of law to morals is far from being simple. The object of this chapter is to explore this relationship more fully in general terms. The succeeding four chapters will then take up more specific features of the problem, namely, first, the natural-law approach, embodying the main conception of a higher law regulating and controlling man-made positive law; second, the positivist theory which regards positive law as enjoying an autonomous sphere within which its validity cannot be impugned by any other law, natural or otherwise; third the problem of law and justice; and lastly the relation of law to freedom. Within the ambit of these five chapters we shall discuss, in its various aspects, the abiding problem of how man-made law (which jurists usually describe as 'positive law', and which will be so designated here) is related to the value-systems which confer on human life its meaning and purpose and give it its distinctively human quality.

LAW AND RELIGION

We have become accustomed in modern times to the purely secular conception of law as made by man for man and to be judged accordingly in purely human terms. Very different was the attitude of earlier ages when law was regarded as having a sanctity which bespoke a celestial or divine origin. Law, morality, and religion were treated as inevitably inter-related. Some laws, indeed, might be traced directly to a divine lawgiver, as in the case of the Ten Commandments; others, while clearly owing their direct origin to human sources, would be given an aura of divine sanctity by attributing a measure of divine inspiration to the human lawgiver. Moreover, lawgivers in ancient times tended to be treated as mythical, semi-divine, or heroic figures. A characteristic view of the ancient Greek approach to law-giving occurs in the opening passage of Plato's *Laws*, where the Athenian puts this question to the Cretan: 'To whom is the merit of instituting your laws ascribed? To a god, or to some man?' To this the man of Crete replies: 'Why, to a god, indubitably to a god.'[1]

This elementary feeling that law is in some way rooted in religion, and can appeal to a divine or semi-divine sanction for its validity, clearly accounts to a considerable degree for that aura of authority which law is able to command and more particularly for the belief, to which we have referred, in the moral duty to obey the law. No one who is persuaded that the gods on high have themselves directly, or indirectly through human agency, decreed the very content of the laws in imperishable letters of fire would be much impressed by the view of a modern jurist such as Austin that the law depends for its validity on having some legal penalty or sanction duly annexed to it. Not that human penalties were lacking in importance in the early stages of law; quite the contrary, for ancient systems displayed a rich ingenuity in devising and inflicting penalties of the most appalling kind, from various forms of torture and dismemberment to such curious inventions as the Roman penalty of launching parricides into the sea bound in a sack and accompanied to their doom by a dog, a cock, a viper, and an ape. And even if the offender were to escape the vigilance of human penalties the gods could be relied upon to inflict punishment in their own way and in their own time. The familiar story of Orestes, so dramatically expounded in the works of the ancient Greek dramatists, sufficiently illustrates the belief in divine intervention for offences against the laws. Orestes, to avenge his murdered father, kills his mother and her lover. The divine

Furies then appear and relentlessly pursue Orestes for the murder, though finally they allow themselves to be appeased by the intervention of Athene. Such a story also emphasizes the degree of flexibility in the administration of divine justice which might result from a system of polytheism, where one god might be set off against another and so mitigate the full rigour of the law. With the development of the Hebrew notion of monotheism the stern inflexible will of God presented far less scope for the easy moral compromises of other faiths based on a belief in a pantheon of squabbling deities.

Although religion thus played a key role in investing the law with its peculiar sanctity it must not be thought that the whole of the law governing a particular state would be necessarily regarded as either directly or indirectly God-given. A distinction would normally be made between those parts of the law which were regarded as fundamental and virtually unchangeable since they embodied the very structure of society and the relation of its members to its rulers and the universe at large, as compared with other laws which were clearly man-made in character and lacking in cosmic significance. No doubt in a society such as that of ancient Egypt where the ruling pharaoh was regarded as the incarnation of God on earth, this distinction would not easily emerge, for every decree of the reigning monarch, however trivial its subject matter, would carry divine authority. For the most part however, ancient societies did not identify their rulers with the gods and so there was a clear-cut distinction between the divine and the merely human in the sphere of law.

HEBREW AND GREEK INFLUENCES

Of the peoples of the ancient world the Hebrews and the Greeks in particular can be said to have brought this contrast between divine and human life into prominence in ways which have influenced the Western concept of law ever since. The Hebrews rejected all systems of polytheism and of divine rulers and set up in their place an unswerving monotheism in which God's will dictated the moral pattern for all mankind, and obedience to that will was secured by the divine punishment of offenders, whether individuals or whole peoples. The Hebrew prophets, in language of unsurpassed sublimity, tirelessly reiterated the imperative character of God's law; the obligatory character of that law upon rulers and people alike; and the condign punishment that God would inflict upon those who disregarded his decrees. Human rulers there might be – and the Hebrews recognized kings who were regarded as lawfully anointed of the Lord and therefore enjoying divine sanctity – and these kings could and did impose laws upon their people by virtue of their kingship. But what if those laws were in conflict with God's will? And how in any event was God's will to be ascertained?

During the great prophetic period of the Hebrew religion, as recorded in the later books of the Old Testament, there is little doubt as to the answer to these questions. Kings might propose but God disposed; no mere kingly decree could prevail against the will of Almighty God as embodied in the Laws of Moses, and the Old Testament is full of stories of the condign punishment meted out to kings and people alike who repudiated those laws in favour of other gods or alien modes of life. Again, God's will, when it was not to be detected directly in the divine scriptures themselves, was declared by the prophets – as remarkable a body of men as any that have emerged in human history. These men, entirely lacking in any official standing either in the hierarchy of the state or the priesthood, by the sheer force of their personal charisma and their burning sense of religious communion with the will of God, were able, ultimately, to establish the idea of a divine order of moral law in the universe, whose scope and decrees rested not on the affirmations of rulers and priests but on the inspiration or intuition of God-intoxicated individuals whom God had chosen as humble instruments to convey his messages to mankind. That the moral law had to be revealed in this way showed plainly enough that the laws laid down by human rulers could and frequently did conflict with the divine decrees that God had laid down for the governance of mankind. It also showed that any merely man-made laws could not stand or possess any validity whatever in the face of divine laws which the rulers themselves were not competent to reveal or to interpret.

The possibility of the laws of man, even where emanating from rulers ordained of God, conflicting with God's own laws brought to a head the moral dilemma in which man finds himself. Law on the one hand and morality and religion on the other may speak with divided voices, and for all the aura that man-made law may enjoy and for all the moral authority that it may wield, it may yet be opposed to the very morality upon which much of its own authority rests. It is impossible to over-estimate the value of this Hebraic contribution to the human spirit in thus rejecting human law as the necessary embodiment of morality, but two observations need to be made on the position thus arrived at.

In the first place the Hebraic view of divine law really resulted in equating law with morality. For the only true law was that which embodied the decrees of God's will and any other man-made decrees were not entitled to rank as law at all. Law therefore really means simply the moral or religious law which is laid down by God or developed by divinely inspired human beings, and the way is thus opened for that theocratic form of rule which is found in the post-prophetic Jewish state and in the early stages of Calvinism, where law and morality are one and no recognition can be granted to any laws which are lacking in divine inspiration. Hence the possibility of conflict between human and moral laws is resolved draconically by treating all valid human laws as nothing but expressions of the moral law. The dangers inherent in this situation may be stressed by referring to our second observation on the Hebraic conception. This is that the source of the moral law, save in so far as it is contained directly in divinely inspired scriptures, rests on the authority of those who can persuade themselves and others of their personal inspiration. Moreover, even the established scriptures will be full of doubts and obscurities of language, and these will need to be authoritatively interpreted if they are to be treated as legislative in character. Hence there is limitless scope for personal interpretations as faith or fanaticism compete to impose their will upon their followers and denounce (and punish if they can) those whose inspiration or inclinations favour other interpretations of the law. Further, as every rejection of an approved construction of the law is to be regarded as a renunciation of the will of God, it is clear that differences of opinion on disputed points will assume a gravity of offence which no dispute on mere man-made law is likely to achieve. Such an approach is likely to result either in the triumph of a rigid orthodoxy imposing its moral tenets on every aspect of the life of the community, as in the Geneva of Calvin, or in a virtual anarchy of individuals each interpreting the law according to his own moral inspiration. This latter situation, indeed, was of frequent occurrence in many places in Germany in the early days of the Reformation when fanatical leaders of such sects as the Anabaptists attempted to impose their passionate convictions upon whole communities, seized by the religious ferments of the period.

The Hebraic approach to the moral law, with its appeal to personal inspiration and the divine afflatus, inevitably stressed the irrational and mystical elements of faith. God's ways were mysterious and not fully understandable by man, as the Book of Job demonstrates, but man must submit lovingly to the divine will even if it passes understanding. 'Though he slay me, yet will I trust in him.'[2] Such an attitude, far from presupposing a rational moral order intelligible to human reason, rather appeals to the very incomprehensibility of the universe as a justification for resort to faith alone. '*Credo quia absurdum*' is apt to be the maxim of this kind of irrationality.

It is at this point that the Greek form of faith in a rational order of the universe, governed by intelligible laws ascertainable by rational investigation, provided so important a countervailing force to that of moral mysticism. Certainly there were strong mystical and irrational elements in both Greek religion and philosophy, as evidenced by the secret

Orphic rites and Pythagoreanism. Also, Fate played a mysterious role in cosmic and human affairs, deciding human destiny in an inscrutable fashion (witness, for instance, the Oedipus legend), and it was beyond even the power of the gods to alter it. But in contrast to these factors in Greek thought there developed a very powerful attachment to rationalism, a belief that both the physical and the moral order of the world were based on rational principles, and that man's reason shared in this rational nature of the universe and was thus capable of understanding it. To this approach is owed much of the modern belief in scientific laws and in the possibility of a rational philosophy which can elucidate the ultimate principles of the physical structure of the world and of the moral order governing human conduct, and also the relation of human beings to one another and to the universe. Such a belief in human reason in the moral sphere clearly entails the idea of a moral law of a rational kind whose imperative character derives from the fact that man's reason must necessarily accept the rational solution as the moral or true one. For the universe being itself ordered rationally, reason requires the acceptance of rules which stand the test of rationality.

The Greek philosophers were aware that human laws which actually operated in different societies differed greatly from one another and that many of these laws were either against reason or certainly not fully justifiable on rational grounds. Necessary identity on the Hebrew pattern could not be asserted between the laws of God and of man, therefore, nor did the Greeks affirm that the validity or existence of man-made law was directly controlled or affected in some way by a higher law of reason. We shall have more to say in a later chapter of the development of natural-law ideas in Greek speculative thought; here it suffices to point out that the tendency of Greek thought was to recognize that human law, whether or not it might owe its origin in part to divine or semi-divine sources, possessed an autonomous position in human society. It did not depend for its validity on any divine origin, though where this existed it naturally would give the law a peculiar sanctity. At the same time human law, autonomous though it might be, could be subjected to moral scrutiny, and such scrutiny meant, in the last resort, comparing it with the touchstone of ideal rationality believed to be inherent in the universe as a whole.

The Moral Duty to Obey the Law

The Hebraic and the Greek conceptions of law had this important feature in common, that they underlined in their different ways the need to face a possible conflict between the obligation imposed by mere man-made law and that required by the moral law. In the Hebraic view nothing could be clearer than that a human law dictating what is contrary to divine law (for instance permitting incest) would be utterly lacking in validity and must be ignored whatever the cost, for no mere human penalties or sanctions could prevail against God's law, and God's justice could be relied upon to manifest itself (though possibly in an inscrutable way) in the final balance of accounts between ruler and subject and their Maker.

Less simple was the Greek position, for here there was obviously a very intensely felt sense of the moral obligation of a man to obey the law of the state even when he believed it to be wrong or immoral. Moreover this view was not weakened, as with the Hebrew prophetic faith, by a belief in the necessary identity of law and morality, nor by any clearly felt assurance that human law, even if contrary to reason, was any the less operative on that account. This is well brought out in that familiar passage of Plato's *Crito* where Socrates explains to his companion why, though his condemnation may have been unjust, he must abide still by the state's decision and would be acting wrongly by trying to escape the penalty:

SOCRATES: . . . Ought a man to perform his just agreements or may he shuffle out of them?

CRITO: He ought to perform them.

SOCRATES: Then consider. If I escape without the state's consent, shall I be injuring those whom I ought least to injure, or not? Shall I be abiding by my just agreements or not?

CRITO: I cannot answer your question, Socrates. I do not understand it.

SOCRATES: Consider it in this way. Suppose the laws and the commonwealth were to come and appear to me as I was preparing to run away and were to ask, 'Tell us, Socrates, what have you in your mind to do? What do you mean by trying to escape, but to destroy us the laws, and the whole city, so far as in you lies? Do you think that a state can exist and not be overthrown in which the decisions of law are of no force, and are disregarded and set at nought by private individuals?' How shall we answer questions like that, Crito? Much might be said, especially by an orator, in defence of the law which makes judicial decisions supreme. Shall I reply, 'But the state has injured me: it has directed my cause wrongly?' Shall we say that?

CRITO: Certainly we will, Socrates.

SOCRATES: And suppose the laws were to reply, 'Was that our agreement? or was it that you would submit to whatever judgment the state should pronounce? ... Since you were brought into the world and educated by us, how can you deny that you are our child and our slave, as your fathers were before you? And if this be so, do you think that your rights are on a level with ours? ... Do you think that you may retaliate on your country and its laws? If we try to destroy you, because we think it right, will you in return do all you can to destroy us, the laws, and your country, and say that in so doing you are doing right, you, the man, who in truth thinks so much of virtue? Or are you too wise to see that your country is worthier, and more august, and more sacred, and holier ... than your father and mother and all your other ancestors; and that it is your bounden duty to receive it and to submit to it ... and either to do whatever it bids you to do or to persuade it to excuse you; and to obey in silence if it orders you to endure stripes or imprisonment? ... That is what is your duty ... In war, and in the course of justice, and everywhere you must do whatever your city and your country bid you do, or you must convince them that their commands are unjust. But it is against the law of God to use violence to your father or to your mother; and much more so is it against the law of God to use violence to your country.' What answer shall we make, Crito? Shall we say that the laws speak truly, or not?

CRITO: I think that they do.[3]

Such was the painful dilemma presented to the citizen of fourth-century Athens by the idea that to live according to the laws was the highest unwritten law, for this might, as Plato himself showed in the case of Socrates, result in those laws requiring the justest man to die. To this dilemma Plato himself later propounded his own solution, that only when the state itself embodied the idea of the good could the life of the individual properly be sacrificed to the state. In other words Plato argued for an identity of law and morality, but an identity based not on blind faith but on human wisdom and reason. Of this more will be said later,[4] but for the present those points in the Greek position which emerge from the *Crito* deserve emphasis. The first is that it is recognized that obedience to the law of the state is itself a principle of the highest morality; and for this purpose it is not very material that Socrates bases his argument largely on a kind of agreement (an early form of the social contract) between the citizens and the state to observe these laws whatever may be the consequences to a particular individual. At the same time, the second point arises that there is a moral law, independent of state law, by which a particular decree of the state may be shown to be immoral or unjust. Thirdly, however, this moral law in no way overrides the law of state so far as the individual citizen is concerned, for his duty is confined to trying to persuade the state of its moral error, and if he fails then his inexorable duty is to obey the law of the state. For the law of God itself requires obedience even to an unjust law.[5] Nothing could indicate more vividly the contrast with the Hebraic idea that not only must the law of the state yield to the law of God, but that God's decrees, however inscrutable, cannot uphold injustice against justice.

The Hebrew view then insists that human law is to be obeyed only when it corresponds with divine law; the Greek view, on the other hand, is that human law may conflict with moral law but the citizen must still obey the law of his state though he may and indeed should labour to persuade the state to change its law to conform with morality.

THE RELATION OF LAW TO MORALS

Of these two views, the Greek seems nearer to the prevailing opinion of the modern world, with certain modifications. Certainly there are those who argue that the duty to obey the state is in all circumstances overriding. In the philosophy of Hegel (which has proved so influential in relation to later totalitarian doctrines) the individual is treated as submerged in the higher reality of the state, whose superior wisdom could hardly be expected (as Socrates thought) to be open to the persuasion of an individual citizen that it was in error, or that its courts were unjust or immoral, since the state itself represents the very embodiment of morality. But among democrats and anti-totalitarians generally, while they might go some part of the way with Socrates in recognizing a moral duty to obey the law, greater emphasis would be placed on the limitations of this doctrine in those cases where morality was in conflict with the provisions of positive law.[6] For although even in many such conflicts the overriding moral duty might be to obey the law (as Socrates thought) until persuasion is effective to bring about legislative changes, there may still be extreme situations where the law dictates acts of such patent immorality (as in the case of Nazi laws, under which death and the most appalling tortures were inflicted upon millions of innocent people) that, whatever the position in positive law, the moral duty is that of rejection of rather than obedience to the law.

The distinctive feature of this approach is the recognition that while law and morality may, and normally do, occupy much ground in common there is no necessary coincidence between the dictates of law and morality. And though there is a moral duty to obey the law, whether its specific content is or is not in accordance with morality, in the case of an acute and fundamental conflict of principle between the two, morality both requires and justifies disobedience. The implications of this approach, which raises issues of the first importance, not only for lawyers and moralists but for ordinary citizens everywhere, will be discussed in the next chapter. For the present it will be in place to say a little more about the respects in which law and morals may be expected to coincide and the reasons why modern jurists are justified in rejecting the idea of a total identity between these two spheres.

The relation of law to morals is sometimes described as two intersecting circles, the part inside the intersections representing the common ground between the two spheres and the parts outside representing the distinctive realms in which each holds exclusive sway. This picture however is misleading in so far as it suggests that where there is common ground between the two, there is a kind of identity. This is not generally the case. The law of murder may be said, for instance, to concern prohibitions rooted in common morality but none the less there may be considerable divergences between what the law and morality would regard as amounting to murder. In English law if death supervenes more than a year and a day after the act which causes the killing there is no murder, yet morally it may be said there is no valid distinction between acts resulting in death in 366 and 367 days later. Yet legal systems may be justified in drawing distinctions, and even in some cases arbitrary lines, on grounds of practical expediency whatever may be the precise dictate of morality to the contrary.

Still the reason why there remains a broad territory common to law and morality is not far to seek. For both are concerned to impose certain standards of conduct without which human society would hardly survive and, in many of these fundamental standards, law and morality reinforce and supplement each other as part of the fabric of social life. If we do not refrain from physical assault on others and from misappropriating what belongs to others there can be no security of life or of the transactions which further life and well-being in human society. Moral codes, by recognizing that we ought generally to refrain from such acts, supplement the force of the law which equally forbids them. And the moral reprobation which such acts inspire is reinforced by the criminal and other sanctions imposed by the law. The moral code itself largely presupposes the existence of a legal system underlying its precepts, for a moral rule requiring respect for the property of others necessarily assumes that there are rules of law which define in what circumstances property exists (for 'property' is a legal conception implying rules as to what is capable of ownership; how one becomes or ceases to be owner; how ownership is transferred; and so forth).[7] And because it is a presupposition of legal systems that they exist, broadly speaking, to uphold the moral standards of the communities to which they apply, the moral duty to obey the law is generally accepted, and plays an important role in establishing the authority of the law and ensuring obedience to it, in the majority of cases without actual recourse to coercive measures.

The close parallelism between codes of morals and of law is sufficiently brought out by the similarity of normative language that each employs. Both are concerned to lay down rules or 'norms' of conduct for human beings and this is expressed both in moral and legal language in terms of obligations, duties, or of what is right or wrong. Both laws and morals lay down that it is my duty to do this or that, or that I ought to do so and so, or refrain from doing something else, and that I have a right to act in a certain way, or that it is wrong to do so. This correspondence of language, though it brings out the interrelation of the two spheres, is also dangerous in that it tends to trap the unwary into thinking that law must necessarily connote moral obligation (there seems something of this confusion in Socrates' speech quoted above) or that moral obligation needs must be translated into law.

WHERE LAW AND MORALS DIVERGE

This leads us naturally, therefore, into a consideration of the divergences between law and morals and the reasons for such divergences. Let us start with one or two simple examples which may indicate how law and morals, even where starting from similar premises, may yet develop along different and indeed contrary paths. The law may condemn and even punish sexual immorality in various forms, but it may refrain from attaching legal consequences to some kinds of immorality such as prostitution, the keeping of a mistress, fornication lacking in any element of violence between adults of opposite sex, and so forth. Again the moral duty to save or preserve life may in many instances not give rise to an equivalent legal duty. A parent may be under a legal duty to care for and protect his infant child, but under no legal duty to go to the rescue of another person who is drowning even though this might be done without risk to himself. And a person who has borrowed a knife from a friend may not have the 'right' in law to refuse to return it on request, even though he has good reason to suspect that his friend intends to use it later to make a violent assault upon a third person. In all such cases, the law shrinks, for one reason or another, from pursuing what may nevertheless be recognized as the authentic path of morality.

The reasons for such discrepancies are various and not all may be of equal validity. There are many instances where the higher ethical attitude may not be sufficiently embodied in popular sentiment to be productive of legal action in conformity with it. Here law may reflect popular morality though the latter is slowly being made to yield to a more refined or humanitarian approach. Much of the activity of the early criminal law, with its savage penalties for trivial offences and the gradual move (still far from complete) towards a more humane penal system, reflects this kind of relation of law to popular feeling and the gradual improvement of both moral and legal standards, each reflecting and interacting upon the other. In such cases the impulse to reform the law generally depends upon a relatively small section of determined individuals who have the moral force to produce a sufficient change in popular sentiment to bring about changes in the law. The development in this country of the law relating to the protection of children and animals against cruelty has been almost entirely due to this kind of pressure, and illustrates how new moral duties may come to be recognized and in due course translated into legal duties, and how such legal duties may themselves be productive of the spread of more humane moral sentiments and standards.

On the other hand there may be fields of human activity where the law deliberately prefers to abstain from supporting the moral rule because it is felt that the machinery is too cumbersome to engage upon the particular task and that more social evil may be created than prevented by its intervention. Examples in modern times are the refusal to penalize fornication or drunkenness in private. In fact in some places (as in certain states of the United States) where adultery is treated as a criminal offence the law is virtually a dead letter and so tends to do harm by bringing the law generally into disrepute. Much of the argument propounded recently by the Wolfenden Committee[8] urging that the offence of homosexual relations between consenting male adults in private should be removed from the statute book[8a] was based on the belief that such a law is exceedingly difficult to enforce, and when enforced is likely to do more harm than good by encouraging other evils such as blackmail. Reliance was also placed on a further and more abstract argument in favour of the non-intervention of the law in such cases: namely the libertarian proposition, traceable to John Stuart Mill, that the law should not intervene in matters of private moral conduct more than necessary to preserve public order and to protect citizens against what is injurious and offensive. In other words there is a sphere of morality which is best left to the individual conscience, as for instance in the case of liberty of thought or belief.

This libertarian view has been strongly criticized on the ground that the criminal law depends for its effectiveness on its incorporating the moral standards of the community and that failure to give expression to these standards must weaken the moral authority of the law and the society it exists to uphold. Failure to recognize this compelling need is thus stigmatized as 'the error of jurisprudence' in the Wolfenden Report.[9] Yet when one pauses to ask how these moral standards are to be ascertained the reply given, that we must appeal to what the law calls the 'ordinary reasonable man', the man (or woman) in the jury-box, or as he has been facetiously described, the 'man on the Clapham omnibus', seems a good deal less than adequate. For this fictitious paragon, if he exists at all, may be a bundle of prejudices, ignorances, and unresolved conflicts, though the plain man's view on some questions of simple morality (if morality is ever simple) may provide as good a touchstone as any. The fact remains that many such questions require a degree of detailed knowledge, painstaking investigation, and sophisticated reasoning which can hardly be expected of the common juryman.

The Nature of 'Cruelty' as a Ground for Divorce

A ready illustration of this sort of difficulty may be found in our modern law of divorce. For instance, English law allows a spouse to claim a divorce if he or she can satisfy a court that the other spouse has been guilty of cruelty.[8b] Cruelty on the face of it may seem a simple enough conception, but the courts have experienced very great difficulty in distinguishing the sort of conduct which may be regarded as part of the ordinary wear-and-tear of married life from conduct of so serious a character as to justify divorce. In particular, English courts have been very greatly exercised by the question whether it is necessary to show that the spouse who has been guilty of the conduct complained of (and whom we will call, for convenience 'the husband') has acted deliberately or intentionally towards his wife with the aim of injuring her, or whether it is enough that his conduct, in an objective sense, was such that she could not be expected to tolerate it.

It is easy enough when a husband has behaved aggressively towards his wife by assaulting her, or deliberately humiliating her, or making her life miserable. But what of the case where the husband displays no aggression or unkindness towards his wife but is simply lazy or ineffectual, and does nothing to assist her financially, so that the whole burden of maintaining her family falls upon the wife, and as a result she is made ill? Or, on the other hand, suppose a wife shows a complete neglect of her duties, by getting up late, neglecting to prepare meals for her husband or their children, and generally behaving in an indifferent and sluttish way, though without any desire or aim of making her husband ill or miserable, but simply because this is the type of person that she is. Can it be said that such a husband or wife has really treated the other spouse with cruelty?

For some time the English courts took the view that in cases of this kind, the husband's conduct must in some way have been 'aimed at' his wife, in the sense at least that he must have realized that conduct of the kind in question was likely to have a serious effect upon the wife's state of health. Recently, however, the House of Lords has decided that in cases of cruelty it is not necessary to show an intention on the part of the husband to injure his wife.[10] The aim of the law of divorce is thus recognized as being primarily concerned with protecting one spouse against intolerable behaviour on the part of the other, and the test of cruelty is whether the conduct is so bad that the other spouse should not be called upon to put up with it. If, therefore, conduct of this kind is established it will be immaterial whether it was 'aimed at' the other spouse or merely due to unwarranted indifference, selfishness, or laziness.

It might be felt that an easy way out of this sort of difficulty would be simply to leave it to the good sense of a jury to say in any particular case whether cruelty had occurred. Undoubtedly, this would afford some kind of solution, and one which probably, in the majority of cases, would lead to much the same result as is already produced by the more deliberate judicial determinations which occur at present. The fact is, however, that one of the aims of the legal process is, so far as possible, to try and achieve a general uniformity of result in cases of a similar kind, and it endeavours to achieve this by attempting to arrive at rational tests and criteria by means of which disputes may be resolved. It may be that the conclusion ultimately arrived at by the House of Lords in this particular instance is still open to some criticism, but it illustrates that the courts, by a process of applying various types of criteria to actual cases which come before them, are able gradually to develop rational principles which can be applied in a multitude of differing situations and which can yet achieve a substantial measure of justice. In this way society is provided with a more subtle and sophisticated means of bringing the law into contact with the needs of current morality than it would be by simply leaving each matter to be dealt with according to the common-sense judgment or moral insight of the ordinary juryman.

The history of law reform is not likely to be a very illuminating one if no move can be made, however desirable it may be demonstrated to be, until popular sentiment can be fully mobilized in favour of the change, lest the whole authority of the law be whittled away. Indeed, as we have seen, it is often only with the change in the law itself that popular opinion is gradually re-moulded to a more enlightened viewpoint. It is doubtful, for instance, whether the numerous cases to which capital punishment applied would ever have been reduced or that this penalty would ever be ultimately abolished if a popular majority had first to be ensured.

The 'Ladies' Directory' Case

The notion that law should be directly related to conventionally established standards of morality is one which is not lacking in practical consequences. Recently, in a case generally referred to as the *Ladies' Directory* case, the publisher of a booklet giving information as to the addresses, telephone numbers, and other particulars of various prostitutes was held guilty of conspiring to corrupt public morals. His conviction was upheld by the House of Lords and approving reference was made by the judges to the role of the court as the custodian of public morals and its duty to preserve the moral welfare of the state.[11] The House of Lords did not shrink from the fact that this was in effect to confer on judge and juries a discretion to create new offences in accordance with the exigencies of public morals as these might vary from time to time. The part that judicial legislation plays in law generally will have to be discussed at a later stage, since it represents a vital facet of the whole functioning of law, especially in a developed community; the *Ladies' Directory* case also has important implications in the realm of liberty and the rule of law which will be referred to when the relation of law to freedom comes to be considered later on. In connexion with this case, it is sufficient to point out that the ascertaining of the requirement of public morals at a given moment is in effect entrusted to the particular jury which happens to be charged with any particular case. In accordance with English procedure, however, the law is previously expounded to the jury by the trial judge, who will no doubt endeavour to convey his own insight as to the content of public morals operative in the community. This hardly seems an ideal machinery for developing the criminal law. It is only surprising that judges who have in other fields repudiated judicial legislation as a means of 'usurping the function of the legislature'[12] should accept with such equanimity the prospect of creating new crimes by judicial decision based on the somewhat tenuous findings of juries as to what public morality dictates.

CRIME AND PUNISHMENT

The difficulty of reaching any agreement as to the true demands of morality has in some quarters led to a reaction in favour of trying to eliminate moral judgments from the criminal law, and concentrating on achieving its social purposes: to protect society and reform the prisoner, rather than to aim at the somewhat nebulous goal of establishing the guilt of the prisoner and the degree of his moral responsibility for the crime. It is argued that the degree of moral responsibility for wrongful conduct is something which is beyond human power to allocate and that if the law were to confine itself to the more limited sociological objectives which it is capable of attaining, then much of the present confusions relating to the vexed subjects of crime and punishment would disappear.[13]

It is not of course an answer to this thesis that for legal purposes finding a man 'guilty' of a particular offence involes merely a legal judgment, viz. that he has committed conduct falling within the scope of the crime as defined by law. For this omits consideration of three vital respects in which morality impinges upon law. Firstly, the whole idea of 'guilt' in criminal law is linked with the idea of moral responsibility and in this way morals reinforce the authority of the law and the duty to render obedience to its decrees. In the second place, 'responsibility' in law is treated as excluding the possibility of guilt if there exists some circumstance of excuse which causes us to adjudge the accused as not morally implicated in the deed which constitutes the offence. For instance, he may have been so insane as not to realize that what he was doing was wrong (e.g. if he kills a policeman under the insane delusion that the latter is a foreign soldier engaged in an armed invasion of his country), or he may have been coerced by overwhelming force into committing the act, or have done it during a blackout or in a state of mental 'automatism'.[14] The *raison d'être* of all such defences is that responsibility for a crime entails a certain mental element (called by lawyers '*mens rea*' or a guilty mind) and that circumstances which negative this mental state may relieve the accused of legal responsibility. There are exceptions to this principle – for example, crimes where a man may be liable absolutely, whatever the state of his mind – but this generally applies only to relatively minor offences. In a recent decision of the House of Lords,[15] the House, somewhat surprisingly, even recognized an exception in regard to the most serious crime of murder, by holding that a person could be convicted of murder if he so acted towards the deceased that a reasonable person should have realized that his acts were likely to inflict serious injury on the deceased, and that the actual state of mind of the accused, as to foresight of injury to the deceased, was immaterial. This decision has indeed been seriously criticized both in England and abroad, as blurring the need to establish the personal responsibility of the particular offender.[15a]

The third way in which morals impinge on legal responsibility is in deciding upon the punishment to be inflicted.

T–c

As to this, it is argued that by eliminating the idea of moral responsibility for crime a more rational form of sentencing policy can operate than where (as now) courts are concerned to assess the incalculable factor of the degree of moral guilt. Although this is certainly an attractive argument[16] it seems to be open to the objection that it ignores the factor (perhaps over-emphasized, as we have seen, by the 'moralist' school of thought, but nevertheless of great significance in the functioning of the legal system) that law needs, in order to enjoy its full authority, to be buttressed by the moral convictions of the community.[17] Moreover, it is not easy to see how the idea of moral responsibility can be eliminated from the question of legal guilt for the offence charged without undermining the whole basis of mental responsibility for crime and substituting for it an inquiry into whether the accused did the acts in question and if so what is the best social solution to be applied to his case. It seems improbable that, at any rate in the present stage of human society, such a substitute for the morally based criminal law would be either intelligible to the community as a whole or that it would appear to be in accord with the sense of justice of ordinary people upon which the effective administration of the law so largely depends.

Perhaps a compromise might eventually be found by retaining the conception of guilt and responsibility in relation to the actual commission of the offence, but eliminating it from the consideration of punishment. In this way the court would be able to avoid embarking upon the invidious if not impossible task of determining degrees of moral responsibility, in favour of considering the effect that punishment is likely to have upon the particular convicted person, having regard to such psychiatric evidence as is available, and how far he is likely to benefit from punishment. It must not be thought, however, that this method would inevitably mean that if a convicted person was regarded as incapable of benefiting from punishment, he would automatically have to be released. For the court would also have to have regard, as it does at the present day, to the protection of the public, and if it appeared that the condition of the accused was such that his release would involve serious peril to other members of the public, then the court would be entitled and obliged, as it is now, to require him to be detained. The ultimate release of the prisoner would then depend upon whether his condition was regarded as no longer constituting a danger to the public, a position similar to that of criminal lunatics under the present system.

It may well be that if such a sentencing procedure was introduced, and was found to work successfully without endangering the public welfare to any greater extent than does the existing system, this might perform an educative function and adjust peoples' minds gradually to the idea that the whole of the criminal law could be transmuted into an inquiry into the facts of a particular crime and the social, mental, and other aspects of the background of the accused person, without need to introduce the notion of responsibility at all. If this were so, then it might well be, as Barbara Wootton has argued,[18] that the concept of responsibility could be allowed gradually to 'wither away'. There are even signs of a gradual move in this direction in some advanced social democracies, more particularly in those of Scandinavia. All the same it must be admitted that this approach still rests on a number of unproved assumptions, such as the capacity of modern psychiatry to make a substantial contribution to the rehabilitation of criminals or social misfits. To many minds the risks involved in eliminating or reducing the sense of moral responsibility of the individual remain markedly greater than the obvious imperfections of the existing system.

CONFLICTS BETWEEN POSITIVE LAW AND THE MORAL LAW

What, it is suggested, emerges from the foregoing discussion is that law and morality are inter-related and interact upon one another in a highly complex way. Moreover there remains always the possibility of serious divergency between the duty imposed by law and morality in a given situation. We have seen that there are three main attitudes which may be adopted towards the possibility of such divergency and these may conveniently be recapitulated here.

In the first place, it may be said that law and morals must necessarily coincide either because the moral law dictates the actual content of human law, as in the case of the Hebrew or Calvinist theocracies, or alternatively because morality is itself merely what the law lays down. The first alternative leads to the proposition that in effect only the moral law is valid and that nothing which does not conform to the moral law itself can properly be regarded as effectively binding law. The second alternative has been propounded by various philosophers. Thomas Hobbes, for instance, argued that morality really means nothing more than obeying the law, so that an unjust law is a contradiction in terms. Hegel's mystical theory of the moral superiority of the state over the individual also recognized that the individual could claim no higher right than to obey the law of the state of which he formed an insignificant part.

The second attitude is to recognize that man-made law and the moral law each enjoys a realm of its own, but that the moral law is a higher law and thus provides a touchstone for the validity of merely man-made law. Conflicts therefore need to be resolved, at least in the last resort, in favour of the moral law, though the consequences which may be drawn from this solution vary a good deal. For instance, it may be suggested that the human law is, in case of conflict, certainly nullified and so the citizen is relieved of his moral duty of obedience. On the other hand, it may be said that this is a matter which must be left between God and the unjust ruler, but that the citizen's duty is still one of simple obedience. Obviously there are many other variants which may be and have been propounded at different times with a greater or less display of logic or authority. Broadly speaking, however, this theory of the two laws, has, from the time of the Hellenistic Greeks up to the present day, been discussed in Western jurisprudence mainly in terms of a so-called law of nature, or natural law, which is regarded as containing precepts of a higher order, whether ordained by God or part of the natural order of the world. This doctrine at various times, and particularly in the modern period, has been linked with the important idea of the 'natural rights' of man, which have played so large a role in democratic thought since the days of the American and the French Revolutions.

Thirdly, there is the approach which treats the autonomy of each of the spheres of law and morality as exclusive, so that neither can resolve questions of validity save in its own sphere. This theory is commonly referred to at the present day as 'legal positivism'. It insists that the validity of a legal rule can depend solely on legal criteria, just as moral validity must be ascertained by applying such criteria as are necessary or appropriate in relation to a system of morality. Those who support this view generally take a pragmatic view of the moral law, basing it on some such principle as utility, expediency, tradition, or social custom. For them any conflict between the two spheres cannot impugn the legal validity of man-made law or alter the duty of legal obedience, though it gives rise to the moral problem whether the law as it stands ought to be changed. And, in extreme cases, a conflict between legal and moral duty may have to be resolved in accordance with the dictates of the conscience of the individual and his moral courage to defy a law which he believes to be contrary to what is morally right or just.

It is proposed in the next two chapters to examine in more detail both the background and the implications for our present-day society of the two opposing theories of natural law and of legal positivism. The theory of the identity of law and morals will be left for later discussion under the heading of Hegelianism,[19] which is the main form in which it has been of significance in modern times.

4   Natural Law and
       Natural Rights

The idea of the two laws, one resting solely on human authority and the other claiming divine or natural origin and therefore entitled to supremacy over mere human law, has a long and chequered history, and still possesses vitality in the twentieth century. Indeed, it may be said that while the scientific and technological advance during the nineteenth century and the present age has played a key role in the rise of positivism and the rejection of natural law ideas, the turmoils, revolutions, wars, and barbarisms of recent history and their close association in many minds with those technological improvements which seem to have served the purposes of cruel tyranny as much if not more than of advancing human happiness, have led to something of a revival of natural-law thinking.

The aim of this chapter will be to explore briefly the significance of natural-law thinking in the past; to summarize the forms in which it manifests itself at the present day; and to attempt to evaluate the contribution it may be capable of making to the problems of law in the modern world.

THE MEANING OF NATURE

In early society as well as in early forms of civilization no clear distinction is made between the natural world, animate or inanimate, and the world of human beings and human affairs. Gods and supernatural spirits direct, if they do not actually embody, the powers and forces governing everything in the universe including man and the conduct of his affairs on earth. No distinction is made between those physical laws of nature which govern the order of the universe and the decrees of the gods or of their representatives on earth which determine the order of human society. The gods or the supernatural powers reign over everything, and it lies just as much in their power to suspend or alter the normal physical course of things, to turn night into day or change the course of the heavenly bodies, as to intervene in human affairs, to change the results of battles, to destroy rulers, empires, and peoples, to set up one nation and throw down another, to pursue peoples or individuals with divine wrath or vengeance, to kill and to restore to life.

On this level of thought, so far as we can translate it adequately into modern terminology, nature is really contrasted with the supernatural and is both inferior to the latter and subject to the latter's constant control and capricious decrees. It may, for instance, be the nature of the sun to rise and revolve in a certain way but if God wishes he may upset this natural progression and cause the sun to stand still in order to achieve his particular purpose, as he did to aid Joshua to win his battle with the Amorites.[1] Nature, therefore, at best, is how things or peoples may normally be expected to be or behave, but as the supernatural may intervene at any stage it is the gods and the supernatural powers that must be looked to for the true explanation of the course of events both divine and human.

Few peoples attained an approach to nature differing essentially from that described above in general terms. Even the Chinese, for instance, despite their tremendous development in civilization and culture extending over many centuries, did not arrive at the notion of fixed physical laws of nature governing the universe. The Chinese did not accept the idea of a personal divine lawgiver who could lay down laws for the universe or for man, but relied rather on the idea of harmony as the governing principle. This harmony, in the realm of the physical world and in human affairs, was not to be attained by natural or positive law. It would either arise spontaneously or by dealing with the particular situaiton on its merits. There were therefore no pre-ordained laws in either sphere, but justice and harmony could be preserved if the appropriate ritual and customary observances were followed. It is for this reason, it has been suggested, that the Chinese never succeeded in developing a scientific outlook on the Western pattern, which presupposes the acceptance of pre-ordained causal laws.[2]

The example of the Chinese demonstrates that if the idea of the will of the gods as a perpetual and capricious force tends to diminish the status of nature in contrast with the supernatural, the link between God's will and nature may also under other conditions serve to place nature itself upon a pedestal. This development may be connected especially with the emphasis on monotheism in the Judaeo-Christian religions. For the elimination of polytheism served to remove much of the capriciousness of divine intervention and to substitute for it the notion of a divine pattern or purpose gradually being unfolded in human history. This in turn encouraged the belief in a natural order of things divine and human inexorably established by God's decree. God could thus be conceived as a divine lawgiver who has on the one hand laid down once for all the fixed order of the physical universe and on the other provided the laws to govern human affairs. It is true that scope still remained for occasional divine intervention, but these miraculous interpositions, frequently though they might occur, could still be treated as exceptional and not such as to interfere with the divine plan or ordering of the universe but rather indeed as in furtherance of that plan.

This new approach had a number of important consequences. It rendered possible the scientific approach to laws as fixed principles governing the physical world, though it was only at a much later date that the question of the source or origin of these laws came to be treated as a distinct question from their existence and operation, thus ruling off science from theology. It also put nature into the centre of the stage as a fixed order and one which was entitled to peculiar reverence, since it was God-given. Moreover it draws no clear line of demarcation between the unchangeable order of nature laid down by God for the functioning of the universe – as, for instance, the revolution of the earth and the planets round the sun, the position of the fixed stars, and so forth – and the pattern of human conduct equally laid down to all eternity as God's law to man.

THE EARLY GREEK PHILOSOPHERS

The scientific approach to nature also received a vital contribution from the so-called pre-Socratic philosophers. Although some of these were undoubtedly influenced by mystical and theological attitudes their main objective was to explore the world of nature in order to find some principle or principles governing the universe which would explain its structure and functioning. Such inquiries were partly what we would call nowadays philosophic speculation and partly scientific investigation, but their uniqueness lay in the fact that these philosophers did not just rely upon inspiration or intuition to guide their thought but believed rather in the power of human reason guided by observation to attain a true understanding of the world. Hence arose that belief in rationalism, that is, the idea that the universe is governed by intelligible laws capable of being grasped by the human mind, which has played so large a part in subsequent Western science and philosophy. Moreover this approach also had important consequences regarding man's place in the world, for since the universe was to be regarded as rational and man's reason partook of that rationality, it should be possible to determine rational principles to govern man's conduct both as an individual and in society.

This Greek tendency to seek for the structure of the world in terms of nature alone obviously conferred a peculiar aura on the natural order of things both in the realm of physics and in human affairs, for what was natural could be identified both with truth and rightness.

When, however, this reasoning was applied to human conduct difficulties immediately arose. By examining the course of physical bodies it might be possible to determine what natural law these should and did obey; but what was 'natural' for man himself? It could be argued for instance that nature enables the strong to prevail over the weak; is therefore the rule of the former over the latter what nature lays down as what is right for man? Or it could be argued that the attempt by each man to prevail over his weaker brethren can lead only to anarchy and therefore that nature requires, in the interests of self-preservation, that each man shall renounce his power to inflict harm on his neighbour, and that laws shall protect the weaker against the stronger. Again it could be said that there are really no rules governing human conduct which are natural to man since these differ markedly from community to community; therefore laws are a mere matter of conventional arrangement and there is nothing in nature which lays down what these laws should contain. Nature in man is no more than instinct and much of human law is directed not to giving scope to but rather to curbing man's instincts, for example, his sexual urges.

These and other opinions became part of the current coin of discussion in fifth-century Greece. An entirely new turn was given to the controversy by the two principle philosophers of the ancient Greek world, Plato and Aristotle.

PLATO AND ARISTOTLE

Plato's answer to these problems was in terms of his idealist philosophy. For him the direct experience of our senses is no more than a shadow world, a pale reflection of the reality which lies in the realm of absolutes beyond the ken of immediate sense-impressions. This somewhat mystic philosophy was, however, linked with a characteristically Hellenic belief in the power of rationalism, for Plato believed that it was possible for the wise man suitably educated in philosophy (his own, of course) to attain a vision of the perfect realm which lay beyond the world of the senses.

This idealist approach, which regarded the 'idea' as a kind of absolute thing-in-itself enjoying a higher degree of truth and reality than the mere physical appearances of an immediate world, was applied by Plato to the realm of moral as well as of physical phenomena. Indeed his most famous work, the *Republic*, is directed to expounding the 'idea' of justice so far as it can be grasped by the idealist philosophy. Justice is presented as a kind of absolute which can be apprehended only by the philosopher and can be fully realized only in an ideal state ruled by philosopher-kings. Justice as represented by the laws of particular states can amount at best to no more than a pale shadow of real justice. It is clear, therefore, that Plato has moved far from the position of his former master Socrates with his reverence for the laws of his native land. Yet Plato did not conceive the higher idea of justice as a form of law decreed by nature to which man-made law was subordinate. It is true that in his old age he endeavoured to show in detail in his book, the *Laws*, how an approximation to ideal justice might be realized by actual laws to be laid down for governing an actual state. But there was no question of regulating the validity of existing laws by such a set of ideal laws, which had indeed to be swallowed whole. Moreover Plato's static view of justice, like that of most Utopians, involved a totalitarian conception of law and government of the most rigid and inflexible kind.

Aristotle began as a pupil of Plato, though he gradually rejected the idealist philosophy of his teacher. Aristotle, while intensely concerned with theology, was also conspicuous for his attempt to develop the realms of knowledge in a scientific spirit, relying on observation and experience. As a naturalist, he arrived at a dynamic view of nature as the capacity for development inherent in particular things. This he expressed in terms of the end or purpose of a thing and, like Plato in this respect, he applied his approach to the phenomena of the moral as well as of the physical world. In the realm of human affairs Aristotle recognized that justice might be either conventional, varying from state to state according to the history and needs of particular communities; or natural, that is, common to all mankind, because based on the fundamental end or purpose of man as a social or political being. Aristotle does not however enlarge greatly on this theme, though he makes the important observation that though among the gods nothing can change, among human beings everything is subject to change, including even natural justice.

One contrast emerges between the Platonic and the Aristotelian positions which was to prove of great importance in natural-law thinking right up to the present time. The notion of natural justice or natural law may, broadly speaking, take up two divergent attitudes towards 'nature' as a conception. On the one hand, nature may be looked upon as an ideal expressing the fundamental aspiration of man if his full potentialities are attained. On the other hand, nature may be regarded as simply the way man behaves by reason of his psycho-physical make-up. In the former view nature operates normatively as an ideal standard against which the non-natural or purely conventional may be measured. The latter is more essentially factual, being based on a study of man as he actually is, rather than as speculation or intuition might conceive him as capable of becoming ideally. Yet at the same time even the second view contains implicitly a normative element because, in examining man's actual behaviour, some standard will inevitably have to be applied in order to decide what is natural and what is non-natural to man. For this purpose various criteria may be adopted such as health, physical or mental well-being, or, on the social plane, things like social harmony or welfare. But all such conceptions involve values of various kinds and therefore are intrinsically normative in character.

From the point of view of eliciting the content of natural law, however, there is still a good deal of difference between the approach which regards such a law as purely an ideal standard to be elicited by reasoning, revelation, intuition, or some such process, and the factual approach which starts primarily from man's behaviour. For the latter is likely to regard as the best evidence of what is natural for the governance of man in society the rules and standards which are found to be common to mankind in all types of society. If, therefore, such a natural law exists at all, comparative study of humanity may be expected to provide important clues to its content. The former view, however, has often, as in Plato, tended towards a purely idealistic view of natural law as something which may be glimpsed by rational intuition and yet may never have been and perhaps never will be realized upon this earth.

It will be found that most later conceptions of natural law have oscillated between these two differing ideas of nature as fact or as ideal, frequently seeking to derive some sustenance from each of these approaches. Indeed in Aristotle we can already see signs of the blurring of the two approaches, factual, in so far as he regards natural justice as based on rules actually common to mankind, yet ideal, in so far as he regards as natural to man that which best enables him to fulfil his purposes as a social being.

THE STOIC PHILOSOPHY

The subsequent history of natural law owes a great deal to the stoic philosophy which arose after Aristotle. Although Aristotle had referred to natural justice as common to all men, his conception of ideal justice as well as Plato's was essentially linked with the idea of the relatively small Greek city-state. So far indeed was Aristotle from thinking in terms of universal law governing all men alike in virtue of their common humanity, that he justified slavery as a natural institution based on the fact that some men are slaves by nature. Ideal justice at best was something which could apply to free Greeks but not to slaves or barbarians. With the break-down of the old Greek world of independent city-states due to the conquests of Alexander the Great, a less exclusive view began to prevail in Greek philosophy. Two principal doctrines arose, the Epicurean and the Stoic. The former had much in common with utilitarian positivism, which will be discussed in the next chapter. Stoicism on the other hand stressed the universality of human nature and the brotherhood of man. An important feature of this doctrine was its emphasis on reason as the essential characteristic of humanity.[3] Accordingly when in the later

Stoicism the doctrine of the two laws was propounded – that is, the law of a man's city, the *polis*, and the law of the universal city, the *cosmopolis* – the latter was regarded as a purely rational law and as such entitled to claim moral superiority over the local and conventional rules governing particular states. For the Stoics therefore there was a universal law of nature ascertainable by reason which provided a touchstone for determining the justice of man-made laws. It was not as yet adduced, however, that conflict between the two must result in the rejection of the latter in favour of the former.

This later Stoicism coincided with the spread of Roman power over the Mediterranean world, and the philosophical speculations of the Stoics became associated, though by no means identified, with an important Roman legal conception, that of the *jus gentium*, the law which was applied in the Roman state both to the Romans themselves and to foreigners. The idea of a common law applicable to all mankind, at least within the confines of the very extensive Roman world, clearly afforded some concrete shape to the hitherto rather abstract Stoic conception of a universal law of nature. The Roman lawyers, however, made little or no direct use of the idea of natural law, though references to this idea, both in the corpus of Roman juristic writings and in those of rhetorical writers such as Cicero, provided the vehicle by which the natural-law speculation of antiquity was passed on to later ages.

CHRISTIANITY AND NATURAL LAW

The extent and peacefulness of the Roman *imperium* in its heyday allowed the spread not only of the universalizing doctrines of Stoic natural law and of the *jus gentium* but also of the new universal faith of Christianity. It was really the combination of Christian theology, working upon a substratum of Greek philosophy and Roman law, that fused into the medieval scholastic doctrine of natural law, which has played so important a part in the legal philosophy of the West ever since.

One great difficulty was however inherent in the Christian approach to law and was only overcome by a long and painful process. The Judaic view of law, as we have seen, was that it represents God's will on earth. Accordingly it was supremely good. The early Christians however were taught to despise the things of this earth and to expect the destruction of the world and the ultimate reign of God's kingdom. Hence while the earthly rulers had to be obeyed until they were overthrown by God's decree, earthly laws were mere evils arising out of man's sinfulness, which derived from the Fall of Man. Therefore although the early Christians took up the Stoic belief in the brotherhood of man they were indifferent to the idea of a universal law of reason upon this earth. The impact of Christianity on Platonism is revealed in St Augustine's famous work, *The City of God*, in the fourth century, where he equates the Platonic realm of ideal justice with the conception of the City of God on earth, when Christian justice will at last reign supreme.

At the same time Christian writers recognized that even in the imperfect states of this world there was need for justice as decreed by God. 'Without justice,' remarks St Augustine himself, 'what is a state but a robber-band?'[4] Such justice is really a part of divine law, which God has laid down to govern mankind so long as our sinful earthly existence endures. It is therefore part of the divine order of things, though an inferior form of that ultimate divine justice which will reign in the City of God. All such human institutions as law, property, and slavery are imperfect on account of sin but still form part of the necessary order of things here below. Natural law is thus equated with divine law, partly miraculously revealed, and partly ascertainable by reason, but the defects in man's existing nature due to sin call for a natural law which lacks many of the features of ideal justice. At the same time the link-up between natural law and Christian theology vastly increased its authority compared with that of the older Stoic law of nature. For natural law was now imposed by God and was expounded by the head of the Catholic Church, the Pope, who, as the Vicar of God, was

invested with the power to expound and interpret the law
of God, which was binding on all men, rulers and ruled
alike. Hence we see the idea gaining currency that mere
human law is subordinate to natural law and moreover
cannot stand if it conflicts with it. Furthermore machinery
now existed, in the power of the Pope and the Catholic
hierarchy, not only to expound that law so that all men
might know what it permitted or prohibited, but also to
require kings and emperors (as the mere secular arm of the
spiritual order) to recognize and enforce its decrees. Also
the Church could impose its own ecclesiastical sanctions,
especially the drastic one of excommunication.

AQUINAS AND SCHOLASTICISM

An important element of Catholic philosophy in the later
Middle Ages was the re-discovery of Aristotle's writings
(though in a rather garbled form through Arabic sources)
and the attempt to assimilate these into the fabric of Christian
theology. Thus was created scholasticism, of which the
supreme exponent was St Thomas Aquinas. St Thomas,
under the influence of Aristotle's view of man as achieving
his natural development in a political society, rejected the
earlier notion that law and government were rooted in sin
and therefore necessarily imperfect. A distinction had to be
made between divine law, which could be known only by
revelation, and natural law, which was wholly rational and
which could be understood and interpreted by the light of
unaided human reason. The scholastic philosophy was thus
a highly rationalistic one in the sense that it relied heavily
on truth as elicited by logic and deductive reasoning, but at
the same time its premises were not chosen on rational
grounds but were given by the beliefs of Christian theology.
Rationalism could thus dispute the validity of inferences
drawn from these premises but could not venture to reject
the premises themselves. The Inquisition was a perpetual
reminder of the limits of rationalism, whether scientific or
merely heretical.

Aquinas set the pattern of modern natural-law thinking in another vital respect. Natural law was not a system of rules which covered the whole sphere of human affairs. There were many matters which needed regulation by law and yet which were morally indifferent, as Aristotle had pointed out. The rule of the road affords a typical instance, for the important thing is to insist on adhering to one side, but it is morally indifferent which is chosen. Moreover Aquinas recognizes that nature was not an absolutely rigid conception, so that certain parts of natural law (admittedly not very clearly defined) were destructible and could be replaced to meet the exigencies of changed conditions.

Human law then was at last fully reinstated as entitled to play a major role in human government, both by filling the gaps left by natural law, and by developing further the implications of natural-law rules in relation to the many intricacies of human relations for which natural law has not directly legislated but merely provided a general guide. But what if human law were found to conflict with the dictates of natural law? In such a case human law was clearly overridden, but Aquinas remained ambiguous on how the subject was to act when his ruler imposed upon him a legal obligation contrary to natural law. On the whole Aquinas seemed to think that obedience might still have to be rendered in order to avoid scandal and disorder, and that it should be left to God to resolve the situation in his own way.

THE RENAISSANCE AND SECULAR NATURAL LAW

The new humanism which emerged from the Italy of the fifteenth century carried important implications for the future history of legal thinking. While the Catholic Church adhered to the scholastic philosophy, a new scientific approach arose which largely ignored or evaded the claims of theology and concentrated on observation and experiment aided by human reason. The Reformation in countries under Calvinist influence saw an attempt to re-create the theocracy of the Old Testament, under which the priests directly interpreted God's will for the governance of mankind. Ultimately, however, the Reformation, with its emphasis on national Churches controlled by the state, led to a secular revolution in which the new scientific approach became dominant.

This new age, far from leading to the rejection of natural law, may be regarded as the Golden Age of the law of nature, and endured until the end of the eighteenth century. The whole emphasis now was placed on the rational character of natural law. It may be, in the remote sense that God created the world and everything in it, that natural law was God-given, but even this was not essential, for Grotius, one of the leading exponents of the law of nature and the founder of international law on a natural-law basis, argued that natural law would still apply even if God did not exist. This was because the unique quality of man lay in his reason and this rational element is shared by all mankind. Hence reason dictated a rational order in human affairs, an order which could be elicited by reasoning alone, and which, at any rate in broad outline, should operate everywhere. A system of natural law could therefore be rationally constructed which could be regarded as universally valid. It is true that on the plane of national law this approach had comparatively little effect save among theoretical jurists, though it did ultimately lead to important attempts at codification, of which the French Civil Code of 1804 was the most conspicuous product. In the field of international relations, however, the idea prevailed that the independent nations were in a state of nature towards each other and were therefore governed by natural law. In this way the seeds of the modern view that the relations of states *inter se* should be governed by international law became gradually established.

What was the relation of this new, secular, purely rationalistic, natural law to human law? The position remained, as may be suspected, somewhat ill-defined. Human law should give effect to natural law and might be presumed to do so unless a conflict was clear, which was very rarely the case, since there was little agreement as to the actual tenets of the law of nature. Theoretically, in a case of conflict natural law prevailed, so that the great English Chief Justice, Sir Edward Coke – who with patriotic zeal regarded the common law of England as the embodiment of human reason and therefore co-terminous with natural law – was able to declare that the common law could even treat a statute as void if contrary to reason.[5] This was, however, never really a practical doctrine either in this country or elsewhere, though Blackstone paid lip-service to it as late as the eighteenth century. More important for national law was the contribution of natural-law thinking in developing law as a rational scientific body of rules designed to achieve justice in the prevailing social and economic conditions. This created a spirit which was hostile to archaic and feudal survivals in law, but it must be admitted that in the absence of revolutionary upheavals the process of ridding European law of these excrescences was a painfully slow one. In this respect, however, the new secular natural law possessed within itself certain revolutionary implications which bore fruit, especially in the United States and France.

NATURAL LAW AND NATURAL RIGHTS

Although the earlier natural law was a distinctly conservative force encouraging obedience to established rulers who enjoyed authority by reason of a natural order decreed ultimately by God himself, there was nothing inherent in natural-law thinking which compelled support of monarchy or existing rulers. Even in the Middle Ages such writers as Marsilio of Padua argued from natural-law premisses in favour of democracy not only in the state but even in the Catholic Church. After the Renaissance such arguments became more pervasive. The notion gradually gained currency that man possessed certain fundamental rights in a state of nature, and that when civil society came into being he took over those rights into his newly gained civil status and these still remained protected by natural law. In England, Locke gave this approach a valuable impetus by arguing that by the terms of the social contract (which most writers of this period regarded as the origin, at least in theory, of civil society) the power of government was conceded only on trust by the people to the rulers, and that any infringement by the latter of the fundamental natural rights of the people put an end to the trust and entitled the people to re-assume their authority.

This view of natural rights clearly depended upon belief in the existence of natural law, for such rights could only be valid and binding by reason of the law of nature. None the less, a distinct change of emphasis emerged, for in the past natural law was largely conceived as imposing duties and prohibitions whereas now it was looked to as the source of fundamental democratic rights restricting the freedom of rulers, hitherto treated as enjoying virtually absolute authority. The American Revolution was strongly influenced by Locke's philosophy. The United States Constitution is essentially a natural-law document setting out the fundamental authority of the people under natural law and guaranteeing the natural rights of the citizens. This Constitution indeed, carried a large part of the heritage of natural law into the modern world, even at a time when natural-law ideas were tending to wane. Not only did it indelibly associate that law with the idea of liberty but it also enshrined the unique idea, so influential in modern times, that natural rights could be the subject of legal guarantees and that these could be adjudicated upon like any other rights and duties conferred or imposed by secular law. Moreover, because they were embodied in the Constitution, these rights were given a special priority which enabled the courts to treat them as superior to and thus prevailing over any legislation or other legal rule which conflicted with them. Thus was created for the first time an actual machinery whereby natural rights might be brought into the fabric of the law and enjoy recognition and enforcement as legal rights.

The other important influence on the revolutionary consequences of natural law was that of Rousseau. Rousseau, however, started from different premises from those of Locke. For Rousseau natural law, far from creating imprescriptible natural rights in favour of individuals, conferred absolute and inalienable authority on the people as a whole, who were regarded for this purpose as constituting a somewhat vague and mystically conceived entity, the 'general will', which differed from the mere sum of the individual wills of the citizens. This general will was, by natural law, the sole and unfettered legal authority in the state, and any actual ruler was such only by delegation and could be removed whenever rejected by the general will. This doctrine was, from one point of view, a good deal more revolutionary than that of Locke, since it implied that the people were the real rulers and could overthrow at their discretion any reigning monarch. It was in the light of this philosophy that the French revolutionaries ultimately overthrew the *ancien régime* and sought to impose the natural law of reason in its place. Unfortunately, however, at this point the limitations of Rousseau's doctrine became apparent for it enabled almost any demagogue who could seize power to claim that he represented the 'general will' and so impose his authority. Moreover even in a properly organized democracy Rousseau's approach really implied little but the tyranny of the majority: the recalcitrant minority, in Rousseau's ominous phrase, must be 'forced to be free'.[6] Nor was there any provision in this system for natural rights to be retained by individuals to protect them against the authority of the state itself. And the mystic character of the 'general will' as an entity distinct from the citizens also enabled this doctrine to be assimilated to the later Hegelian idea of the deification of the state as an entity more rational and more 'real' than the mere citizens which composed it.[7] Thus, ironically enough, Rousseauism, which arose out of a faith in democracy and liberty, became an instrument of totalitarianism.

MODERN APPROACHES TO NATURAL LAW

The nineteenth century witnessed the nadir of the natural-law school. Its place was largely taken by legal positivism which was closely connected with the rise of scientific positivism (which we shall discuss in the next chapter) and by the historical school which was linked, at least in its German form, with Hegelianism.[8] Various forces doubtless combined to dampen enthusiasm for natural law; significant among these were undoubtedly the reaction against the excesses of rationalism in the eighteenth-century philosophy of the Enlightenment, as well as the feeling that natural law was devoid of any scientific or empirical basis and that it ignored the vital role of historical processes in the development of law. In addition, the association of natural rights of the people (if not of individuals as such) with the French revolutionary upheaval gave this doctrine what may be called a 'bolshevik' flavour for the reactionary ruling circles of the early nineteenth century.

Nevertheless the natural-law idea was by no means extinguished (indeed it seems to possess almost inextinguishable powers of survival) and in our own century it has manifested itself in a variety of forms. It has also, owing to the impact of the horrors of the two world wars and their barbarous accompaniments, shown signs of a distinct revival. A little will first be said here about the main types of natural-law theory encountered in our own day and then something of the character and significance of the more recent revival of natural law, especially on the continent of Europe and in America.

Theories of natural law may be conveniently divided into the three categories of Catholic, philosophical, and sociological. Catholic theories, which remain especially influential in countries where the Catholic Church exerts considerable authority, still take the form laid down by St Thomas Aquinas, though the attempts to adapt his tenets to the conditions of modern times are usually referred to as neo-

Thomism. The philosophical forms of natural law have been prominent on the Continent and have generally taken the form of neo-Kantism, that is attempts to develop Kant's view of the realm of the moral law. Kant treated this as involving the categorical imperative that we should always act so that our norm of conduct might be translated into a universal law. This imperative Kant held to be a principle whose absolute truth was known by intuition but it remained a formal principle without specific content. Neo-Kantian legal philosophers, such as Stammler and del Vecchio, have striven to deduce by logical principles a fabric of actual rules which they hold to be implicit in Kant's universal law. Stammler, however, has recognized that such rules cannot be immutable in all times and conditions and his approach has been described as 'natural law with a variable content'. This sort of philosophical approach, with its undue emphasis on logic, has had little if any appeal in common-law countries with their leaning towards empirical solutions.

Both the types of theory already referred to may be said to take an idealist view of natural law, treating nature as something imposing an ideal standard and resting largely on rather arbitrary assumptions about man's common rationality. The sociological theory of natural law, on the other hand, adopts a more factual approach. The important development here has been an attempt to apply scientific methods derived from the emergent social sciences in order to elicit the primary data of man's fundamental drives, urges, or needs, and the norms of conduct which may be shown to be inseparable from the realizing of these human factors in society. The strong emphasis on the social sciences in the United States has led to a greater development in this sort of approach in America than elsewhere. Here we see natural law being defended against the attacks of positivism by using weapons out of the armoury of positivism itself. The further discussion of the validity of this attempt to justify natural law scientifically may thus most conveniently be considered later in the context of positivism.[9]

It should be added that it is quite common at the present

day for distinguished lawyers to express in public addresses a general approval of natural law, but these assertions tend to be so vague that they are more in the nature of rhetorical flourishes, rather in the manner of the ancient Roman orators, than a serious attempt to give content to natural-law thinking and assess its potential contribution to law in the modern world.

THE POST-WAR REVIVAL OF NATURAL LAW

The reasons for the more recent revival of natural law are not hard to seek. The rise of Nazi and Fascist dictatorships, the spread of totalitarianism, the appalling savagery of the massacre of millions of innocent people in the name of racial ideology, and the deliberate repudiation by large and powerful nations of all the norms of morality and culture which have been regarded as the indispensable elements in human civilization have led to much heart-searching and re-examination of the principles of human law and government. Can it really be true, as the positivists so consistently urged, that human law must be regarded as valid and entitled to obedience whatever its moral content and to whatever extent it imposes conduct contrary to all received moral or civilized standards?

These questions became particularly acute in the aftermath of the overthrow of Nazism in Germany. In the trials of the Nazi leaders by the International Tribunal at Nuremberg, as in the more recent trial of Eichmann in Israel, consideration had necessarily to be given to the position of those responsible for organized massacres in concentration camps which were carried out under the laws of their own state. Is there a higher law which could render such acts punishable whatever might be the decrees of the particular state to which the accused owed allegiance? Clearly a natural-law approach might seem to afford a way out of this kind of dilemma. However, a certain reluctance to base actual decisions on this rather nebulous foundation tended to cause such proceedings to seek a more solid legal basis. Thus the Nuremberg trials were treated, rightly or wrongly, as a development of customary international law. The historical foundations of that law in natural-law theory undoubtedly played a part in rendering such a development respectable in the eyes of many statesmen and lawyers as well as of the informed public at large. Again, the Eichmann trial was based on an actual Israeli law passed retrospectively, though many of its provisions, such as those dealing with 'crimes against humanity', had a distinctly natural-law ring about them.

The newly constituted Federal German Republic has also had to wrestle with the problem of the validity of former Nazi laws in relation to situations which occurred during the Nazi régime. Should, for example, an accused man be entitled to rely upon a flagrantly immoral law as legal justification for having caused grave injury to another? Cases have occurred, for instance, of one spouse having denounced the other to the Gestapo for anti-Nazi sentiments expressed in privacy; should it now be treated as a defence that the denouncing spouse was only acting under the compulsion of Nazi law? Some German courts have shown an inclination to resolve this type of case on a natural-law footing, though more generally they have avoided this in favour of other solutions, such as interpreting the Nazi law in a sense unfavourable to the accused.[10]

It has to be borne in mind that in the nineteenth century when natural law was at so low an ebb, there existed a substitute for it – a deeply rooted belief in human progress, both material and moral, and a firm conviction that the established blessings of civilization were being consolidated and gradually spread universally among mankind. Whether or not, therefore, human laws could be said to rest upon the basis of the law of nature, those laws could still be assumed to be aiming so far as practicable at the realization of man's higher purposes in their social context. Admittedly discordant voices were already being heard, such as that of Nietszche, doubting the whole fabric of traditional morality and wishing to transform morals into the cult of the superman; or at the other end of the scale, the cult of Tolstoyism, repudiating all law and government in favour of a personal vision of the duties of primitive Christianity. These, and similar views, were signs of the new irrationalism which was beginning to invade every aspect of human society as a re-action to the rationalistic and scientific empiricism of the eighteenth and nineteenth centuries. Readers of Thomas Mann's masterly novel, *The Magic Mountain,* first published in 1926, will recollect how in the discussions between the ex-Jesuit, Naphta, and the Italian child of the Enlightenment, Settembrini, the forces of rationalism and irrationalism are weighed against each other with so inconclusive an out-come. But both natural law and positivism have shared in their different ways a belief in rationalism and this no doubt accounted for the relatively smooth transition in the nine-teenth century from natural-law rationalism to the rational belief (as it was then widely assumed to be) in the law of human progress. It is rather in this century with the over-whelming development of anti-rational ideologies, such as Nazism and Fascism,[11] that the rational faith in natural law has felt the urge to re-assert itself, though it has chosen for this purpose as its main opponent the belief in positivism, which is equally founded, as we shall see, in rationalist assumptions. Nevertheless this counter-attack of natural law upon positivism is by no means illogical since it was positiv-ism which historically played an important part in under-mining its authority.

THE RELEVANCE OF NATURAL LAW TO THE MODERN WORLD

What can be said at the present day for or against natural-law thinking must be postponed until we have had an opportunity to review the background and present status of positivist thought in relation to legal theory. But the question still remains, what actual contribution this doctrine has made to the legal and moral problems of the modern world and whether it has a particular relevance, as many appear to think, to the acute conflicts which affect mankind at the present day both in the sphere of national and international affairs and, indeed, even in outer space.

It has already been pointed out that the natural-law idea received one of its most fruitful developments in the incorporation of a Bill of Human Rights in the written constitution of the United States, with the result that such rights have been given not only a specific content but also legal recognition. Undoubtedly this owed much to natural law in its inception; and moreover natural law has often been invoked in the interpretation of such schemes of natural rights both in America and elsewhere.[12] All the same, once a scale of values is accepted and duly incorporated in specific legal provisions in a constitutional code, the judicial authorities will have to construe and interpret these provisions just as with any other legislation, though admittedly they will probably seek to do this in as broad a manner as possible, giving full weight to the spirit rather than the letter of the constitution. It is difficult to see how such interpretation can be materially assisted by further reference to the vague and disputable content of a system of higher law whose very existence is open to question and whose actual dictates have either been correctly stated in the code (in which case they are of no further relevance) or they have been incorrectly stated, in which case they are equally irrelevant. For the duty of the judges will be to interpret the actual constitution and not their own conception of some higher system of law from which they may or may not believe it to be derived.

Apart from constitutionally guaranteed rights, there are many other claims that are made for natural law. Some sponsors of this doctrine are prepared to attribute every recourse by a legal rule to such notions as what is reasonable, fair, or just, or whether something has been done in good faith, as resting on a foundation of natural law. But there seems no reason why legal systems, which all need to employ conceptions of this kind, should imply more by their use than reference to certain norms prevailing in the community, without reference to the remoter concept of a higher law superior to human law and binding on all mankind. It is true that there are cases where a legal system may invoke 'natural justice'; for instance, English law may set aside a decision of a domestic tribunal (such as that of a trade union, a club, or a professional association expelling one of its members) if the decision is contrary to natural justice, or may refuse to enforce a foreign judgment on this account. But this phrase really means no more than the need to comply with certain standards which English law (reflecting to the extent to which it does established English norms of behaviour) considers essential. A fair hearing is thus obligatory in the case of expulsion of a member from his club or trade union, [13] and a foreign judgment will not be recognized which was obtained by fraud or without due notice being served on the defendant. [14] Here again such rules do not necessarily presuppose the existence of a higher law either to explain or justify the attitude of English law, which is entitled to and does form its own view of what justice requires.

What then of those grave and uncertain problems which lie on the borders of law and morals and which create so much doubt, controversy, and perplexity? The law is obliged to require some solution to problems concerning human life – for instance, euthanasia, suicide, and abortion – either by prohibiting or permitting them, with or without conditions. Again, whether the law should impose or forbid capital punishment creates acute moral controversy. These are exceedingly difficult and delicate moral problems which impose severe strains on any legal system and many arguments moral, social, practical, and juristic can be adduced for or against permitting acts of these kinds. However it seems in the highest degree doubtful whether reference to a higher moral or natural law affords any real assistance in such controversy, so long as there remains no agreement either as to its existence or its actual content. Who is to say for instance whether natural law does or does not prohibit abortion or capital punishment? Of course if all mankind accepted one authoritative body as the expounder or interpreter of this law, such as the Catholic Church, the answer to this problem would be ready-made, though it could still be pointed out that this solution would really only substitute one system of legislation for another. Since the Reformation, however, there has seemed but little prospect of this occurring, and indeed in our own day the division of the world by the Iron Curtain makes this appear even more improbable.

Can it be said, when we turn to the international sphere, that the existence of many conflicting systems of law, of competing nations all asserting their individual needs and claims, demands that we recognize some higher system of justice by which all these sources of conflict could be satisfactorily resolved? The need for some such system has never appeared more vital than in the present state of the world with its division into so many conflicting regions, factions, and ideologies. Moreover the recent intrusions into outer space and the possibility in the relatively near future of interplanetary travel stresses the imperative need for some rational way of developing an international society and establishing its standards of conduct to meet the requirements of peace, justice, and human welfare. To state the existence of the problem, however, is not to postulate the availability of any ready-made solution in the way that some natural lawyers seem to think. International law has attained so far only a relatively primitive stage of development compared with the legal systems of many national states, but it does aim, in a gradual and piecemeal way, at achieving solutions to these problems by a variety of methods. These include developing existing rules (e.g. the traditional rules regarding the freedom of the seas might be applied with modifications to outer space); creating new rules by means of international treaties to which most if not all civilized nations adhere; and by the creation of new international institutions, such as the United Nations and the Permanent Court of International Justice. This system of rules, ill-developed though it may be, owes a good deal historically to a general belief in a rational and universal law of nature. However, it is not easy to see how the problems which beset the international community can be materially assisted by reference to a vague system embodying a higher order of justice whose actual dictates can neither be identified nor authoritatively interpreted by any human power. How, for instance, does it help to assert that natural law decrees that outer space shall be free? For not only does this precept mean very little without a detailed code of specific rules, which could hardly be said to be dictated by natural law, but it is scarcely conceivable that even the broad proposition itself would be accepted unless the most powerful nations of the world were satisfied that it was expedient and desirable in their national interests to accept it. Accordingly an effective role for natural law seems as dubious on the international as on the national plane.

Perhaps the final test of the usefulness of natural law as a means of resolving the tensions between law and morality arises in those contexts where one section of a community is imposing a régime of terror or oppression on another section in pursuance of an ideology. Such situations have arisen in the modern world in Nazi Germany, where a majority oppressed and sought to destroy a distinctive minority of the population, or in South Africa, where in this instance a white minority, possessed of all the positions of command, military, social, economic, and governmental, directs its laws towards the perpetual subordination of the black majority, with the declared aim of preserving white civilization. In such contexts it is often urged that natural law alone can resolve the legal predicament. But before examining this crucial type of case, it is necessary first to put the standpoint of positivism before the reader.

Legal Positivism

PHYSICAL AND NORMATIVE LAWS

Although there are traces in earlier periods of what might be
regarded in modern terminology as a positivist approach –
for instance the views of the great rivals to the Stoics, the
Epicurean school – the real impetus in this direction can be
traced to the Renaissance with its emphasis on the secular
studies of science and humanism. The empiricism associated
with observation as a means of ascertaining the laws of
science was attended with increasingly spectacular achievements and cast its influence over every field of human endeavour. In England a strong movement was set on foot,
which is still far from exhausted, to base philosophical speculation on a more solid and empirical basis comparable in
method to that which had attained such success in the realm
of pure science. Inspired by the sceptical beginnings formulated by Descartes, this movement was given powerful
impetus by John Locke and his successors, of whom the most
important was David Hume.

One outcome of this movement was of particular significance for legal and moral philosophy. This was a clear demarcation between the laws of the physical universe, which
were regarded as governing the behaviour of all physical
entities, animate or in-animate, human or non-human, in
accordance with the inexorable principle of physical caus-
ation; and normative laws, legal, moral, or of any other kind,
which laid down norms of human conduct.

Until the eighteenth century no clear line was drawn
between the physical laws which dealt with propositions
about the world, and which could be refuted by empirical
evidence showing their non-applicability, and normative
rules laying down standards of human conduct. As indicated

in the previous chapter, the theological background of natural law, which interpreted both physical and moral laws as traceable to God's will, effectively blurred this distinction, for if either could be attributed to an act of divine volition there was no difference in kind between them.

'Is' and 'Ought'

Hume pointed out that there are really two realms of human inquiry, one in the field of facts, which is concerned with what is actually the case, and whose proposition can be treated as either true or false, and the other in the field of 'ought' – that is, what ought to be the case. Hume argued that we cannot ever demonstrate what ought to be, for instance, the rule of moral behaviour, as an inference from something that is in fact the case. This we can see clearly if we consider the simple illustration of a world in which capital punishment has always been inflicted. This is a fact, but its existence in no way compels us to infer that we ought to permit capital punishment or precludes us from querying the morality of such a practice. It has become common in modern terminology to refer to those subjects which deal with 'ought' propositions – that is, which do not state facts but lay down what 'ought' to be done – as 'normative', and the actual propositions of such subjects are often called 'norms', referring to standards of conduct. This convenient terminology will be adopted in this work.

Hume's discussion was principally concerned to distinguish between fact and moral obligation. It is clear, however, that although important distinctions exist between human law and morals, as has already been explained, human law shares with morals the characteristic feature of being normative, since it lays down rules of conduct rather than stating facts. For instance a rule of law that murder is prohibited and punishable by death does not state a fact as to the behaviour of persons subject to the law, who may still continue to commit the acts described in the law as murder. Nor does it predict the conduct of the authorities of the state, since many murders may be committed with impunity. What the law does is to lay down standards or norms of conduct for citizens or officials and (usually) to indicate what sanction should or ought (as a matter of law) to follow a breach of the provisions. Such a law therefore does not state any facts as such, but neither is it in any way refuted (as is a physical law) by its breach or non-observance. Law, however, differs from moral norms in this further respect that it calls for a certain measure of regularity of observance, for without this feature it would hardly be entitled to rank as law at all. A moral rule on the other hand may still be held to be valid even if it is never or scarcely ever observed: for instance, the rule that we should love our neighbours as ourselves. This distinction, moreover, does not apply solely to rules of what may be termed the 'higher morality', for in considering the ordinary moral code of a community the position may well be similar. For instance a community may well acknowledge rules of sexual morality as valid even though such rules are more honoured in the breach than in the observance. It is clear therefore that law raises rather special problems as to the circumstances in which we would regard an individual law as binding, for instance, where it has become totally disregarded with the passage of time, and also the circumstances in which we might treat a whole legal system as invalid, either because it has been superseded by revolution, or on account of the virtual anarchy or lawlessness which reigns in the territory.[1]

The demarcation between 'is' and 'ought' also carried with it serious implications for natural-law thinking since it seemed to dispose of the idea that the truth of particular rules of natural law could be demonstrated, even if the rules were shown to be universally observed. Natural law thus began to look not like a higher system of law or justice whose truth was self-evident or demonstrable by reason, but rather like a mere pretentious name for moral rules. And the justification for such rules of morality was, as Hume indicated, to be sought in certain ends or aims of human life which were determined not by reason at all but by the desires of mankind, or what Hume designated as 'the passions'. Hume, who rejected natural law, made various suggestions as to the way in which the human passions come to create moral norms. But the question remained whether any rational standard could be found which could provide the means of judging between right and wrong. If such a standard could be found then it might provide a substitute for natural law, though with important differences, as we shall see. Kant attempted at the end of the century to provide an answer to Hume by recognizing the two realms of 'is' and 'ought', but asserting that the latter contained the absolute rule of morality which he called the 'categorical imperative'. The difficulty with this principle was that not only was it not provable – or at least it was unproved (*pace* Kant) – but that it failed to provide an effective test for the actual solution of particular problems.

There was, nevertheless, another line of approach which was very much in the air in the eighteenth century and this was the principle of utility. It fell particularly to Jeremy Bentham to develop and popularize the principle which became so influential in the nineteenth century. And it was from the seeds sown by his school of utilitarians that much of the later harvest of the legal positivists was reaped.

THE UTILITARIANS

The idea of the utilitarians was that the behaviour of mankind was dominated by the influence of pain and pleasure. By increasing pleasure and diminishing pain human happiness would be extended. Utility therefore really meant no more than what served to increase human happiness, the sum of which was to be assessed by calculating the stock of pleasure and pain which resulted from a particular course of action. For this purpose numerical standards were adopted, each man's happiness being considered the equal in value of that of any other man, so that the test of utility was what served the happiness of the largest possible number. Bentham's principle was aimed at 'maximizing' human happiness according to the slogan 'the greatest happiness of the greatest number'. Although Bentham rejected natural law with scorn – for him natural rights were not just nonsense, but 'nonsense upon stilts' – he was nothing if not a rationalist in the spirit of the Enlightenment, and his arguments in favour of utility were based squarely on the fact that human reason could find no other rational justification for preferring one course to another. Ironically, Bentham's own principle that one man's happiness was of equal worth to another's, owed much to the widely established 'natural' right to equality. Moreover, as Bentham himself conceded, the principle of utility was itself a metaphysical principle whose truth could not be demonstrated for 'what is used to prove everything else cannot itself be proved'.[2] But Bentham was not so much concerned with establishing the philosophical unassailability of his principle as with showing how it would work in practice, though he also appeals in support of it to the experience of mankind, whose conduct has been universally moved by the twin factors of pain and pleasure which lay at the roots of his system.

Despite a certain naïveté in his belief that happiness could be virtually quantified in almost arithmetical terms, Bentham's work laid a solid juridical foundation for much of that reform of the law which was one of the most crying needs of the early nineteenth century. The notion of utility might, as was perceived by Bentham's follower, John Stuart Mill, be less easy to maintain philosophically than his master fondly believed, and of less universal scope in the fields of morals and aesthetics, but still it provided an impressive rationalization of the factors which were increasingly accepted by liberal thinkers as the goal of legal and social reform. For after all, in an age of progress, what purpose could appear more self-evident than that of increasing the sum of happiness of the population as a whole, though there remained infinite scope for disagreement as to what means might most effectively attain that end?

THE MOVE TO LEGAL POSITIVISM

The utilitarian school provided not so much the necessary

logical foundation but rather the appropriate climate for the move towards legal positivism. This had two aspects, both of which must be referred to here. First, the firm distinction between law as it *is* and as it *ought to be*; and second, the tendency to treat law as a *science* deserving to be ranked with the other sciences both in its aims and its methods.

LAW AS IT IS AND AS IT OUGHT TO BE

Bentham linked his discussion of morals in terms of utility, and his rejection of all natural-law thinking, with the firm conviction that law could only be properly understood if it was treated as an autonomous field of study free from all issues of morals, religion, and the like. The great criticism of natural law was not only that such a law was really mythical (except to those who accepted a certain type of theology and even among them there was no agreement as to its actual precepts) but that it led to muddled thinking by confusing legal with moral issues. Whether a rule was law within a given state was a purely juristic question to be decided by those criteria which the particular legal system accepted. This was a completly different question from that which might be raised by those who were considering whether the law as established was good or bad. What the law is, and what the law ought to be, are entirely different issues and each is the proper subject-matter of inquiry of a distinct field of study which Bentham himself designated as expository and censorial jurisprudence (or the science of legislation) respectively. It follows that in deciding whether a legal rule is valid or not, the point whether it is good or bad, just or unjust, is irrelevant, since these questions are concerned with the moral worth or expediency of the legal rule which remains none the less legal, whether good or bad.

It must not be thought, as some critics of positivism have suggested, that what Bentham and his followers were here asserting was that law and morals are totally unrelated or that a bad law is just as deserving of obedience as a good one. Indeed this would have been a patent absurdity, especially for Bentham himself, whose whole active life was devoted to ridiculing the then state of English law, attacking the complacency of the legal profession and the ruling class in England, and pressing strenuously for reform of the law in all its branches. There have been writers, the best-known of whom is probably Thomas Hobbes, who have sought to argue that whatever the law decrees is synonymous with morality. This opinion, however, had little influence and certainly no school rejected it more decisively than the utilitarians and their positivist successors. For Bentham, the question of the goodness or badness of any given law was to be adjudged by his great principle of utility, the essential weapon to be wielded in the critical struggle for law reform. The great advantage claimed for this method was that it made for clear thinking by distinguishing between legal and moral obligation. Where these conflicted to a decisive degree (which the application of the criterion of utility would reveal) then the citizen could bring the whole weight of moral argument to bear to promote a change in the law. Bentham did not pay much attention to the further issue as to whether, when a law stood morally condemned, the citizen was entitled to disobey it. This hardly seemed a practical issue for Bentham,[2a] who, as a rationalist, considered that the walls of reaction must ultimately yield to rational persuasion, particularly as the constitution became more democratic and so made increasingly effective the claim of the population as a whole to its due share of human happiness. Experience, so far as Western democracies are concerned, has on the whole justified Bentham's optimism in this respect, for the history of the nineteenth century and the growth of the modern welfare state has provided impressive evidence of the effective pressure of public opinion in favour of the reform of the law, much of it inspired by the criterion of maximizing human happiness so dear to Bentham's heart. Of course in despotic régimes (and even sometimes in democratic ones, for instance, in the case of conscientious objections to military service) the conflict between the ruler and the ruled may present itself in a more acute form, where the subject may have to decide

whether to obey a law he considers totally immoral or withhold obedience and take the legal consequences. There is no
doubt that the Benthamite approach to this is that the legal
duty does not cease to be a legal duty because the citizen is
persuaded of the moral iniquity of the duty, but that whether
he chooses to comply or obey is a question for his own
conscience. This is certainly the view that an English court of
law would adopt, on the basis that courts exist to uphold the
law and are not concerned with the goodness or badness of
that law. Accordingly appeals to a higher morality are treated
as irrelevant in convicting suffragettes or nuclear disarmers
for their breaches or defiance of the law, though it is always
open to a court, in deciding what is the appropriate penalty
to inflict, to take into account the moral urges which affected
the accused.

The positivists attack the natural-law idea not merely
because it makes for muddled thought but also because, by
regarding a certain inherent moral quality as an essential
feature of law without which it is no law at all, it tends to
confer on established law a sanctity to which it is not always
entitled, and so creates a barrier against law reform. We
have seen that the moral claim of obedience to law plays an
important role in conferring authority upon the legal system,
and this no positivist would deny. It is plain, however, that in
a period such as that when Bentham lived, when the law
contained a mass of meaningless archaisms and was a
machine of harsh repression, a theory identifying law and
morals in this close manner was liable to lead either to a
reactionary claim by those it benefited that the law was the
acme of reason and perfection, or to its total rejection by the
oppressed on the ground that it offended the first principles
of natural justice. Both positions were for Bentham fraught
with peril and were likely to act as severe barriers to the
rational advance of mankind in the interests of progress.
Only by a cool-headed evaluation of existing law by the
standard of utility and by unflinching pressure by rational
persuasion for its amendment could the ultimate goal of
reform be attained. It must be admitted that such an argu-

ment stems from the belief of the Age of Enlightenment in the
ultimate force of human reason and might well appear devoid
of reality to a person of liberal persuasions living in a Fascist
state. However, even in such a melancholy situation, the
legal positivist would argue that there is no advantage in
confusing the legal and the moral issue. Indeed he would
urge that the very separation of the legal and moral duty of
the citizen makes plain the nature of the conflict and the
spur to moral action.

Suppose for instance we take the position of those in
present-day South Africa who are persuaded that the repressive racial laws of apartheid are fundamentally immoral.
Those among them who think on the lines of the natural-law
school will urge that these laws are contrary to the dictates of
a higher law binding on all mankind and therefore lack legal
validity.³ The legal positivist on the other hand will, provided these laws are formally valid within the constitutional
framework of the country, accept their juridical validity but
condemn them on moral grounds according to whatever
criterion of morality he accepts. The moral dilemma is
surely revealed as clearly by saying, 'It is law but I won't
obey it because I believe it to be wrong', as by saying, 'It
isn't law at all in any fundamental sense, and therefore I am
not bound to obey it'. Moreover the great weakness in the
position of the natural lawyer rests on the premiss that he can
establish, as conditions precedent to his plea, not only that
natural law exists but that it contains the specific precept of
racial equality and that this nullifies any human law to the
contrary. Apart from the uncertainty involved in the first and
third of these conditions, he will find himself faced in South
Africa with other natural lawyers who will declare with equal
conviction that the law of nature decrees racial inequality.
How this dispute is to be resolved on the level of pure
reasoning is indeed difficult to perceive.

The Judge and His Conscience

What of the judge or other official of the law who is called
upon to administer a system of law which seems to his moral

conscience to be manifestly unjust? Take, for instance, an anti-Nazi judge in Hitler's Germany, or an anti-apartheid judge in South Africa. In the natural-law view, such a judge, if he performed his true legal duty, should refuse to apply the unjust laws as being invalid. This, however, both theoretically and in practice, seems to place him in an impossible situation since he would have, so to speak, to declare himself *ex cathedra* as an authoritative exponent of natural law, and to decide that its decrees compel him to ignore his own municipal laws. To such a pronouncement, apart from its impracticability, the legal authorities might well point out that natural law is a matter of keen controversy, even on a theoretical basis; that even if the authorities accept its existence they take the view that racial segregation is in accordance with and not contrary to nature; and that in any case the judge is appointed and paid to apply municipal law as laid down by established organs of law-making and not to indulge in or to apply his own personal speculations as to systems of higher law. The legal positivist, on the other hand, would submit that the judge's legal duty under the laws of his state was clear, namely to apply that law according to its letter and spirit; if he was persuaded of its moral unconscionability, then his moral duty clearly conflicted with his legal duty. What action he should take would be a matter for his own conscience, but at the least he should presumably resign his judicial office. Here again such a solution seems both more intelligible and more sensible than that propounded on the other side. It may, however, be asked how it comes about that if Nazi judges were only doing their legal duty by staying on and helping to enforce the monstrous laws of the Nazi state they could be validly tried and punished by courts set up either in Germany or elsewhere after the last war for their behaviour in their judicial office. This question raises an entirely different problem, and one which is of a purely juridical character, namely, under what law such judges are being tried and punished. So far as the municipal law of Germany or of other states is concerned the law would either have to be one in existence at the time when the conduct of the judges (now complained of) occurred or it would have to be a law passed subsequently and given retrospective effect. Retrospective legislation, especially in the sphere of criminal law, is generally regarded as objectionable,[4] though it is occasionally accepted as justifiable even in modern democratic states. It would no doubt be easier to justify where it meets an altogether exceptional situation such as was created by the rise and fall of Nazism in Germany. Moreover it would also be more easily accepted where there is ground for saying that, even at the time, the accused must have realized how morally reprehensible was the course he was pursuing under the aegis of state authority. There is, it will be noted, nothing contrary in this to the positivist view, for this fully acknowledges that a man may, in fulfilling his legal duty, knowingly be acting contrary to the dictates of morality.

LAW AS A SCIENCE

The tendency of the legal positivist to proclaim the autonomy of his subject and to assert its right to be treated as a science had an important influence on the future of legal theory, which in turn, as is usual in such cases, has provoked its own reaction. It was in the nineteenth century that science assumed that mantle of prestige to which its remarkable achievements, both in the realm of theoretical knowledge and technology, seemed to entitle it. Every field of study, it came to be felt, must organize itself on a scientific footing if it was to contribute to the general march of progress to which the methods of science pointed the way. Darwin's demonstration of how evolution could have accounted for both the present state of the animal world and of man's own development by emphasizing man's continuity of evolution from the animal world not only cast grave doubt on man's unique stature in the universe but also seemed to point the way to treating the affairs of mankind as open to scientific investigation just as in the case of other phenomena of nature.

The word 'positivism' was devised by the French philosopher Comte in the first half of the last century to designate his own particular philosophic system, but this was in fact largely derived from philosophic attitudes which were part of the climate of the period and which may be described as positivist in a more general sense. These attitudes derived from a belief that adequate knowledge could be attained only by employing the scientific method of investigating reality by observation and subjecting its theories to empirical investigation. Validity was thus denied to *a priori* knowledge or to metaphysical questions lying beyond the realm of observation. Comte argued that there were three steps in the development of man's approach to the world, the religious, the metaphysical, and finally the positivist, which Comte believed man to be at last attaining in his own day. To assist in this process Comte turned to the study of man in society and endeavoured to create a new science of 'sociology' (the term was also his) by which the whole of man's social activities might be viewed in the light of scientific principles. Unfortunately in his later work Comte deserted his own scientific tenets in favour of unsupported *a priori* assertions about human social activities, and so extreme a form did his final dogmatism take that he even devised a new 'religion of humanity' to support his authoritarian conception of the new 'positive society'. On this, John Stuart Mill, once Comte's admirer, wrote that, 'Others may laugh, but we would rather weep at this melancholy decadence of a great intellect.'[5] Such fantasies tended to bring the whole idea of positivism into disrepute but it must not be overlooked that the extravagances of Comte's own philosophical development had little bearing on the fundamental core of positivist thinking, derived not from Comte himself but from the scientific spirit of the age.

So pervasive indeed was this scientific spirit that it was to be found infiltrating the citadel of the arts and of literature. The school of naturalism and social realism in the nineteenth century novel, of which Zola was the leading protagonist, was an attempt to create a new type of fiction based on scientific investigation and written by scientific methods, which would recapture some of the prestige surrounding the great scientists.[6] And many significant developments in landscape painting were stimulated by similar objectives. John Constable, for example, endeavoured by the direct study of nature to transfer to his canvases a truly realist and scientific interpretation of what he beheld. 'Painting,' he urged in 1836, 'is a science, and should be pursued as an inquiry into the laws of nature. Why then may not landscape painting be considered as a branch of natural philosophy, of which pictures are but the experiment?'[7] Again Courbet's realist painting has been said to reflect Comte's new science of sociology,[8] and the great French Impressionist painters, were concerned to attain a scientific truth to nature, aided by a study of the theory of vision and the structure of light.[9]

It is hardly surprising then, in an age when science and scientific method were acquiring such unique prestige, and when serious thought was being given to the development of such sciences as sociology, social anthropology, and psychology, that jurists should be persuaded that legal theory also both could and should be capable of development on scientific lines. Bentham had already pointed the road towards this achievement by demonstrating (at least to his own satisfaction) the way in which the principle of utility could be developed in a scientific spirit and applied to the problems of criminology and of criminal and civil law in his new science of legislation. Although Bentham was less interested in what he termed the expository branch of jurisprudence, in the course of his writings he gave many indications and clues to how he thought the general pattern and structure of law could be examined scientifically and freed from the preconceptions and biases of past ages. It was left to his follower, John Austin, to develop these chips from the master's workshop into a new kind of legal theory which Austin called 'the science of positive law'. Such a science placed in the forefront the distinction between positive law, that is man-made law as it actually *is* (or was, if viewed historically), and law as it ought to be. Only the former is the appropriate subject-matter of this science, the latter constituting a distinct field of its own to be investigated not by the jurist but by the theologian or the student of ethics.

Austin's 'Science of Positive Law'

Unfortunately Austin's view of the scope of this particular science was by no means clearly thought out. Austin was mainly impressed by the fact that law as a self-contained body of rules applicable to human society operated by means of a system of conceptual thought, and his aim seems to have been to examine, in the dispassionate spirit of science, the essential features of this conceptual system. This involved not only endeavouring to determine the actual structure of law and of the functioning of a legal system but also giving a scientific exposition of all the fundamental notions which provide the framework for the articulation of such a system. This framework is supplied by means of such key concepts as rights and duties, persons, property, ownership, possession, crime, civil wrong, contract, and so on, and accordingly Austin's science developed very largely on the lines of an analysis of fundamental legal concepts. Being scientific, however, involved selecting one's data for research on the basis of actual fact acquired by observation. Austin recognized that such data would have to be gleaned from actual legal systems, past or present, and he recognized also that the inquiry might be confined either to a single legal system or to legal systems in general. On the whole, however, he was persuaded that there was sufficient in common in the conceptual systems of all legal systems to justify a general jurisprudence by which conclusions of general validity might be attained, though he limited his scheme of inquiry to what he termed, rather vaguely, the 'more developed' legal systems.

Whether Austin himself would have been satisfied with a science of law directed purely to conceptual and analytical inquiries of this kind may be open to doubt but his many followers showed themselves very ready to adhere to this purely conceptual attitude towards legal theory. Legal positivism has thus tended to be associated with a conceptual approach to jurisprudence, which has brought it into a certain amount of bad odour in recent times. There are several reasons for this.

The 'Conceptual' Approach

In the first place the criticism is raised that a legal theory confined to analysing fundamental concepts tends to induce a frame of mind where legal concepts are regarded as possessing a certain inherent structure and that any developments of law which disregard this structure are illegitimate. This may impose an undue restriction on the legal process in adapting the law to new and changing social and economic conditions. For instance, if analysis of the concept of contract shows that its essential features include the characteristic that by agreement parties to the agreement are able to affect their rights and duties *inter se*, but not so as to affect third parties, this may act as an impediment to creating contractual rights in favour of third parties, even though such rights would meet a social need. Or again, if juristic theory decrees that only an entity possessed of legal personality can enjoy legal rights, this may impede the recognition for legal purposes of unincorporated groups or associations, such as clubs or trade unions.[10]

The second criticism of the conceptual approach attacks the attitude that legal problems can be solved by means of logical analysis disregarding the role that policy plays in arriving at legal decisions. The conceptual approach to legal theory leads, it is said, to the notion that the answers to legal problems can be arrived at by working out the logical implications of legal principles, so that, for instance, the courts merely have the task of working out and applying on rational lines the given principles of the law. Hence the judiciary can regard itself as isolated from all questions of policy, its duty being merely to apply mechanically the principles supplied to it by the law.

It is extremely doubtful whether Austin himself would have subscribed to the view of jurisprudence aimed at in these criticisms.[11] Still, the conceptual approach associated with positivism has certainly laid itself open to the accusations that it tends to an excessively logical approach, and also tends to underestimate or unduly diminish the law-creating functions of the courts. To these matters we shall return later in a little more detail.[12] The third criticism, however, to be heard among modern jurists can probably be directed with more justice even against Austin himself. Austin seemed to overlook that the level of investigation on which he contemplated that his science of positive law would operate was really only that of what we may call second-order facts, namely the rules of law as contained in the statutes, recorded cases, and law-books associated with given legal systems. Behind such second-order facts lies an enormous mass of 'first-order' or primary facts consisting of the actual behaviour of legal officials, judges, and others (including ordinary private citizens) in relation to these complex legal rules. It is really this complex mass of primary facts which gives meaning and purpose to the structure of rules and principles which overlay these facts, and the investigation of the intricate and delicate interplay of these two orders of facts may be said to form an essential key to the understanding of law in society. Thus any theorizing on a purely conceptual basis which ignores the factual substratum of the concepts in question is likely to be an arid and unrealistic inquiry and not one which is calculated to yield principles of scientific validity. Neglect of this factor, in Austin's day, when the new infant science of sociology had attained little more than its baptismal name, is understandable enough, but in our own day, with the considerable development of the social sciences, especially in America, the need for a more sociologically oriented science of jurisprudence has been increasingly felt, and attacks upon the purely conceptual approach of Austinian positivism have usually been regarded as the appropriate prelude to initiating a new attitude to legal theory.

In this connexion the sociological jurist also assails the positivist axiom that law as it is and as it ought to be are two distinct and watertight compartments for, it is pointed out, the law is not a static but a dynamic and developing body of doctrine, and many of its developments are produced by judges who are either consciously or subconsciously reaching decisions on the basis of what they think the law ought to be. The scientific jurist therefore cannot ignore the fact that there is built into the law the seeds of its own development on the lines of some value system acceptable to the community, and the way in which the value system directs or controls the changing complex of legal decision forms a vital constituent of a legal system. It should be added however that this, true though it may be, does not in any way vitiate the main proposition of the legal positivist that the validity of an established rule is not impugned, as a matter of legal obligation, by its conflict with some value system established by religion or morality or any other non-legal source.

WHERE POSITIVISM STANDS TODAY

Positivist legal theory is usually associated today with a disbelief in the possibility of finding an absolute standard or norm outside the legal system itself by which the validity of a rule may be tested and, if necessary, found wanting. Logically, it is true that the positivist is not bound to be a moral relativist claiming that moral systems are relative to time and place and that there is no way of deciding between them save on the footing of personal choice. For a positivist may still insist that the validity of law is distinct from the question of its moral rightness even while adhering to some system of absolute moral values. In practice, however, it must be admitted that the positivist usually adopts a relativist approach to moral values and for this reason: if it could be shown that some absolute system of moral values was demonstrably of universal validity then the argument in favour of subordinating the validity of man-made law to this system would be extremely persuasive. The attack on positivism therefore tends to be launched today in two ways. First, it is alleged that legal positivism, by its refusal to acknowledge an absolute higher morality controlling legal validity, has made it possible for totalitarian dictators to bend the laws and those who administer them so as to perpetrate, under the guise of legal authority, appalling injustices such as have been carried out in recent European history. Secondly, attempts have been made to show that absolute moral values do exist and can be demonstrated to exist by various means.

The first argument really seems both misconceived and based on a false assessment of the facts. It is misconceived because the legal positivist, in asserting, for instance, that a court is concerned with what the law is and not with what it ought to be, is in no sense suggesting that the law is not subject to moral condemnation if it deserves to be condemned. Nor is there any reason to suggest, because the positivist denies that value systems can be proved true, that he is any less attached to the moral values which he believes to be right for his time and age, even though he knows no way in which he can demonstrate their rightness. Moreover, the notion that legal positivism has led to dictatorships in modern times is palpably false, for it is in the Anglo-Saxon world of the common law that this legal doctrine has held, and still holds, widest sway, and democratic value systems have attained as high a standard of legal recognition and enforcement there as anywhere in the world. In pre-Nazi Germany and pre-Fascist Italy on the other hand the main influence was that of Hegelianism, which, by its treatment of the State as the highest value, did much to encourage an ethic and a legal theory peculiarly adapted to the spirit of totalitarianism.[13]

As to the second argument, appeal is usually made to revelation, to intuition, or to a belief in human reason common to all mankind by which it is possible to arrive at unassailable moral truth. Unfortunately it has so far not proved any more possible today than in the past to achieve agreement either as to revealed sources of morals or religion, or as to the truths yielded by intuitive insight or by rational inferences. Some sociologists, especially in America, have striven to overcome these obstacles by trying to establish, by means of scientific investigation, that there are certain basic human needs and drives which can be shown to require certain basic norms of behaviour to give adequate effect to them. If it could be shown that such norms in one form or another prevail universally in human society then, it is argued, we will have gone a long way towards establishing a universal value system natural to man and therefore entitled to prevail over human arrangements which conflict with or are at variance with its requirements. The operative idea of this approach is doubtless that human nature is every-where and at all times pretty much the same and if you dig down deep enough you will find a fundamental core of moral rules which have always operated and always will operate.

No doubt there is some substratum of truth in the idea that all human societies everywhere have needed to impose cer-tain restraints, for instance against certain kinds of killing and stealing, to enable them to exist as societies at all. But when one leaves a few points of common ground of this kind, and contemplates the enormous variations in standards between different societies it is difficult to see that this argu-ment is likely to carry one very far. In some societies killing a slave or a newly born child has been treated as morally indifferent, and the killing of a member of a rival tribe as positively meritorious, just as in modern society we still approve killing the enemy in war, and Nazi persecutors regarded killing Jews as either a sport or meritorious in itself. And for the medieval knight war and fighting represented the only worthwhile activity of the ruling orders of society. Moreover, those who hope to elicit by this method some sort of *de facto* support for the scale of Western values of liberty, equality, and democracy in which they believe must find it somewhat daunting to contemplate the actual form of human societies which have prevailed in most ages and still prevail widely at the present day, where differences of status are regarded as part of the built-in order of the universe.

The positivist, if we may return to him, does not deny that rational arguments may be applied to the moral evaluation of law as to other subjects and his leaning is often (though not necessarily) in favour of law reform and moral progress. He does, however, recognize in the last resort that if the Athenian

believes in freedom and the Spartan in discipline as the highest value there is no way in which reason can decisively
resolve the controversy.

On the whole the positivist shares with the natural lawyer
(whether actuated by religious, ethical, or sociological
motives) a rationalist approach to the moral values of his
society, an approach which is rooted in the historical foundations of European ethical thought. In this respect both are
rational creeds which may be contrasted with the various
forms of irrationalism which have emerged in modern times.
Nazism and Fascism were both irrational systems relying on
such factors as blood, race, and destiny. So too, the modern
Existentialists reject reason in favour of the inner liberty of the
individual as the source of true morality.

The positivist, then, while retaining his faith in systems
which can be subjected to rational scrutiny, prefers to concentrate on studying the values that are inherent in our present
stage of civilization and on exploring how these may best be
realized in the conditions of today, rather than to postulate a
series of absolute and unprovable values claimed to be valid
for all places and all times. The positivist believes that a
clearer understanding of human social problems can be
attained by keeping the questions of legal validity and of
moral worth distinct. But he does not insist, as did some earlier
legal positivists, that the lawyer is concerned solely with
analysing legal principles and applying them logically or
systematically to fresh situations as these arise. There is, as
has already been pointed out, nothing in positivism which
compels so narrow an outlook and at least the more progressive positivist of the present day recognizes that the law,
while entitled to regard itself as an autonomous field of study,
has many close and intimate relations with other aspects of
human activity. For law cannot be considered or rightly
understood apart from the aims which it seeks to achieve,
even though these aims may be only transient and variable
and not absolute *sub specie aeternitatis*. Consequently the
lawyer needs to come to grips with the value system inherent
in his society and to wrestle with the many problems which

arise in developing the legal system as machinery for achieving justice within the framework of that value system.

Accordingly, the next two chapters will explore first, the various ways in which law is related to justice, and secondly, how attempts have been made to incorporate the value system which has developed or is developing in Western society, and in those non-Western countries subject to its influence, in the fabric of a modern legal system.

In the previous chapter an attempt was made to show how law needs to be related to the system of values recognized in the particular community in which it operates. Such a system of values may and in fact does differ from place to place and from period to period. Though it may be impossible, as the positivist is disposed to think, to demonstrate the absolute superiority of any particular system over all others, actual or possible, nevertheless if a community believes that its values are the highest attainable it will clearly judge the existing law in accordance with those values and try to amend or adapt it where it falls short of them.

It may be said, however, that this is all very well as an approximate description of how law tends to function, at least in enlightened communities which enjoy a fair degree of harmony as to their basic aims, but there is a more general purpose that the law everywhere aims, or should aim, at achieving, and that is 'justice'. The idea of law, it may be urged, has always been associated with the idea of justice, and if it is agreed that this represents the ultimate goal to which the law should strive, then we can arrive at the purpose of law more directly, without becoming entangled in the values of particular societies with all their conflicts and uncertainties. For, after all, are not those values themselves, so far as they seek to be embodied in the laws of the community, merely an individual expression of the general striving towards justice itself?

This question is clearly one of fundamental importance in an understanding of law, in view of the wide acceptance of the view (symbolized by the statue of Justice holding the scales erected over the Old Bailey, the Central Criminal Court of London) that law must be assimilated to justice and that law without justice is a mockery, if not a contradiction. Some attempt will therefore be made in this chapter to clarify what is meant by the term 'justice', and its relation to law, before attempting to come to grips in the subsequent chapter with the problems which are encountered in seeking to give effect by legal machinery to the particular set of values prevalent in our own Western society.

WHAT IS JUSTICE?

One point must be plain at the outset of this inquiry, and that is that justice, whatever its precise meaning may be, is itself a moral value, that is, one of the aims or purposes which man sets himself in order to attain the good life. If all the moral purposes of human life are classified as 'the good' then the idea of justice is no more than one of the various 'goods' which morality sets before mankind. A particular 'good' may function either as a means or as an end in itself. For instance we may regard happiness as an end in itself and liberty as a means of attaining happiness, rather than as something good in itself. In other words we may classify the various 'goods' or 'values' of human society in a hierarchy so that some of these are merely means to attain higher values, all leading to some ultimate good. Thus under the utilitarian system the ultimate good is 'the greatest happiness of the greatest number' to which all other 'goods' are subordinated.

As we have already argued, what *is* the ultimate good is a matter not of demonstration but of choice, and we could if we wished place justice itself upon this pinnacle. Indeed some lawyers, and even some outstanding philosophers, such as Plato, have placed justice at the summit of the moral world. The Hebraic attitude to ethics and law, to which we have already referred, also seems to share something of this approach.

What meaning then can be ascribed to this pervasive idea of justice? We have already mentioned the central role that justice plays in the Platonic ethic, so perhaps a good starting point for our discussion would be to refer briefly to Plato's conception of justice and see whether this seems to provide the answer we are seeking.

PLATONIC JUSTICE

In his famous dialogue, now called the *Republic*, Plato sets out to explain what is meant by justice. For Plato the microcosm of the just man is a reflection of the pattern of the just society. He therefore seeks to arrive at the meaning of justice by depicting what a just society, conceived as an ideal society, whether attainable on this earth or not, might be like. Such a society will be just, in Plato's view, because it will conform to his conception of justice. This conception seems to be that every thing or person – for Plato thinks justice applies to objects as well as people – has its proper sphere and that justice means conforming to that sphere. For instance, a tool, such as a saw or an adze, has its proper sphere of use in carpentry, which Plato regards as 'just'; so, too, the carpenter or the physician has his appropriate sphere, namely carpentry or healing the sick, performance of which to the best of his abilities represents 'justice'. In the same way, only the wise man is fit to rule, so that in a just society he alone will act as ruler.

This view of justice will hardly commend itself to modern libertarian patterns of thought. For it is obviously based on the aristocratic idea that every person is inherently adapted to some specific function and that if he departs from that function he is guilty of injustice. This somewhat resembles the feudal idea of the three orders of society, priests, warriors, and labourers, each with their own self-contained function, which was not to be overstepped. Plato does of course go far beyond the feudal idea in arguing that the potential rulers are to be selected not by birth but by attainments, coupled with an elaborate and prolonged course of education, before being qualified to rule. All the same Plato's system seems based on the fallacy that each man is by nature fitted for one specific job or function and that there is such a job or function adapted to each person's natural attainments or aptitudes. Moreover, even the division between freeman and slave is fitted into this pattern, for, as Aristotle subsequently argued, some men are slaves by nature, and therefore only fitted for servitude. Nor did Plato find any room in his just society for such emotional factors, which many would regard as of the essence of moral values, as charity, benevolence, or philanthropy. On the whole then Plato's conception of justice is unacceptable in principle apart from being, by modern Western standards, a quite inadequate criterion of any ultimate good which our own society may aim at achieving.

FORMAL JUSTICE AND EQUALITY

Conceptions of justice may vary from age to age. This is sufficiently illustrated by the fact that for the Greeks justice essentially embodied the idea of inequality, since the very lack of natural equality between human beings (as well as physical objects) called for different treatment, whereas it may be ventured that in modern times equality has been regarded as the very essence of justice. It is indeed the attaining of equality, not the preserving of inequality, that modern moral and legal philosophy treat as the vital function of justice.

This idea of justice being linked with equality of treatment undoubtedly owes much to the association of justice with legal proceedings. The law is supposed to be applied equally in all situations and to all persons to which it relates without fear or favour, to rich and poor, to powerful and humble alike. A law which is applied without discrimination in this way may be regarded as the embodiment of justice. What needs also to be noted is that justice in this sense is really no more than a formal principle of equality. Nor can it be regarded even as a principle of equality without qualification. Justice cannot mean that we are to treat everyone alike regardless of individual differences, for this would require us, for instance, to condemn to the same punishment everyone who has killed another person, regardless of such factors as the mental incapacity or infancy of the accused. What this formal principle really means is that like shall be treated as like, so that everyone who is classified as belonging to the same category, for a particular purpose, is to be treated in the same way. For example, if the vote is extended to all citizens of full age by the franchise laws of a given state, then justice requires that all persons qualified in this way shall be allowed to exercise his or her vote, but justice would not be infringed by the exclusion of aliens and infants from the list of voters.

In other words formal justice requires equality of treatment in accordance with the classifications laid down by the rules, but it tells us nothing about how people should or should not be classified or treated. It follows that formal justice is a rather empty category, resembling somewhat Kant's categorical imperative, since if it is to be given a specific content other principles than mere formal equality will need to be appealed to. A franchise which confers the right to vote only upon males, or persons belonging to a particular racial or religious group, may be justly applied in the formal sense that all those classified in this way are treated equally; whether we are prepared to acknowledge the justice, in a concrete sense, of a classification on these lines, is a very different matter. Clearly, however, no purely formal principle of treating like as like will suffice to resolve this sort of problem since we need further principles for deciding which differences are to be treated as relevant. On the ground of equality alone we do not know whether or on what basis we are to have regard to or ignore differences of sex, race, religion, birthplace, physical prowess or mental attainment, or wealth or influence. People are not in fact born equal either physically, mentally, or in other respects, so that the classification of equality between human beings remains of necessity a mere formality until we have proceeded to indicate how we are going to divide people up into further sub-groups according to what are regarded as the moral or social needs of the particular society. Moreover even treating people equally may involve special arrangements in favour of the poorer or humbler sections of the community, to enable them to seek justice on an equal footing with those who possess natural, social, or economic advantages, which otherwise would weigh heavily in their favour. A cynical English judge of the Victorian era once remarked that 'the law, like the Ritz Hotel, is open to rich and poor alike'. A notional equality of this kind is of little service to the impecunious, and modern legal systems have tried to bridge the gap by providing a state-financed system of legal aid to enable people of modest means to litigate on a basis of equality with their richer opponents.

We shall say a little presently about how the gap between formal and substantial or concrete justice has to be filled.[1] For the moment we will examine in rather more detail the attributes of justice in the purely formal sense. The idea of justice embodied in the principle of treating like cases in the same way, seems, when expanded, to involve three related conceptions: first, that there shall be rules laying down how people are to be treated in given cases; second, that such rules shall be general in character, that is to say, that they shall provide that everyone who qualifies as falling within the scope of the rule shall be governed by it. (In other words, it must be applied either to persons generally, or to certain categories of persons as defined, and not merely to random individuals.) In the third place, justice requires that these general rules shall be impartially applied, that is to say, that the agencies concerned in administering them shall apply them without discrimination, or fear or favour, to all those whose cases fall within the scope of the rules. If, for instance, it was a rule of a trade union that any male worker over eighteen was entitled to be admitted as a member, it would not be in accordance with formal justice to refuse someone who qualifies with the requirements because he is an alien, any more than it would be just to admit a female worker or a male who is only sixteen.

SUBSTANTIAL JUSTICE

It will be apparent from this expansion of the ideas involved in formal justice that such justice amounts to little if anything more than working out the logical consequences of what it means to apply a system of rules. The very idea of treating like as like, if it means anything, means that there is a system of rules applicable to like cases; a rule can hardly be said to be a rule at all unless it applies generally to whatever persons or situations fall within it; and if the rules are not applied impartially in accordance with their terms then there is really no system of rules at all. It is hardly surprising therefore that a conception of justice which amounts to no more than giving effect to the logical implications of rules deals with little more than the procedural aspects of justice and tells us nothing about how we are to assess whether the actual rules themselves are just. To achieve substantial or concrete justice the formal requirements of justice therefore need to be supplemented in two ways.

(1) *Concrete Justice :* How are we to decide whether the actual rules are themselves just ? A franchise which is conferred only on males over twenty-five may, if impartially applied, satisfy the requirements of formal justice, as we have seen, but we also want to know whether it is substantially just that the franchise should be limited in this way and not extended to females or to males who have not attained the specified age group. In his *Ethics,* Aristotle refers to what he calls *distributive* justice, which deals with the distribution of honours and rewards by the state to persons according to their deserts. This same idea of justice is also expressed by the Roman Emperor Justinian in the codification of the Roman Law associated with his name, when he asserts that justice consists in 'giving to each man his due'. But what is due ? How do we assess merit or worth ? Suppose the state establishes a fund upon which all the citizens are entitled to make claims according to what is 'due' to them. Suppose also that for this purpose 'due' refers not to a legal claim in respect of some

debt owed by the state (in which case decisions would have to be made in accordance with law, rather than justice, whether these coincided or not) but to what each individual may be able to show he is *justly* entitled to. It is obvious that some criteria would have to be established by which one claim might be preferred to another. The administrator of the fund would have to decide whether he is to reward actual achievements (and how these are to be evaluated), or effort, or work, or triumph over adversity, or to compensate for physical or economic deficiencies, and so on. In other words, he would have to establish a scale of values which would guide him in discriminating between the various competing claims. Is it not then obvious that these values will have to be based on something other than justice itself? Justice can tell us, as a rational principle of coherence and regularity, that an administrator who has chosen to prefer achievement to effort has or has not been guilty of applying that principle unjustly between two competing claimants. Again, justice can tell us whether a person has been unjustly excluded from exercising his vote in accordance with the franchise laid down. What justice cannot tell us is whether it is right to prefer achievement to effort as a subject for reward, or to limit a franchise to males, to the exclusion of females. The criticism or justification for these decisions has to be sought in some wider criterion or principle than justice can itself afford.

This conclusion is indeed hardly surprising when we consider that justice is little more than the idea of rational order and coherence and therefore operates as a principle of procedure rather than of substance. (This is not to denigrate procedure, which is, as we shall see, of enormous importance in attaining legal justice.) What values we care to affirm are a matter not of logical necessity but of choice. This does not imply, of course, that our choice is absolutely free, for in the first place it will be deeply conditioned by our history and traditions and by our social and economic environment. Moreover, there seems no reason why a choice of values, like other choices, should not be capable of being justified by rational argument.[2] All the same, the truth of scales of values cannot be logically demonstrated but has in the last resort to be accepted or rejected, because we feel that we cannot do otherwise. This is what Hume had in mind when he remarked that it is 'not reason but the passions' which impose our moral criteria.

It should be understood that though the criterion of equality operates in the idea of justice purely as a logical and formal principle and not as an ultimate value to which society must be directed, this is not because equality is in itself incapable of being erected into a higher value of this kind. On the contrary, as we shall see when we discuss the relation of freedom to law, equality takes an important place in the scale of values which operates at the present day. But in this sense it is not the merely logical principle of treating like as like within a framework of rules, but rather consists in the deliberate value-judgment that certain differences between human beings are not appropriate grounds for discrimination. This applies especially to such differences as sex, race, colour, and religion. Adherence to a value-judgment of this kind is clearly one of conscious choice and moral conviction which cannot be deduced from the formal criterion of equality incorporated in the idea of justice.

(2) *Equity:* There is yet a further difficulty in looking to formal justice as a means of adjudicating fairly between man and man. For, as Aristotle pointed out, the general nature of rules means that not every individual situation can be forseen or provided for adequately, and therefore formal justice may press very hard in individual cases. This is why in all legal systems a need has been felt to correct the rigour of the law. This corrective is generally introduced by conferring a certain discretionary power to interpret the laws in the spirit of equity rather than insisting on their strict letter, and to limit or control their operation in cases of hardship. This last point is well brought out in the saying that 'justice should be administered with mercy', which means that legal justice should be tempered to the individual case in a spirit of equity. This principle allows a fairly free and ready appli-

cation in the sphere of criminal law, for though justice may require a conviction, as only the maximum penalties are fixed flexibility in sentencing is allowed for, so that the punishment can be adjusted to the particular case. Capital punishment, when fixed as the sole penalty, does not lend itself to equitable administration, and on this account has sometimes resulted in a guilty man being 'unjustly' acquitted by a jury which feels that he does not deserve the death penalty. In civil matters, however, the question is a more difficult one, because if hardships were regarded as a ground for avoiding one's legal obligations this might introduce great uncertainty into the law. This is no doubt why the system of equity, contrasted in England with the common law, has tended to grow increasingly rigid and more like a supplementary system of law than a means of tempering the strict dictates of justice according to law. On the other hand, however, there has been a considerable growth of discretionary powers conferred on courts, tribunals, and administrators by modern legislation, and these constitute a kind of equitable principle built into the rule of law itself. In English law the concept of 'reasonableness' is often invoked for this purpose, as for instance where a court is empowered to order the eviction of a tenant of a rent-controlled dwelling-house only if satisfied that it is 'reasonable' to make the order.

LEGAL JUSTICE

Justice is a much wider conception than law and may apply wherever there is a code of rules, legal or non-legal. For instance a private club or a school may govern itself by rules administered in accordance with formal justice, whether or not strictly legal rules apply. We have so far considered justice in this wider context. It is now necessary to carry the inquiry into the specific province of law and for this purpose we have to consider both the relation of law to justice and what specific meaning we can give to the idea of legal justice or justice according to law.

If we compare the formal attributes of justice with the

features usually regarded as characteristic of law we can see that these, broadly speaking, correspond. Indeed so close is this correspondence that there seems to be good reason for supposing that the very conception of formal justice has been largely derived from or modelled upon the conception of law itself. In an earlier chapter we have already stressed the interaction of law and morality and pointed out the extent to which morals may be said to be derived from legal rules; here again we see the great influence that legal conceptions exert over ethical modes of thought in providing a framework within which an ethical concept of justice has been able to develop separate from, but closely related to, the formal structure of a legal system.

To what extent can it be said that a legal system partakes of the three features of formal justice to which we have referred, namely, the existence of rules, their generality, and their impartial application? In the first place it is plain enough that a primary characteristic of a legal system is that it shall contain rules for regulating human behaviour and for settling disputes. Moreover, these rules will almost necessarily, though perhaps not invariably, be general in character, for the whole purpose of law is to classify acts and situations, and to provide general rules for dealing with them. It is conceivable, and indeed has sometimes occurred, that laws have been passed which deal only with one person or with a single situation, as for instance a penal enactment such as the old Act of Attainder, providing for the infliction of penalties upon an individual, or an Act of Parliament dealing exclusively with the administration of a particular estate.[3] However even seemingly non-general enactments of this kind are often general in their implications: for instance the rights of third parties in relation to any property falling within the scope of the statutes in the above two examples would be affected by them. The fact remains that even if very special examples can be thought of, which amount to laws lacking general application, these remain so exceptional that they do not cast serious doubt on the broad proposition that legal systems are composed of rules which are general in their application. Some jurists indeed have sought to argue that nothing can qualify as a law unless it possesses the attribute of generality, but this seems a needlessly arbitrary limitation on our definition of law, and creates an awkward problem of terminology in the case of a non-general enactment validly passed by a legislature, for it is hardly likely that lawyers would wish to refer to it by any other name than that of a law.[4]

Coming now to the third feature of justice, the need for the impartial application of the rules, the situation is a little different. For here it may be said that impartiality is generally closely associated with law in the sense that it is regarded as a highly desirable attribute or aim of any legal system, but the practice, save in the most well-regulated of states, and not invariably in those, is often very different. It would seem that the question here is to some extent one of degree, as are so many questions in human affairs. If all legal systems fall short to some extent of achieving complete impartiality we cannot regard the universal preservation of impartiality as an essential attribute of law itself. On the one hand, a state or country which is governed in theory by rules which are so capriciously applied that it is impossible to predict even in the most straightforward cases how individual decisions are to go, in view of the likelihood of corruption or of personal factors influencing decisions, could hardly be said to possess a legal system at all. On the other hand, we would not necessarily refuse to recognize that a legal system operates where the law is generally applied with regularity but where certain sections, classes, or individuals can usually rely on favourable treatment both from the courts and other legal authorities; we would probably prefer to say that there is a legal system but it operates very defectively in certain cases.

Be this as it may, the fact remains that a certain measure of coherence and regularity is a vital feature of any legal system but no exact standard can be laid down by which this measure is to be judged. Moreover the general state of social development of the particular society in question would have to be taken into account and compared with the state of development in other societies of the same epoch. We would not judge the operation of the law in a feudal country in a period of general feudalism in the same way as we would the conditions in a backward country in the contemporary world.

In addition to the features already considered, which are common both to law and justice, there is also the equitable element to which reference has been made. Here again the importance if not the actual derivation of the idea of equity stems primarily from the operation of this idea within the framework of the law. Aristotle discusses equity mainly as a means of mitigating the apparent rigours of the law, and in the later Roman law many examples could be given of the way the spirit of equity was invoked to enable the law to be developed in a juster and more humane manner than was permissible within its strict letter. English law in turn developed a separate system of equity administered by a separate court in order to turn aside some of the harshnesses of strict law and this institution has spread to all common-law countries, including the United States, and still survives in a modified form in English law today. Here again we see the close correspondence between formal justice and law in that both have felt the need for softening their respective rigours to meet individual cases of hardship. And just as, in the case of justice, we could not say there was no justice because appeals to equity were ignored – let us recall the distinction, already mentioned, between 'justice' and 'mercy' – so we cannot deny the existence of law when it admits of no softening of its asperities on equitable grounds. Law might lose its character of law by an excess of caprice in its administration but it could hardly cease to be law because of its rigid application according to its tenor. The law of the Medes and Persians – 'which altereth not' – might have been harsh but none the less it was still law.

*

LEGAL INJUSTICE

So much then for the correspondence between the two conceptions of law and of justice. In view of the closeness of the formal attributes of these two concepts the question arises in what sense we can condemn the law itself of injustice.

It would seem that there are three distinct types of case in which injustice in relation to law may arise and which need to be distinguished. First, the law is, as we have seen, so closely linked in the general opinion with the idea of justice, that it may itself be, and frequently is, treated as synonymous with justice; it is for this reason that we often refer to ' Courts of Justice' as a synonym for ' Courts of Law', even though the latter may in practice often fall far short of the ideal standards set by the former. Legal injustice then may be done when a case is decided in a sense contrary to what the law itself lays down. Of course whether what the law lays down coincides with what is regarded as substantial justice is quite another matter. For instance, the law may permit a person to inflict severe loss or injury on another without that other having any right of redress. A decision to this effect is legally just though it may be regarded (even by the court itself) as morally most unjust. On the other hand, if the court were, contrary to established law, to decide in favour of the plaintiff notwithstanding, this might be morally just but it would still amount to legal injustice. These examples naturally assume that in the case in question the law is clear, but has been misapplied. In practice, however, the complexities of most legal systems are such that they are full of uncertainties as to what is their correct interpretation in a great many situations and a decision of a lower court may be corrected by a higher court on appeal. Where a particular lower court has simply taken what has proved to be a mistaken view of the law the word 'injustice' is not very appropriate and is a good deal less likely to be used. The close association of justice with morality would generally require some deliberate 'wrenching' of the law to arouse a condemnation of injustice, rather than a mere *bona fide* misinterpretation of the law by a court doing its best to discharge its duty. There is also the further complication that the decision of the higher court may not in the eyes of the legal profession seem to be soundly based as a matter of law and, moreover, under some systems, even the highest court may subsequently be entitled to overrule its previous decisions as being wrong in law.

The second form of legal injustice is perpetrated when the law is not duly administered in that spirit of impartiality which it requires. If, for example, a court finds facts in favour of a powerful litigant, not because it is genuinely persuaded of their truth but because it wishes to show favour to the powerful either out of fear of the consequences of an adverse decision or on account of bribery or hope of future benefit or advancement, then a legal injustice has been committed. Such an injustice will also necessarily be unjust from the point of view of abstract justice as well as law, for whatever the merits of the case and whether the relevant laws are or are not in accordance with substantial justice, a lack of impartiality still remains a fundamental breach of the conception of formal justice. The point may be reinforced by considering the case of a court showing similar partiality to a humble litigant because it feels that he deserves particular sympathy. Take the type of case, which not infrequently occurs in our modern society, where a person of small means has suffered some physical injuries in a road accident or at his place of work and brings an action in which the real defendant is an insurance company or some wealthy company which was his employer. A judge or jury who decided the facts in favour of the plaintiff contrary to the fair assessment of the evidence out of genuine sympathy for the hardship to the plaintiff and because the financial loss would fall much less heavily on the defendant would undoubtedly be guilty of committing an injustice, both legal and moral, however well-meaning such a decision might be.

The third kind of injustice will arise when the law, though perfectly impartially administered according to its tenor is itself unjust if judged by whatever value system may be

applied to test the substantial justice of the legal rule. The
philosopher Hobbes propounded the rather startling thesis
that the only standard of justice is the law itself, so that
whatever rule the law lays down must *ipso facto* be just.[5]
This argument appears to be totally untenable for there
seems no conceivable reason why we should not be entitled
to evaluate the substantial justice of a legal rule by some
external criterion, though this does not necessarily imply, as
we have already seen, that such a criterion must be one of
absolute, universal, and unchanging validity. Hobbes is
really seeking to treat all laws as just by definition, but this is
a purely arbitrary piece of terminological legislation which
has been rightly rejected by most philosophers and lawyers
and by the verdict of common sense. It is true that a celebrated English Chief Justice, Sir Edward Coke, once
attempted to equate the law with moral principle and
natural law, when he described the common law as 'the
perfection of reason'[6]. This however was no more than a
rhetorical flourish which in any event was peculiarly inapt,
in view of the barbarous state of the common law in the
seventeenth century.

An unjust law, then, in this sense, is a perfectly intelligible
conception if we understand it as meaning simply a law
which, valid in itself, conflicts with the scale of values by
which we choose to judge it. Moreover this idea may be
perfectly properly applied not only to individual laws,
which offend our sense of human values, but also to a whole
legal system which may be condemned, for example, as
being directed solely to furthering the interests of a particular group, or as outrageously repressive towards other
groups, whether constituting a majority or a minority of the
population as a whole.

Is it a further ground of distinction between law and
justice, that whereas it makes perfect sense to speak of unjust law, it is really meaningless or a contradiction in terms
to refer to 'unjust justice'? On the face of it this sounds a
senseless and contradictory expression; nor is it a phrase
that is commonly encountered except perhaps when used

with an ironical implication. Here again, however, it is necessary to contrast the formal and the substantial aspect of justice. If justice is treated as embodying the purely formal rule of equality previously discussed then justice which exemplifies this principle cannot be unjust by definition. For justice limited to this meaning is a formal and logical principle and if regularly applied cannot contradict itself. Equity, on the other hand, as we have seen, operates not as the expression of a logical rule but by shaping itself to the individual case – even, it may be said, erratically. For this reason in the early days of English equity, it was criticized as 'varying with the length of the Chancellor's foot.' In its formlessness it therefore resembles charity, which is spontaneous and uncalculating, aiming to relieve suffering without regard to any rules whatever. Equity therefore in this sense is the antithesis of formal justice, or at any rate a supplement to it, rather than part of the concept of justice. However, in a broader sense we may regard equity itself as a kind of justice and formal justice may then be intelligibly treated as unjust if it complies with the rigid logic of its own requirements but fails to temper its conclusion in a spirit of equity with the particular circumstances of the case. Thus a decision of an association or club to expel a member for his conduct may be perfectly just within the scope of its rules providing for expulsion but may still be 'unjust' because it ignores the special circumstances which palliate the offence. It will be seen therefore that this type of case corresponds to that in which the law is administered in accordance with the letter rather than in a spirit of equity, or where legal justice is not tempered with mercy,

Apart from this case, formal justice, like law itself, may fail to result in substantial or concrete justice. There is here an exact analogy between abstract justice and law. A father may, for instance, lay down a rule that he will disinherit any child of his who marries a Roman Catholic.[7] The application of this rule with regularity and without regard to individual favour would comply with formal justice, but tells us nothing as to the substantial justice of the rule itself. In the same way a rule of a particular state excluding members of particular races or religions from participation in elections might be applied perfectly justly in relation to those subject to this rule, but the substantial justice of the rule itself still remains entirely open to question. It will be apparent therefore that we have here arrived at the same fundamental distinction encountered in considering the meaning of an unjust law, namely that a rule may be perfectly justly administered according to its tenor and yet may itself embody the most profound injustice. And when we speak of injustice in this sense we refer to that scale of values which, on whatever basis, we choose to accept as providing the criterion by which we judge all human rules of conduct, whether legal or non-legal, as being good or bad, just or unjust. Indeed, in this broader connotation of what we have called 'substantial justice' there is little if any important distinction which can be drawn between 'the good' and 'the just', though goodness remains a far wider category than justice even in this sense.

LAW AND 'SUBSTANTIAL' JUSTICE

It is not enough then for a system of law to comply with the formal attributes of justice even though tempered with a spirit of equity. For in addition law needs to possess a just content, and this can only mean that its actual rules must themselves by their provisions aim at and endeavour to conform to some criteria of rightness which repose on values exterior to justice itself in the sense that no merely formal idea of justice can dictate to us the basis upon which we are to prefer one set of values to another. The assertion therefore that law aims at justice cannot provide a substitute for a scale of values, for without these the most appalling forms of substantial injustice may be perpetrated in the name of justice itself. We will therefore conclude this chapter by saying a little in general terms about the way in which a legal system may endeavour to give effect to the particular scale of values which obtain in a given society. This will lead, in the next chapter, to some consideration of the scale of values dominant in our present Western society and the diverse ways in which these values function as operative factors in the legal systems of Western democratic countries and of other countries which reflect a similar outlook.

There are two principal ways in which a legal system may aspire to attain not merely formal but also substantial justice so far as this is reflected in the value system operative in the particular community. Of these two, the first is more limited, but perhaps in some ways more pervasive in the long run. This is by imparting a certain flexibility in the rules applied by the courts or other organs of legal administration so as to confer on the judges and other legal officials the possibility of developing the law and adapting it to the needs of the society in which it operates. Naturally there is no guarantee that this flexibility will be used in this way. A narrow-minded and rigid legal profession may fail to come to terms with the values of the society in which it lives, especially where that society is in a transitional state with substantial currents of social and economic change gradually transforming a more traditional community.[8] It may be said that to some extent a society gets the legal profession and the judiciary that it deserves, and that social pressures will eventually be effective in these spheres as in others, though resistance to change in some societies may be stronger in the realm of legal traditionalism than in most other fields. It is also partly a question of education, not merely legal education in the narrow sense, though this is not without an important influence, but also the extent to which the general educational system of the country succeeds in propagating a scale of values and provides both the background and the impetus for an informed and alert public opinion.

This method then – allowing flexibility in the rules – does not so much provide a set of values for the law to apply but rather gives the judiciary scope within the established rules to have regard to the dominant values accepted in the society in question. There is room for a positive approach even if this is not always recognized or adopted. On the other hand, the need may be felt to give the judiciary and other officers of the law, as well as the legislative organ itself, more specific guidance as to the values they should adhere to in arriving at decisions or expositions of the law or in framing new legislation. In every legal system it may be said that there is, at least implicitly, built into it some kind of value system which the law reflects. In a system such as the common law the principles expressing the inherent values of English society are not contained in a specific legal document but are to be distilled out of a long historical tradition manifested in certain institutions, constitutional principles and conventions, and decisions of the courts, which have been treated as embodying in a special degree the spirit or values of the English way of life. Educated in this tradition, those whose function it is to develop and apply the law can generally be assumed to be cognizant of the spirit of the community expressed in these various forms. In this way the built-in values of the system are generally adhered to and developed. If this, unhappily, is not always the case, then the various organs of public opinion may have to be, and frequently are, used to make the public aware of any threats to those values which may arise within the framework of the law.

Such an approach may serve for a country with a long tradition of ordered government and with a fairly homogeneous population which is broadly in accord as to the essential values which embody the spirit of the community. Less integrated or more recently established states may require something more explicit than the rather haphazard repertory of law and tradition which has served England reasonably well up till now. Here the United States, with its written Constitution established in 1776 and its Bill of Rights appended almost immediately thereto, set a pattern which has been repeatedly followed in recent history, namely, to incorporate by positive enactment in the constitution certain value-judgments or principles. These principles were regarded as representing, in the historical context of the eighteenth century, essential natural rights, and

in our own day, when the natural-law idea is more controversial, essential human rights. The value of this approach
is not only that it makes explicit some of the underlying
assumptions of the legal system, but also that it may render
these into obligatory and overriding legal norms capable of
being enforced by legal process. Thus in the United States,
subsequent legislation which encroaches upon such fundamental provisions of the Constitution is declared to be invalid.
However, in some modern written constitutions broad statements regarding human or natural rights are inserted without conferring upon them specific legal force or empowering
the courts to give effect to them.[9] In constitutions of this kind
the declarations of human rights really amount to little more
than exhortations and slogans, and accordingly in many new
constitutions established since the Second World War, as for
instance in India and Western Germany, the American form
of a compulsory Bill of Rights has been adopted.

When some of the fundamental values of a legal system
are embodied in the constitution it may be thought that
these will make unnecessary any further search for underlying
values either on the lines of natural law or on some other
acceptable ethical basis. For where the courts are given
power to apply these provisions of the constitution it may
be said that they stand as agreed statements of natural-law
positions or supersede any that might otherwise be arrived
at on general reasoning alone. To a large extent this is
certainly the case, for the courts will henceforth consider
that their function is to give effect to the stated principles of
the constitution rather than to embark on theoretical or
personal inquiry as to the fundamental values of the constitution, whether inferred from natural law or some other
basis. This matter is, however, less simple than might appear,
not only because natural-law ideas are still widely current
even at the present day, but also because the precise meaning
and implication of general value principles, such as freedom
of speech, may be extremely controversial and give scope for
many varying attitudes. Moreover, the fact that fundamental
rights of this kind can only be stated in the constitution in

very general terms, subject either to very general specifically stated limitations or to implied limitations of an indefinite kind, leaves ample room for conflicting interpretations, even at the judicial level.

A written constitution embodying a bill of rights which expresses in general terms some of the main assumptions of the scale of values to which it is to give effect may go some way towards closing the gap we have discussed between formal and concrete justice. But that this solution is merely a beginning rather than a final solution of this problem will be manifest in the discussion, in the ensuing chapter, of the relation between law and freedom.

Law and Freedom

Law functions as a means of directing and imposing restraints upon human activities and it must therefore seem something of a paradox that the idea of freedom can be embodied in the law. The answer to this seeming paradox is to be gleaned by directing attention not on man solely as an individual living in an unfettered state of nature, but on man as a social being living a life of complex inter-relationships with the other members of his community. Rousseau's celebrated *cri de cœur*: 'Man is born free; yet everywhere he is in chains,' may have derived from the romantic notion that the savage lives a life of primitive freedom and simplicity, but in practice – as Rousseau realized – man is never isolated and free in this sense but always part of a community, and the degree of freedom he enjoys or the extent of the social restraints imposed upon him will depend upon the social organization of which he is a member. Nor, it should be remembered, is a restraint necessarily an encroachment upon liberty. The law restricts physical assault by one person on another, but if indiscriminate assault were permitted no human society could survive, for there would not even be that minimum degree of security without which human calculation for the future would be vain. Hence universal restraints of this character play an essential if indirect role in securing the freedom of all.

In most previous ages when inequality, rather than equality, was regarded as the fundamental law of human society, freedom operated in law as little more than a concept whereby a man was to be guaranteed, so far as the law could achieve, security in the station of life in which Providence had placed him, together with the privileges, if any, to which law or custom had established his entitlement.

Indeed, in a society which recognized slavery or serfdom, the slave or serf might enjoy no protection whatever by legal process or even custom, but such is the traditionalism of human society that even here quasi-legal acceptance of certain arrangements tends to become obligatory, as for instance in the Roman law of slavery or under feudalism. In modern times, however, where freedom has become closely linked with an egalitarian conception of society, the whole idea of freedom has assumed a central position and a more positive function in the scale of values set up as the operative ideals of a genuine social democracy on the Western pattern.

'OPEN' AND 'CLOSED' SOCIETIES

It has become common at the present day to distinguish between two types of society, the 'open' and 'closed' types respectively. In the former type there is said to be a wide field left for personal decision and for the assuming of individual responsibility, whereas in the 'closed' society there is an almost tribal or collectivist pattern, where the community is completely dominant and the individual counts for little or nothing. This contrast is usually made between a Western democratic society on the one hand and a totalitarian society, such as that of the Soviet Union or the former Nazi Germany, on the other. However, it must always be borne in mind that this contrast is by no means an absolute but only a relative one, and it may be said, indeed, that these two types of society are really 'ideal types,' in the sense employed by Max Weber.[1] Thus Western democracies may regard the open society as a pattern to which they aspire to conform, but at the same time there are tremendous developments even in Western society, in the direction of a more collectivist society. This emerges in the increasing role of the state in matters concerning social welfare. Also, the tendency of the mass societies of the West has been in the direction of increasing conformity in patterns of social behaviour and of repressing or discouraging what are regarded, rightly or wrongly, as individualist aberrations. Moreover, one cannot

ignore the Marxist argument that without control of wealth
and the pattern of its distribution, the genuine scope for
equality and individual initiative remains extremely
limited.

POSITIVE AND NEGATIVE FREEDOM

Another distinction which has also been emphasized in recent years is that between what is called 'positive' and
'negative' freedom. The latter is concerned with so organ-
izing the pattern of society, that despite all the restraints and
limitations that are placed upon individual action for the
benefit of society as a whole, there nevertheless remains as
large a sphere for individual choice and initiative as is com-
patible with the public welfare. Positive freedom, on the
other hand, is very much more in the nature of a spiritual
conception, implying as it does some kind of maximum
opportunity for the 'self-realization' of every individual to
his full capacity as a human being. The law, by its very
nature, must necessarily be concerned with the externals of
conduct, rather than the inner state of spiritual development
of the citizens subject to the law; it is therefore hardly surprising that so far as legal freedom is concerned, the emphasis is on guaranteeing the maximum degree of 'negative'
freedom – it is not the direct concern of the law how the
individual makes his choices within such freedom as the
law permits. The object of this chapter then, will be to try and
indicate the various ways in which, both on the national and
the international plane, attempts have been made in our
modern society to try and give effect to those values which
are regarded as enshrining in one form or another freedoms
which modern man has come to accept as an indispensable
feature of 'the good life'.

BASIC HUMAN RIGHTS

Since the American and the French Revolutions in the eighteenth century, attempts have repeatedly been made to ex-

press the fundamental values of Western society in terms of basic human rights. As we have already seen, this approach has a distinctively natural-law origin. Although the tendency at the present day is to endeavour to formulate these values in specifically positive-law terms, the natural-law origin of this mode of approach still remains fairly apparent, and on occasions intrudes itself into the discussion of fundamental rights as formulated in constitutional or supra-national documents, or even in the actual discussion of such rights in the judgments of constitutional courts.[2] Two outstanding contributions may be attributed to the constitution-makers of the United States and to the early judicial interpreters of that constitution. In the first place it was the founders of the American Constitution who evolved the idea of expressing in the written constitution of their new state a declaration of what were accepted as the fundamental legal human rights of the citizens. It was left to the judges to determine, in later decisions, what the legal effect of this Bill of Rights might be in terms of legal enforcement, and it was Chief Justice Marshall, in the early part of the nineteenth century, who introduced and established the then revolutionary doctrine that it was for the courts, and ultimately for the Supreme Court, to determine the scope of these constitutional provisions. It was Marshall who laid down that the court was authorized, and indeed bound, to treat these rights as 'overriding,' in the sense that any legislation or legal rulings or decisions which disregarded them, were to be treated as invalid.[3] Thus for the first time a pattern of legal machinery was provided by which fundamental rights could be treated, no longer as mere empty formulas, but as genuine legal norms governing actual legal relationships.

Yet a further development, in more recent times, has been the various attempts to express in a supra-national form the basic human rights which are regarded as the legal entitlement of all human beings. In this connexion must be mentioned the Universal Declaration of Human Rights of 1948, the European Convention of Human Rights, and the Declaration on the Rule of Law sponsored by the International

Commission of Jurists in 1959. Some reference will be made to this development after consideration has been given to the internal constitutional approach.

THE MAIN VALUES EXPRESSED IN LEGAL FREEDOM

For convenience these can be grouped under the following headings:

(1) *Equality and Democracy:* Human beings are far from equal either in physique, attainments, or capacities. Moreover, no modern society has considered it desirable or indeed feasible, to enforce a rigid egalitarianism in all spheres. Legal equality therefore tends to be regarded as an expression of the democratic organization of society, to be insured so far as practicable, by a universal franchise, the recognition of equality before the law,[4] and the principle of non-discrimination in regard to such matters as colour, race, or creed.

In recent years the question of non-discrimination is the one which has given rise to the greatest difficulties and controversy. The fundamental notion here is that a difference of sex, religion, race, or colour is not to be regarded as a valid principle of discrimination between one citizen and another in relation to legal rights. Far from accepting this principle, it is well known that some modern states, such as Nazi Germany and the present Union of South Africa, have erected racial or religious discrimination into an article of faith, and applied to it the full rigours of a repressive legal system of unparalleled extent. Moreover even in such a country as the United States, where the fundamental idea of equality is built into the Constitution, tremendous difficulties have been experienced in giving effect to this principle. The outstanding illustration is, of course, the recent decisions of the United States Supreme Court,[5] laying down that segregation between whites and negroes in American educational establishments is contrary to the Constitution, and that the provision of separate though equal institutions for this purpose is still contrary to the legal principle of equality.

These decisions, however authoritative in law, have encountered resolute and so far largely effective resistance in many of the Southern States of America, and it is well known that throughout the United States, a very large number of discriminatory practices against different races and religions and other groups are widely and effectively practised whatever the law may say to the contrary.

Two very important lessons, it may be thought, emerge from this situation from the point of view of the relationship of law to society. In the first place it is apparent that rules of law which are not expressive of the *mores* or standards of conduct which prevail in a given community are likely, notwithstanding all the panoply of legal process, to remain dead letters, through passive or even active resistance of the citizens. The second consideration is that if law is to be an effective focus for giving expression to fundamental values, it cannot content itself with merely aiming to reflect, in all respects, the common level of morality or accepted standards of social behaviour prevalent in the community; it must be regarded as a positive directing force, which can be used as an instrument of social progress.[5a] Of course we are faced with the fundamental dilemma that this inevitably appears to involve the non-democratic procedure of an 'enlightened' minority leading the recalcitrant majority in a direction in which it does not wish to go. Unless, however, it is recognized that, in a dynamic and progressive society, there must be scope for impetus to come from minority groups, rather than simply yielding to mass prejudices, it would seem that democracy must necessarily be inimical to all progress. It is here that the element of free discussion and the possibility of influencing public opinion by reasoned argument form so vital an element of democratic equality. In this respect the employment of legal norms as a means of controlling, developing, and changing public opinion on vital issues is strongly brought out by the present clash between the decisions of the United States Supreme Court and mass opinion in the Southern States. Of course, in this instance, the authority of the law is greatly assisted by the fact that there exists a widespread conviction among large numbers in America, especially outside the Southern States, that non-discrimination is a value of fundamental importance in a democratic society. It seems self-evident that if the weight of public opinion throughout the whole of the United States was in favour of segregation not only would the recent decisions have been far less effective even than they have proved to be, but the decisions themselves would in such a context have been almost unthinkable.

(2) *Freedom of Contract:* During the heyday of the régime of *laissez faire*, which could be said to run from the beginning of the nineteenth century to the outbreak of the 1914 War, the idea of freedom of contract was in some ways regarded as one of the supreme values of a developed society. State interference, especially in the economic sphere, was treated as a great evil, and it was thought that the economy of a free society could best be allowed to develop through the right of the citizen to make his own contractual arrangements. In the United States this doctrine was treated with peculiar reverence, and it was applied, significantly enough, not merely to the right of the individual citizen to make his own contracts free from state interference, but was also accorded to the great commercial corporations and enterprises which grew up rapidly in that country during the latter part of the nineteenth century. The startling abuses which resulted from so unfettered a system led to a counter-move in favour of state control, even though this could infringe the contractual freedom of individuals. The first decisive move in this direction was the legislation against monopolies and restrictive trade practices introduced in the United States at the turn of the century, but the courts on the whole were slow to modify their adhesion to the older doctrine. Accordingly the Supreme Court displayed marked hostility towards social welfare legislation, such as the control of the working hours of women and children in industry which they frequently struck down as being unconstitutional and in conflict with the vital value of contractual freedom. In

England this type of legislation, inspired by the Benthamite philosophy, was already well established as the nineteenth century passed into the present age. Moreover, there were no entrenched provisions in a written constitution in England which could be used as a weapon to enable the doctrine of contractual freedom to resist the flow of social legislation. In the United States on the other hand, this doctrine was still much used by the courts against the legislation introduced by President Roosevelt in the course of his New Deal, and it was not until the 1940s that the Supreme Court came to recognize that freedom of contract was no longer the pillar of the community that it had once been thought to be.

It was usually overlooked by those who regarded freedom of contract as the foundation of a free society that without equality of bargaining position such freedom was likely to be entirely one-sided. To say, for instance, that the factory workers of mid-Victorian England were free to accept or decline the terms and conditions of work offered to them by the employers, and therefore should be left to make their own bargain, was to ignore completely the underlying economic realities. With the rise of the trade unions in recent times something like genuine equality of bargaining power has transformed the character of industrial relations, though this does not mean that there is not still scope for state intervention in these matters, as will be pointed out later on.[6] Moreover, the modern state has found it increasingly necessary to recognize that many classes of persons, such as purchasers of goods (especially under hire-purchase agreements) are in need of protection against traders and suppliers who seek to impose unfair terms and conditions on those who are unable to bargain effectively in their own interests. The widespread growth of so-called 'standard-form' contracts has further exposed the unreality of freedom of contract in the economic world of today. In some instances legislation (such as Hire Purchase Acts) has been passed to remedy the more palpable of the abuses which have emerged as the inevitable economic consequence of unfettered freedom of contract.[7]

(3) *The Right of Property:* There have been few societies in which the preservation of property has not been regarded as one of the supreme purposes of law. The power of the state or the sovereign to tax the citizens certainly seemed to involve some encroachment upon this right, but a reconciliation was found here by the introduction of the principle that taxation was permissible provided there was consent to it, and this has meant, in the modern democratic state, that the taxation has been authorized by a duly elected representative legislature. At the present day, in all developed communities, the level of taxation has been established at a height which in previous ages would have been regarded as nothing less than confiscatory.

Although the inviolability of property still remains an important value in Western society, the fact remains that very important inroads have been made upon this principle. The nationalization of whole industries, the extensive control by planning legislation of the uses that land and buildings can be put to, sweeping powers of compulsory acquisition enabling authorities to acquire land from private owners without their consent; these are accepted today as essential features of the state machinery for controlling the welfare of the community. It is true that under a Marxist or semi-Marxist system, such as that of the Soviet Union, the social function of property may be treated as of even more far-reaching importance. In Soviet Russia the protection of private property is accorded only to property acquired by work and is confined to articles of personal use and not, for instance, the means of production or land. Thus, the objects of ownership are far more strictly limited by Marxist theory, though, as compared with the modern welfare state, the difference is perhaps only one of degree.

At the present day the fundamental belief in the recognition of private property remains, in the notion that property should not be arbitrarily acquired from private persons without adequate compensation. Even here however there may be marked differences in the view of what constitutes adequate compensation. In England, under a Labour government after the end of the last war, legislation was introduced under which compensation was to be based upon the existing-use value of land without regard to the value that land might fetch in the market, having regard to its potentialities for development. More recently a Conservative government reversed this legislation, by providing that compensation should be related to the full market value of the land, including the development value.[7a] Here then we see an effective illustration of the fact that while a certain freedom may be universally accepted as valid its precise interpretations may lead to very different consequences.

(4) *The Right of Association:* Under this heading many types of group activity may be considered. There is the question of the right of various types of groups, whether social, political, or economic, or of any other kind to organize themselves and to conduct their affairs. This extends to such questions also as the right of business enterprise to organize itself and how far it may be legitimately restrained in order to protect the public against monopolies, restrictive practices, or fraud. Thus much of modern company law is concerned with various measures to protect the investor against improper or deceitful practices which might arise in the course of share flotations or the conduct of company affairs. Then there is also the question of the right of labour to organize itself in trade unions and to deal on a collective basis with employers or associations representing them. Last but not least, there is the right of people to hold public meetings, for the purpose of making protests or attempting to influence public opinion and so forth.

The right to hold public meetings has given rise to acute controversy in modern times, and has also posed considerable problems both for the legislator and for the courts. Clearly the state has a right to preserve public order, but this may frequently clash at critical points with the right of holding protest meetings. For instance, are such meetings to be permitted, even though they are summoned for the express purpose of pouring abuse upon and arousing hostility towards particular sections of the community, e.g. racial or religious minorities? In England, owing to the outburst of Fascism during the 1930s, it was found necessary to pass the Public Order Act of 1936, preventing the wearing of unofficial uniforms in public places, and also imposing restraint upon the use of abusive language at public gatherings. It is obvious that this right to hold public meetings is closely related to the more general right to freedom of expression, and therefore more will be said of this problem under that heading.

(5) *Freedom of Labour:* This right in modern times has mainly developed in relation to the trade union organization of labour. Many problems have arisen in the external relations of unions either with other unions or with employers, as well as internal problems concerning the organization of trade unions and their relations with their own members or with non-members. After having long been treated as outlaws, the trade unions have now established themselves in their rightful role as essential organs of the modern democratic community. Yet even to this day, it cannot be said that the fundamental right of a trade union to be recognized as the organ of collective bargaining, by the appropriate employers, is fully established. Moreover this question is now decisively linked with the problem of the so-called 'closed shop' or 'the union shop'. For the unions now regularly maintain that collective bargaining is not an effective proposition unless they are able to insist that all the workers in a given industry or factory are to be members of a union, thereby excluding non-union labour. There is undoubtedly great force in this argument, and so far as England is concerned, there has been no obstacle placed in the way of trade unions establishing a closed shop.[7b] On the other hand this can place in the hands of the unions very great powers in relation to their members or even over non-members of the unions, since it enables them in effect to exclude non-union workers from particular types of industrial activity. Moreover, in English law, there appears to be nothing to stop a union imposing the most rigorous

restrictions upon the qualifications of a workman for entry into a union,[8] and the union may have virtually unfettered power to expel a member for some conduct which the union disapproves, provided only that the union gives the man a fair hearing of any charge that is made against him in accordance with the principles of what is called 'natural justice'.[9]

A further vital aspect of the right of labour in the modern state is the established right to strike[9a] where the workers consider their interests are at stake. It is undoubtedly true that without the strike weapon the power of labour to assert its independence would have been drastically curtailed, but since the earlier days of labour struggles other factors have come to the fore. There is, for instance, the problem of unofficial strikes, where bodies of workmen insist on going on strike without the consent and even against the express instructions of their own unions. Moreover the question also arises whether a small body of men with a grievance, whether genuine or otherwise, should be allowed to hold to ransom a whole industry, or even the whole economic life of the country, without being first required to submit their dispute to some form of arbitral procedure. On the whole the attitude in England has been to avoid any form of compulsion in these matters,[9b] but to leave it ultimately to negotiation between the parties concerned in the dispute, with a rather indeterminate right or power of the Government in the last resort to try and intervene in the dispute, not so much by exercising legal powers as by exerting moral pressures. In other countries, such as the United States, Australia, and Scandinavian countries, much greater faith has been placed in some regular form of compulsory arbitral procedure of a judicial or quasi-judicial character. Views have differed a good deal as to how far labour disputes about wages, or conditions of work are genuinely 'justiciable'. To some extent this question really goes to the root of the whole understanding of the scope and purpose of law in a modern community, and the idea that disputes of this kind are not properly matters which can be determined by tribunals on a judicial or a semi-judicial basis stems to some extent from the old *laissez faire* idea that these are really matters for free bargaining in the open market and cannot be determined by a judicial procedure. However, as we have seen, freedom of contract has already been removed from its former plinth, and increasingly opinion has been moving, both in the national and in the international sphere, towards the idea that no type of dispute is in itself inherently lacking in justiciability, but that the question is really whether public opinion is ripe for submitting particular kinds of disputes to judicial arbitration. Experience in many countries has shown that this type of dispute lends itself eminently to semi-judicial arbitration, and even in England many such disputes are in fact determined by an arbitral procedure. It remains true however that the only form of English compulsory arbitral procedure (set up during the last war), by the machinery of the so-called Industrial Disputes Tribunal, was recently abolished by legislation.

(6) *Freedom from Want and Social Security:* The need to protect everyone, not merely against grinding poverty, but also in the enjoyment of a reasonable standard of life whether in or out of employment, has gradually established itself as one of the supreme values of the modern state. In England, for instance, an elaborate system of national insurance has been introduced, which – for all its faults and deficiences – does at any rate attempt to provide comprehensive cover against the risks of unemployment, and of injury sustained in the course of a person's employment, as well as providing pensions after retirement. In addition a comprehensive scheme covering national health has been introduced, which provides free medical services for the whole population. This emphasis upon the need to spread the risks of misfortune among the community as a whole, rather than allowing them simply to affect the particular victim of the misfortune, has led to further attempts to try and extend the notion of insurance to many of the other risks attendant on everyday life.

Most conspicuous of these is the risk of injury on the public highway due to the use of motor vehicles, and the extent of this problem has resulted in wide-ranging schemes of compulsory third-party insurance, so that a person who is injured by negligent driving may be certain of obtaining compensation from an insurance company if the individual negligent driver is lacking in sufficient means. The value of social security and the belief that it is one of the main purposes of the legal system to ensure this seem to come in conflict at some point with the generally established principle of civil liability, under which a person is only entitled to be paid damages or compensation if he can establish some negligence or other fault on the part of a wrongdoer.[10] This idea, that compensation is only payable on proof of a culpable act, has been to some extent rejected in the sphere of industrial injuries, where a compensation scheme has been established in England and in many other countries providing for compensation on a statutory scale if the injury has occurred during employment. It is true that in England this scheme is in addition to and not in substitution for the ordinary common-law liability, which can still be established if it can be proved that the accident was due to the negligence of the employer or someone for whom he was responsible. In some countries, however, such as Canada, a scheme of compensation for industrial injuries has been established in substitution for the common-law liability. Be this as it may, the insurance principle has not generally speaking been applied to other types of accidents, such as road accidents, for it should be borne in mind that even third-party insurance only operates when the driver is shown to have been guilty of negligence and so causing the accident.

On the whole there is a general feeling at the present day that there may be a need for some more general system of social security which will protect people against the risk of accidents, other than industrial accidents, as a result of which they may be incapacitated, or lose their chance of a livelihood, with grave loss both to themselves and to their dependants. Should the right to recover compensation in such cases depend simply on being able to establish negligence against some particular wrongdoer? This may be exceedingly difficult to do in many cases, and it may be regarded as in a sense irrelevant to the fact that the particular individual has suffered a misfortune for which social justice requires that reparation be made to him by the community as a whole rather than allowing the loss to fall entirely upon himself. It may be said that after all the individual can always make his own provision for private insurance, but this is the sort of argument which has traditionally been used against all types of social security legislation, and rather smacks of the Victorian philosophy of self-help. All the same the law still remains wedded to the notion that compensation for accidents must depend upon visiting the responsibility upon an individual who is liable for his own or someone else's negligence. As the social security aspect of the legal system becomes increasingly extended, this form of thought may become increasingly outmoded and may eventually be replaced by a comprehensive security scheme,[10a] possibly supplemented in certain respects by the existing form of common-law personal liability. Here we see how merely establishing certain types of values as fundamental in a community may still leave many questions of principle in issue, though the acceptance of a new value of this kind does inevitably set up a kind of impetus of its own which tends to create ramifications through many if not all aspects of the legal system.

(7) *Freedom of Speech and of the Press:* In any community where democratic and egalitarian values prevail, it is obvious that the right to free speech and the right of freedom of the Press must be ranked as fundamental values, for without these the possibility of developing and crystallizing public opinion, and allowing it to be brought to bear upon the governmental organs of the state, is bound to be virtually ineffective. Accordingly it is normal to find freedoms of this character put in a central position in the complex of fundamental rights to be found in written constitutions. But even assuming

a constitution which guarantees these freedoms, the question still remains how they are to be interpreted and what they mean in practice. Freedom of speech can hardly be absolutely unrestricted, for in any reasonably ordered society there will exist a law of defamation, which will restrict people from making unwarranted and untrue attacks upon the reputation of others. And there may be other restraints. Even if the state is sufficiently liberal to allow any attacks either in public or in private upon the government of the state, including the character of its fundamental constitution and economic and social structure, the law may still draw the line where attempts are made to incite others to take action to overthrow the government or the constitution by violence. This distinction is attempted in the English law of sedition as it is generally interpreted in modern times, but the line is not always very easy to draw. Again most if not all legal systems usually impose some restraint on publications or representations which are considered to be obscene. The effect of so-called obscenity upon either mature or immature minds is exceedingly obscure and cannot be said to have been established in any precise form by modern psychological research. The fact remains that most communities consider that there is a certain type of obscene publication which ought not to be permitted both as being potentially harmful and also as offending certain established canons of taste. At one time, at any rate, the law of obscenity was used as a means of restraining the publication of much serious literature, such as the novels of Zola and of James Joyce. A far more liberal approach has now become increasingly common and this is certainly indicated in England by the passing of the new Obscene Publications Act of 1959,[11] and the verdict of acquittal in the prosecution brought in 1960 against the publishers of D. H. Lawrence's celebrated novel *Lady Chatterley's Lover*. So far as England is concerned – and this position had already been established in the United States some years ago – it now seems to be accepted doctrine that a book will not be treated as unlawful merely because it contains vulgar words and frank sexual descriptions, provided the book is of a serious character and is not simply aimed at a pornographic type of reader.[11a]

Another aspect of freedom of speech is its relation to censorship. Freedom of speech and of the Press usually implies an absence of initial censorship, that is to say that the works can be freely published subject to any possible legal action thereafter ensuing. Such legal action will then depend upon the general law of defamation, sedition, obscenity, and so forth, and not upon any mere administrative discretion. This is the position which obtains in England so far as book and periodical publications are concerned, but censorship also exists in the United Kingdom in other fields; much of the world of entertainment is dominated by one form of censorship or another. In the case of the theatre, the Lord Chamberlain's statutory power and duty to censor all public theatrical performances prior to actual performance were abolished in 1968.[11b] There is no official or statutory censorship in regard to the cinema, but a substitute for this has been found by a form of self-censorship, in the shape of a Board of Censors which has been set up by the industry and which grants or withholds certificates to individual films, the certificates indicating the class of audience for which the film has been passed. Moreover local authorities possess the power to grant or withhold licences to cinema theatres on such conditions as they care to lay down, and this enables them to control the exhibition of films in cinemas within their areas. Although these authorities usually accept the certificate of the Board, they possess the ultimate power either to permit a film which has in fact been refused a showing by the Board of Censors, or to refuse to allow it to be shown in their area notwithstanding the grant of a certificate. So far as commercial television is concerned, the Independent Television Authority has a statutory power of censorship over the programmes provided by the independent television programme contractors and broadcast by the Authority. The British Broadcasting Corporation is its own censor, in the sense that it has complete discretion to decide what should or should not be shown or transmitted in its programmes; this is still a power of censorship although not exercised by a separate body. These forms of censorship, and more particularly that operating in the theatre,[11b] have come in for a great deal of criticism, some taking the view that there should be no censorship at all, others that the matter should be left to possible prosecution in the event of a performance being in some way contrary to law.

The real difficulty here is to determine what are the ultimate limits of tolerance which may be required by the established value of freedom of speech. For quite apart from questions of defamation and obscenity, there remains the question how far it is permissible to use media of entertainment or broadcasting as a means of propagating doctrines or opinions which may be thought objectionable either by the community as a whole, or by important or sectional interests, or which may be extremely offensive to groups of individuals. If it is once admitted that some restraint is necessary or desirable in relation to matters such as these, it is in a sense only a matter of machinery whether this restraint is to be exercised by some administrative body, or to be dealt with ultimately by the courts of law. In theory this frequently involves questions of taste which are not easily dealt with by legal machinery, though there seems no reason for saying that these are not 'justiciable' issues. Nor does the experience of the attitude of the courts towards so-called obscene literature necessarily indicate that the courts are likely to adopt a more liberal attitude than some administrative board or organ. Perhaps a compromise might be found in favour both of administrative convenience and ultimate freedom of speech, by having such censorship as is needed carried out by an administrative body or official, but with an independent tribunal which can hear appeals from his or their decisions.

There remains however an even more fundamental problem in relation to the so-called limit of tolerance: namely, how far a democratic state should be prepared to permit doctrines to be propagated which are themselves aimed at inspiring intolerance against specific groups. Are Fascists for instance to be allowed to avail themselves of the

tolerance of the democratic state in order to preach intolerance against particular groups whom they hate or despise?
For example, under the English Public Order Act, 1936,
the use at a public meeting of abusive or insulting language
which is calculated to occasion a breach of the peace is an
offence. This enables a successful prosecution to be brought
in the case of a person deliberately using insulting language
in relation to a particular group of persons, where members
of the group being abused may be expected to be present
at the meeting and may be incited to express their hostility
with violence.[12] There is nothing in this law however which
restrains the writing or distributing of, for instance, anti-
Semitic or racialist writings, and it has been suggested that
the law should be strengthened in this respect. One possible
view, which is strongly taken, is that the law should only
concern itself in such matters with public order, and therefore
that it should not attempt to restrain the expressions of
opinion, such as hatred of groups because of their colour,
race, or religion, however objectionable such views might
be and however much hostility they may inspire. Another
view is that tolerance is an essential feature of the values of a
democratic society, and that the very concept of tolerance
involves the seemingly paradoxical feature that such tolerance must be extended towards all persons in relation to any
opinions held by them, save only in the one case of any
person or group which specifically propagates intolerance
against another group. In the latter view it should be recognized that there is both a moral and a legal right to suppress
intolerance of this kind, though it does not follow that it
would always be wise to do so, and the cases in which action
would be necessary would depend upon expediency and other
considerations of public policy at the particular time. Clearly
even this second view does not involve the idea that any
group should be immune from criticism, but only that it
should not be permissible to insult and abuse its members or
attempt to inspire hatred of them for the purpose of encouraging their suppression or their subjection to legal disabilities.[12a]

Censorship problems are generally considered from the

negative aspect, but perhaps their greatest significance at the present day is from the positive point of view. One of the real dangers existing in this age of mass media is the tendency for the organs of public opinon to fall increasingly into a very few hands by reason of newspaper mergers and take-overs of publishing firms and so forth; in addition the facilities for broadcasting, whether sound or television, lie in the hands either of the public authorities or of a very few commercial interests. There is therefore a considerable risk, which is already manifest in this field, that such media will tend to pander to what is regarded as acceptable to rather conventional standards of public opinion, and that the more trenchant and genuinely independent forms of journalism and entertainment will be squeezed out in favour of a general toning down of the material to be put before the public. The law itself can obviously do very little to inspire positive independence of this kind, though some measures may conceivably be invoked by restricting or controlling mergers, and also by ensuring that the organs of censorship are not used merely for the purpose of rigorously enforcing conventional standards of taste and opinion.

Among all these so-called 'mass media' the Press clearly retains a central position because of its unique capacity for serving as a focus of public opinion. Attempts are sometimes made on this basis to treat the freedom of the Press as a supreme freedom which ought to override all other freedoms in the democratic community. This however is to overlook the rather special position of newspapers in the democratic state, by reason of their ownership reposing in the hands of a very small number of 'Press barons'. Moreover the understandable desire to increase their circulations has caused many newspapers to indulge in a highly irresponsible type of journalism of which the frequent invasions of individual privacy, for the purpose of regaling the public with sensational news items, provide a conspicuous and salutary warning example. In the United States the courts have in some instances permitted actions for unwarrantable intrusions into privacy of this kind, and there is also legislation on this matter in some of the states of America. In England the law has not contrived to develop on these lines, nor has the attempt to fill the gap by the creation of a Press Council so far proved particularly effective.[13] The recent distribution by certain sections of the Press of unfounded rumours, in relation to what has become known as the *Vassall* case, has further emphasized the undesirability of conferring unique privileges upon the Press. When, arising out of the Vassall investigation, two journalists were committed for contempt for refusing to give the sources of their alleged information, it was argued that there was an overriding public policy which ought to entitle newspaper reporters to be privileged as to giving their sources of information, but this suggestion was entirely rejected by the English courts.[14] Whether a particular journalist feels it to be contrary to his moral or professional conscience in a particular case to reveal his sources is another matter, and raises the question, already discussed,[15] regarding conflict between conscience and the law. What seems to be unproved is that there is any necessarily overriding public interest which entitles journalists to complete immunity as to revealing their sources of information, although no such immunity is enjoyed by anyone else.[16]

(8) *Freedom of Religion:* In earlier ages, when there was a strong tendency to stigmatize controversial religious opinions as blasphemous or heretical, the question of religious tolerance was the centre of the whole struggle for toleration. Freedom of religious belief however is now recognized as an established value in a democratic society, though the exact implications of this doctrine may appear in a very different light in different communities. Under the United States Constitution no established religion is permitted, whereas in England an established religion is an essential part of the constitution. Perhaps a lack of religious ardour in England prevents this aspect of the problem assuming any great significance at the present day. The main aspects of freedom of religion which are apt to arise nowadays are in

connexion with discrimination against religious groups, which has already been referred to under previous headings, and with the question of religious schools, or the specific teaching of religious faith or doctrine in state or other types of schools. Apart from this kind of problem, which has loomed large in some countries such as France and the United States, religious doctrine sometimes finds itself in conflict with the established public order. Mormons may permit and encourage polygamy – needless to say this is no longer so – and Christian Scientists may refuse medical aid for their children. In this type of case the law generally refuses to regard religious groups as being entitled to any special degree of immunity from legal regulation, and therefore will take action against breaches of the criminal law however religiously inspired these may be. This does not usually cause acute controversy from the point of view of freedom of conscience provided the law is careful only to enforce criminal sanctions in cases which would have the widespread support of reasonably enlightened public opinion. A mother who, from whatever pious motives, allows her helpless child to die without medical aid is unlikely to inspire profound sympathy from the general public on grounds of freedom of conscience.

(9) *Personal Freedom:* Although personal freedom may easily be ranked as supreme among the freedoms of a democratic society, it is not easy to find specific applications which do not more readily fall under other headings of freedom, and can perhaps be dealt with more conveniently thereunder. Thus, such matters as the need for 'due process of law', that is, that no person shall be subject to legal penalty save for a breach of some specific and duly promulgated law and that there shall be adequate safeguards regarding the detention and fair trial of accused persons can be said to form essential elements of the so-called 'Rule of Law' which will be dealt with under the next heading.

Another, and perhaps equally vital aspect of personal freedom, is that everyone should be free to come and go as he pleases, to take up or reject any employment that he may wish, to reside wherever he may desire, and generally speaking to lead the sort of life which, subject to compliance with the law of the land, may seem good to him. These negative but vital freedoms, which provide one of the important antitheses between a totalitarian and a genuinely democratic régime, are not likely to result from any positive lawmaking but rather from the general spirit of the legislator who will refrain from introducing any elements of compulsion in these matters, save when there is some overriding public emergency, such as a state of war. Many of these freedoms may depend largely upon the economic situation of the individual, and so long as the economic structure of the country allows of substantial differences of fortune between classes and individuals, it will follow inevitably that those who possess ample means will have more freedoms of this kind. Here there is clearly an important issue as to the extent to which the state is ready and willing to enforce a high measure of economic egalitarianism. Again, the question of freedom to take up any employment is linked with the matters already discussed under freedom of labour, such as the control of unions over their members and the so-called 'closed shop'. As to the question of the choice of residence, this must to a large degree turn upon economic resources, though the state can do much by providing suitable homes in suitable places for those of the population who do not enjoy the free choice possessed by the wealthy, and also by protecting such persons in relation to tenancies already occupied by them. Any measures of the latter kind, however, will conflict with the belief in the general freedom of property so far as landlords are concerned, and this consideration has no doubt had a good deal to do with the gradual dismantling of the system of rent control which has operated in England since the 1914 War.

Freedom to travel, both within and outside the confines of the territory of the state, raises important issues of personal freedom. This type of freedom has largely been regarded as axiomatic in modern times in Western Europe, but certainly not in Eastern Europe, where restrictions on travel and

residence in particular cities or territories have been traditionally severe. The universal introduction of passports for
the purpose of travel abroad has necessarily placed a considerable power in the executive with or without any express
legislation, since, by the simple expedient of withholding a
passport, the executive can effectively prevent any of its
citizens from going overseas. In England the administration
has not generally sought to take advantage of this situation
though it has done so on occasions. English law provides the
citizen with no remedy whatsoever in such a case. In the
United States attempts have also been made by the executive
to restain individuals from travelling abroad by refusing a
passport, with the object of preventing persons thought to
be undesirable politically from going to other countries. The
United States Supreme Court however has held this form
of executive interference with personal liberty to be unconstitutional if exercised on merely political grounds,
such as the association of the individual with the Communist
Party.

A régime of personal freedom in a democratic society
involves freedom not only for actual citizens but for the whole
community, including friendly aliens resident or otherwise
temporarily present in the country in question. Nevertheless
a state may still be entitled to retain reserve powers to expel
an alien who has seriously misconducted himself, or to return
him to his country under some established extradition
procedure. Extradition treaties traditionally exclude political
offenders, though this is not always so. This has recently
been heavily underlined in the *Enahoro* case, concerning the
deportation of a Commonwealth citizen from England to be
tried as a political offender in another Commonwealth
country, namely Nigeria.[17] A further lacuna in this sphere
of English law was recently brought to light in the *Soblen*
case. In this case it was held that the Home Secretary has
complete discretion to deport an alien back to the country
from which he has escaped, and where he has already been
tried and found guilty of an offence which, having regard to
its political character, would not qualify for extradition,

T–F

provided only that the Minister is satisfied in good faith that such deportation is in the public interest.[18] In this way the alien appears to be effectively deprived of those safeguards against being sent back to stand political trial or answer for political offences which the traditional procedure of normal extradition treaties was designed to protect. No better illustration could be afforded of the danger of making personal fundamental rights subservient to a vaguely defined public interest whose limits are to be resolved solely by executive decree.[19]

(10) *The Rule of Law :* The Rule of Law is here referred to in its narrow sense,[20] as imposing those procedural guarantees which have been found necessary to ensure what in American constitutional practice is known as 'due process of law'. This involves all such matters as ensuring the independence of the judiciary;[21] providing for the speedy and fair trial of accused persons and for adequate judicial control over police and police methods of securing confessions from accused persons; providing adequate safeguards regarding arrest and detention pending trial; and providing adequate legal aid for those whose financial resources are not sufficient to obtain suitable legal defence. Moreover, since the rights of the individual here squarely confront those of the state, the accused must be entitled to refuse to make any statement which is calculated to incriminate himself, and those charged with the duty of advocacy must be free and independent and not subject to any state pressure. Nor must the advocate be regarded as in any way an agent of the state itself or one whose duty is not so much to his client but to the administration of justice, as personified by the state. A further application of this doctrine is the established principle that no person shall be found guilty of an offence which is not specifically laid down in some criminal prohibition established prior to the date when the offence is alleged to have been committed. A doctrine which permits courts of law to recognize new criminal offences from time to time on the ground that these involve a breach of an important rule of established current

morality, as appears to have been laid down in the so-called
Ladies' Directory case,[22] would seem contrary to the spirit of
this principle and has been criticized on this account. For
the same reason penal legislation which is retrospective in
effect is also frowned upon and indeed prohibited in some
modern written constitutions.

It should also be observed that one of the inherent assumptions of the Rule of Law in modern times is the general
recognition of the principle that responsibility is personal
and individual, and that accordingly a person is only to be
answerable for his own wrongdoing and not to be punished
simply because he is in some way connected with or related
to or a member of the same group as the guilty person. The
whole notion of group liability, so familiar in earlier phases
of legal development,[23] is entirely contrary to the spirit of
modern legislation. Few examples of invasion of individual
rights seem more flagrant at the present day than any attempt
to punish a man by inflicting penalties on members of his
family. It is true that, in modern civil liability, the principle
is universally recognized that a man may be held liable for
the acts of his servants or agents acting within the scope of
their employment, but the best explanation of this established principle seems to be that it derives from an accepted
principle of public policy. This is that where risks of injury
are created by the activities of servants or agents, it is right
that such risks should be fairly distributed by imposing
liability on the employer, who is easily able to insure against
any loss, rather than allowing the whole loss to fall on the
innocent injured party. In any event the principle of vicarious
responsibility applies only to civil and not to criminal
liability, though even in modern law there are one or two
minor or special cases where this principle is applicable in
the criminal sphere.[24]

The scope of the modern Rule of Law is not limited to cases
of safeguarding accused persons, but also has a wide and
important sphere of operation in regard to the exercise of
state or governmental powers. All modern states which sub-
scribe to the principle of the Rule of Law have found it

necessary to develop rules of administrative law which enable either the ordinary courts of law, or some special tribunals or officials, to exercise supervision over the administrative or quasi-judicial functions of the executive in all its branches. Some difficulty has been experienced in the past, owing probably to the ramifications of the doctrine of sovereignty, in allowing citizens to bring ordinary actions against the state as such. These difficulties have however generally been overcome, though so far as England is concerned, the situation was not satisfactorily resolved until as late as 1948, when legislation was introduced rationalizing this branch of the law.

More important is the general question of complaints against the state or its executive organs, in relation to its administrative powers, where, for instance, a citizen desires to assert that powers have been exercised in some abusive, improper, or negligent manner to his detriment either individually or as a member of an affected group. Common-law systems on the whole have pinned their faith here upon a general supervisory jurisdiction exercisable by the ordinary courts, whereas Continental countries have, generally speaking, favoured an independent system of administrative supervision operated by a separate set of administrative courts or tribunals, or exercised by a specific official, such as the Scandinavian Ombudsman. The Rule of Law is not as such concerned with the exact technical procedure that is applied to enforce its requirements, save in so far as a fundamentally ineffectual system would not be regarded as complying with the needs of the Rule of Law itself. It is fair to say that some countries have developed a system of administrative law administered by separate tribunals, such as the justly celebrated French system based on the Conseil d'État, which has proved an exceedingly effective instrument for the control of administrative power in many of its aspects. On the other hand the common-law system of controlling executive power by means of supervisory orders issued by the ordinary courts of law to the administrative authorities has proved somewhat inadequate, more especially in dealing with cases where an authority has technically acted within its powers, but where its actual exercise of those powers may be open to question on the grounds of abuse[24a] or negligence. Moreover the English courts dealt a severe blow to the possibility of effective control of administrative authorities and agencies by establishing the rule that the state and its agencies are entitled to claim privilege in regard to the non-disclosure of relevant documents in any case where it is certified by a Minister that it is not in the public interest that the contents of these documents should be disclosed. The English courts even laid down that they could not go behind this certificate by way of looking at the documents to satisfy themselves that the privilege had been properly claimed. Therefore even where an administrative act might conceivably be open to question on the ground of its abusive exercise, the aggrieved citizen was almost inevitably precluded from establishing his claim, since he was prevented from seeing the material documents dealing with the matter in question. However, the House of Lords has recently reversed this ruling by deciding that a court has a duty to satisfy itself that the privilege claimed is justified in the circumstances.[25]

THE PROBLEM OF CONFLICTING VALUES

The foregoing discussion has given some indication of the many ways in which conflicts may arise between the various types of fundamental rights accepted in the modern democratic state, and the values which underlie these. Thus, freedom of speech may conflict with the right of the citizen to be protected against intolerant propaganda; the right to maintain independent religious groups may carry with it consequences involving discrimination; and the rights of organized labour may cut across the claims of individuals to be protected in their particular employments. In addition, the security of the state may be invoked as a value overriding all individual claims. An attempt was made to draw the line beyond which personal freedom would have to yield to considerations of public security by the American judge,

Mr Justice Holmes, when he laid down in 1919[26] that there must be a 'clear and present danger' to public security. The difficulty of applying a formula of this kind however was sufficiently exemplified during the unhappy period in American affairs when 'McCarthyism' held sway in the United States. Some judges of the United States Supreme Court in recent years have also put forward a doctrine of 'preferred freedoms', that is to say, certain freedoms guaranteed by the Constitution are to be regarded as more fundamental than others and therefore should prevail against other less basic freedoms. What this means in effect is that such freedoms are to be treated as the primary values of the Constitution and these therefore will override lesser freedoms when there is a conflict. It is of course entirely open to any judicial tribunal, especially a constitutional Supreme Court, to establish judicially that certain constitutional guarantees are to be treated as more basic than others, but this is not to say that such a judicial ruling or attitude must necessarily be operative at all times. In earlier periods the value of freedom of contract was treated by the American courts as a kind of supreme value, whereas in more recent years this has had to yield substantially to certain social values of a less individualistic character, and is in any event generally regarded as subordinate at the present day to the concept of personal freedom.

Attempts have been made in some constitutional decisions, for instance in recent cases both in the United States and in the German Federal Republic, to try and delineate some sort of natural-law basis upon which a scheme of preferred values might be erected. Thus in some American cases, certain safeguards in relation to federal trials as laid down in the Constitution, such as the principle against self-incrimination, have been treated by some of the United States Supreme Court judges as partaking of natural-law principles because they are 'of the very essence of a scheme of ordered liberty'.[27] However, it is difficult to see how such assertions amount to more than saying that there are certain values which are regarded as deeply rooted in a particular society, or possibly in civilized society as a whole, at a particular phase of historical development. The attempt to distil a whole scheme of permanent values, whether or not arranged in some sort of hierarchical order, encounters many difficulties which have already been fully canvassed and need not be repeated here. What can hardly be disputed is that for the purposes of such a scheme of values as is normally associated at the present day with a democratic form of society, there is perpetual need both for an informed and educated state of public opinion and for a high measure of free discussion in all the organs of opinion which society can deploy. A dogmatically established canon of universally valid standards of conduct, however generally approved, which is not open to free discussion and criticism, is unlikely to form an adequate basis for a truly 'open' society.

HUMAN RIGHTS AND THEIR INTERNATIONAL PROTECTION

It is one thing to lay down fundamental norms, even with all the panoply of a constitutional document, and quite another to ensure that those concerned actually comply with those norms. No more graphic illustration of this distinction could be sought than the attempt to apply the non-segregation principles of the United States Constitution as asserted in leading decisions of the Supreme Court to the reluctant Southern States of America. This unresolved conflict provides a classic example of the respective elements of force and authority in the process of the law, and for the need or these to rein orce each other.

The reluctance or inability of individual states to take adequate measures to protect the individual rights either of their citizens or of aliens resident in their midst has led to a number of attempts in modern times to establish some kind of supra-national authority which can take steps to protect individuals against denials of justice. Customary international law has hardly provided much assistance, particularly in view of the established doctrine that only states are recognized under that system of law, not private individuals, so that an individual has no means of bringing a complaint in the international sphere against his own state unless he can persuade that state, so to speak, to arraign itself, which is hardly likely. Again, a foreign national has to rely on the legal assistance of the state of which he is a national, and it is entirely for that state to decide whether to grant or withhold such assistance. Moreover, customary international law imposes very few restraints upon the sovereign power of a state to deal with its own citizens or resident aliens, and in any event no judicial or other machinery is provided for such issues to be investigated or made the subject of judicial rulings.

For this purpose, therefore, there are at least two requisites, namely, in the first place a clearly laid down code of established human rights accepted by all civilized states, and a system of judicial machinery whereby issues involving alleged infringement of these rights can be investigated and determined by a regular procedure. This still leaves in the air the question of ultimate enforcement but enforcement of judicial or other decisions against states as such does involve problems of very great complexity, some of which have already been referred to in an earlier chapter,[28] and need not be repeated here. The Universal Declaration of Human Rights adopted by the General Assembly of the United Nations in 1948 was an attempt to lay down a code of human rights to be accepted by all states, but this document contained no implementing machinery, and must be regarded as little more than a resounding statement of principle, useful perhaps in influencing public opinion, but not likely to have more than a marginal effect so far as individual grievances are concerned. A further and rather more precise attempt to declare an acceptable code of fundamental rights and freedoms was made as a result of the Convention for the Protection of Human Rights and Fundamental Freedoms, signed by the members of the Council of Europe in 1950. This Convention also contemplated the setting up of specific judicial machinery and this has in fact since been done, by the establishment in 1954 of the European Commission of Human Rights. This represents an interesting experiment in the attempt to give supra-national effect to fundamental rights, and an important aspect of the procedure of the Commission is that the Commission is given competence to hear applications referred to it by individuals against a state which is a party to the Convention, though this competence is only discretionary, so that the Commission is not bound to hear any application that is made. This optional competence has been accepted by most of the signatories to the Convention including the United Kingdom.

Clearly these measures represent only a very tentative beginning,[29] and it will be a long and painful process before states can be persuaded, if they ever are, to renounce their ultimate jurisdiction to be masters in their own domestic territory. Nevertheless these attempts to erode the concept of internal sovereignty represent a useful advance, and point in a significant way to the manner in which the idea of law can be used to give effective expression to the fundamental values existing in civilized society and to translate these from slogans into effective legal norms.

　　　　　Law, Sovereignty, and the
　　　　　　　　State

It is a commonplace in a society with a developed system of law that there must be some authority which is invested with the power of law-making. In a simpler society law may be conceived rather as the customary observances handed down from generation to generation and only gradually modified as new usages come to be adopted and recognized. We shall have more to say of the relation of law to custom in a later chapter; in this chapter it is proposed to examine the way in which sovereignty has arisen as one of the key concepts in the modern idea of law; the extent to which that key concept provides the clue to the autonomy of law as possessing validity not dependent on anything outside positive law itself; and the peculiar problems which sovereignty has created both in the constitutional state and in the world of international relations.

THE ORIGINS OF THE IDEA OF SOVEREIGNTY

Sovereignty, as it is understood today, implies a good deal more than the notion of a supreme ruler. An absolute monarch, a Haroun-al-Rashid, for instance, may have unfettered power to govern and order heads to be struck off, but yet lack legal power to alter, save in points of detail, the established law of the community. The modern idea of sovereignty on the other hand is associated rather with the supreme power of law-making than with the supreme executive or judicial authority to embark on war, impose death sentences, govern the country in its day-to-day affairs, and act as a final tribunal for settling disputes between subjects. The sovereign in present usage is therefore that person or body which is the supreme legislator in a given community. It is by reason of its power to change the law that such a legislator is regarded as possessing the ultimate legal authority in the state, to which other authorities, whether legislative, executive, or judicial are at least theoretically subordinate.

This notion of the sovereign as supreme legislator owes its origin to three main historical sources. In the first place, there was the Roman Emperor, whose will, in the language found in Justinian's *Institutes*, had 'the force of law'. The influence of Roman law on the development of Western law was nowhere more manifest than in the ultimate application of this principle to the several rulers of the national European states which consolidated their power and independence during the fifteenth and sixteenth centuries. Second, during the so-called Dark Ages which followed the fall of the Roman Empire, and the succeeding age of feudalism, the papacy secured for itself the office both in form and, to a considerable extent, in substance of a supreme legislator for all Christendom. During an age when secular law had largely lapsed into a mass of local customs and in which emperors and kings were more concerned with the problem of extending their power over their rivals or over rebellious vassals, the Pope, as Vicar of Christ on earth and as the unique expounder of the divine law, alone possessed the status for fulfilling the role of supreme legislator, and in this he was assisted by a highly developed administrative machinery which was without rival among the feudal kingdoms or even in the Imperial Chancery. When, however, the notional unity of European Christendom was broken up by the events compendiously referred to as the Renaissance and the Reformation, the third, and indeed the most important source of the modern concept of sovereignty, came to the fore. This was the rise of independent nation-states which all through the later Middle Ages had been struggling to shake off the relics both of feudalism and of papal supremacy. Finally these emerged as the successors to the unfettered sovereignty claimed in earlier ages by Pope and Roman Emperor.

SOVEREIGNTY AND THE STATE

A new twist to the older idea of sovereignty was given by its
association with the entity which became gradually known
as 'the state'. In the early days of the new independent
nations the sovereign was still generally regarded as identical
with whatever king or body (for example, the oligarchical
senate of Venice) happened to be their established ruler.
However, as such rulers were not necessarily sovereign in
the legislative sense, it became recognized that every independent country constituted in itself a self-supporting legal
entity, 'the state', and accordingly ultimate sovereignty re-
sided not in any body or person, for these were merely organs
of the state, but in the state itself. As a matter of legal analysis
it then became possible to put forward a general theory of
law and sovereignty of which the first important exponent
was the French lawyer, Jean Bodin, writing in the sixteenth
century. This theory, put at its simplest, was that it was the
nature of every independent state to possess a supreme
legislative power, and this power was supreme in two respects, namely that it acknowledged no superior and that its
authority was completely unfettered. It is true that on this
latter point neither Bodin nor some of his successors were
completely consistent as they accepted that the law-making
power was still subject to certain overriding natural-law
principles. With the increasing secularization of the modern
state, the function of natural law as a fetter on state sovereignty became more and more formal, until, by the end of
the eighteenth century if not before, the national state was
fully recognized as complete master of its own system of
positive law.

The idea that the state itself is the wielder of sovereign
power has not been consistently applied in the constitutional
theory of modern states, so far as internal law is concerned.
In this country, for example, we regard a curious hybrid
body, called the Queen in Parliament, as the possessor of
legal sovereignty. The state is a more general notion than

the sovereign, representing, as it does, the community as a legal organization,[1] and thus symbolizing all the various manifestations of the legally organized community. In this sense all the wielders of official power in the community are organs of the state, whether they are ministers making a general decree, judges deciding a legal dispute, or subordinate officials making an executive decision or carrying out an official order. The state in other words is a personification, for legal purposes, of all the ramifications of legal authority, and though particular parts of that authority, including even the sovereign legislative power, may be reposed in some particular person or body, ultimately that power is regarded as derived from the state itself. This is a point which is peculiarly difficult to appreciate in a state such as England, which has enjoyed prolonged continuity of constitutional development and where, in particular, Parliamentary sovereignty has been accepted for centuries. If, nevertheless, one transfers attention to such a political community as France, where there have been entirely new constitutions introduced at frequent intervals over the last two centuries, we can see the apparent difficulty in attributing ultimate sovereignty to whatever person or body happens to wield this power under the arrangements in force for the time being, and hence the need is felt to rest that authority on some more permanent source, namely the state itself. All the same the state remains a rather shadowy entity more frequently invoked by political scientists than by lawyers, who are less disposed to look behind the immediate constitutional framework to the ultimate sources of legal authority. Still, under a federal constitution this exercise is, as we shall see, less easily avoided.

Internal and External Sovereignty

It is rather in the international than the national sphere, however, that the idea of the unity of the national state, confronting like entities, has been most potent. Sovereignty, in its modern development, really possesses two distinct aspects, internal and external. Its internal aspect which has just been considered is that of the supreme domestic legislator. In its external aspect, on the other hand, the position is very much more like that of the absolute monarch under a customary system of law, who claims not so much power to change the law, as total freedom of action to act as his will or desire may direct. In the same way, the newly established national states claimed total freedom of action in their dealings with one another both in peace and war, for in the absence of any acknowledged superior authority there was no one who could restrict or diminish this freedom of action. Consequently in the sphere of international relations, state sovereignty meant that each state was entirely free to regulate its relations with other states, including the right to declare war and even to annex the territory of the defeated state.

The unhappy state of lawlessness which reigned between these independent nations provided the opportunity for developing natural-law theory as a means of regulating what would otherwise have been a state of international anarchy. The theory became established that nations, like individuals before civil society came into being, were in a state of nature towards one another, and that accordingly they were directly governed by natural law. An attempt was thus made to elucidate the rules that natural law imposed upon independent nations in their relations with one another, whether in times of peace or of war, and from these beginnings were gradually developed the modern principles of international law. It seemed therefore that just as the national state was shaking off the fetters of natural law in its internal legislative capacity it was at the same time subjecting itself to natural law in a new form in the realm of international relations. Hence was created the fresh legal problem as to how the unfettered sovereignty of the national state could none the less be subordinated to international rules not derived from any superior state or authority. But before reverting to this problem something more needs to be said about the legal theory of internal sovereignty.

LAW AS THE COMMAND OF A SOVEREIGN

It was one of the aims of positivist thought, as we have seen, to establish the autonomy of law as a system of positive norms whose validity can be determined within the framework of the legal system itself, without recourse to any other system, whether of religion, morality, or anything else. Moreover the idea of positive law seems also to entail the notion of a rule laid down (*positum*) by some identifiable human lawgiver. The theory that every independent state necessarily possessed the sovereign power of legislation pointed the way towards showing how law was able to possess this autonomy without recourse to some external authority. For sovereignty was itself a legal concept, and if positive law could be defined in terms of sovereignty then here was a self-sufficient pattern by which legal validity could be tested and demonstrated, unhampered by extra-legal considerations.

This line of thought was taken up by a number of jurists from Bodin to Bentham, but obtained its most detailed and influential statement from Bentham's disciple, John Austin; both the command (or imperative) theory of law, and legal positivism are most commonly associated with his name. Accordingly we shall here discuss the command theory mainly in terms of Austin. At the same time it is necessary to point out that positivism in the sense already explained, is by no means necessarily linked to the command theory of law, though the combining of these two theories by Austin has often mistakenly created this impression. Certainly legal positivism, by asserting that legal validity does not rest on and is distinct from the moral order, must explain the significance of legal obligation in its own terms, but this does not mean that it is tied to the command theory for such explanation. We may, for instance, adhere to the basic tenet of positivism and still reject the command theory, as Kelsen does.[2]

The command theory really amounts to saying that the

law is what the sovereign commands, and that, on the other hand, nothing can be law which is not commanded by the sovereign. It follows that legal validity can be simply determined on this view by ascertaining whether the norm in question can be shewn to have been laid down by the sovereign. But this only appears to thrust the inquiry one step further back, for what we now need to know is, how do we identify the sovereign? And here we seem to be faced by an insoluble problem, for if sovereignty is a legal conception it must itself be governed by legal rules. Accordingly, to find out who is sovereign we have to consult the legal rules which fix the location of sovereignty in the particular state. But whence do those rules themselves derive their validity? They cannot derive from some other sovereign body, for *ex hypothesi*, there can be no other sovereign in the state than the sovereign whose identity we are in the process of establishing. We thus seem involved in a completely vicious circle, since sovereignty is invoked to validate law, and then, in turn, law is invoked to create the sovereign.

Some jurists, such as Max Weber, have not shrunk from this conclusion, and have argued that such circularity is really a deliberate feature of the system, enabling legitimacy to be preserved without recourse to value-judgments.[3] Others have sought to regard legal theory as entitled to maintain a kind of self-contained unity like mathematics or logic, and have argued that its purpose is not defeated by the fact that its propositions can ultimately be resolved into identities or tautologies. The relation of the truths of logic or mathematics to real life are controversial, but whatever this may be, it still seems fairly clear that legal theory is not entitled to disassociate itself from the facts of legal life but must be in some way based on these. Of course one way in which this point could be answered is to say that the theory corresponds to the fact that legal systems reflect this vicious circle, logically indefensible though it may be, and that such illogicality is not in itself a fundamental objection, if a practical aim is thereby attained. As Mr Justice Holmes remarked, 'the life of the law is not logic but experience'.[4] This, perhaps, is the root of the justification Max Weber had in mind, though he wrote rather as a sociologist than as a lawyer. Be this as it may, Austin himself did not attempt to shelter behind either of these solutions but proposed another more radical one, which carried with it problems of its own.

WHO IS THE SOVEREIGN? AUSTIN'S THEORY

Austin saw the problem of sovereignty not just in terms of locating the supreme legal authority in the state but as one of determining the source of ultimate power. Adopting an approach already adumbrated by Bentham he therefore interpreted sovereignty as meaning the power in the state which commanded habitual obedience and which did not yield habitual obedience to any other power. In other words sovereignty was not to be derived from legal rules investing some body or person with supreme power but based on the sociological fact of power itself. This certainly served to cut the Gordian knot of circularity, which derived law from law itself, but it still left open the question how the source of actual power in any given community should be investigated, and also how the result of the inquiry was to be transmuted into legal terms to provide a foundation for the legal system.

For this purpose Austin endeavoured to facilitate his task by resting on the postulate of his predecessors from Bodin onwards that in every community possessing a *developed* legal system[5] there must be a sovereign power to which, within the community, unqualified allegiance was paid, and which rendered none to any other power inside or outside that community. For Austin this was the essential mark of an independent state (or 'political society' as he called it). Obedience acknowledged to another outside authority would mean that the society was not an independent state at all but merely a subordinate part of some other state; and absence of a supreme power within the state meant nothing less than confusion and anarchy, the very antithesis of legality. But how was the actual possessor of power to be located? Clearly not by a purely sociological inquiry into the springs of action of the community. Apart from the difficulty in conducting this, it would inevitably lead to sources of power, such as economic or social or military groups or various kinds of power *élites* or *éminences grises*, which, however significant in practice, would afford no guidance whatever in answering the lawyer's question as to how the legal validity of rules and decisions, with which he and everyone else in the state is concerned, is to be determined. Austin, at least implicitly, recognizes this difficulty by accepting the fact that if the constitutional rules for ascertaining the legal sovereign are not final, they cannot be ignored, since he appears to assume they will almost inevitably provide an essential clue to the source of actual power in the state. Thus, for example, in England Austin attributed sovereignty not to the King in Parliament in accordance with orthodox constitutional theory, but to the King, the House of Lords, and the electors of the Commons. In this choice he was particularly exercised by the problem of how, in the case of the Commons which ceases to exist during an election, habitual obedience could be owed to a non-existent body. He therefore sought to fill the gap by substituting the electors for the Commons itself.

The difficulty with this solution is that it is really neither fact nor law; so far as fact goes, it involves a rather facile identification of democratic electioneering with the actual roots of power in the state, and so far as law is concerned, no English lawyer or private citizen for that matter treats as legally binding anything emanating from the arbitrary assemblage of King, Lords, and the electorate, a 'body' which, if it can be so described, has no *locus standi* in the law at all.

The Unity and Illimitability of Sovereignty

Nor did Austin's troubles end here, for he also insisted that the sovereign, to be sovereign, must possess two essential attributes, namely indivisibility and illimitability. Both of these he considered inherent in the logical nature of sovereignty. The sovereign must be a unity (though this could be constituted by a 'body' as well as by an individual).

If sovereignty was divided there could be no habitual obedience owed, for in one matter it might be owed to A, and in another to B. Again there could be no limitations on sovereignty, for such limitations could only result from obedience to an external power (in which case the person or body is not sovereign) or be self-imposed, in which case they could only amount to moral and not legal limitations, and therefore as a matter of positive law could always be disregarded.

This view of sovereignty was applicable enough to a Parliamentary régime such as that of England where the unity of the sovereignty of Parliament has been accepted for centuries, as has the inability of Parliament to bind itself or its successors in the sense that any statute, even if expressed to be unalterable, can always be subsequently abrogated or amended by Parliament itself. But even here some pretty odd consequences are entailed. For Austin claims that all so-called constitutional 'laws' dealing with the structure of the sovereign power are not really legal because who is sovereign is ultimately to be determined by the fact of obedience. He also claims that any attempted restraints imposed by Parliament on its legislative power, whatever moral force these may have, are really nugatory in strict law. This would mean for instance that a provision in a statute that amendment should be effected only by a special procedure – as for instance by a two-thirds majority, or with the sanction of a referendum, or with the consent of some other body – is not really law at all but at most what Austin calls 'positive morality'.[6] Thus the provision in the Statute of Westminster of 1931 which created Dominion status and provided that no legislation affecting the Dominions was to be passed by the Parliament at Westminster without the consent of any Dominion affected is, on this view, not law at all, and can be theoretically ignored, though in fact it is far more imperatively binding than much normal legislation.

In England, for social and historical reasons, we have not so far felt the need for any 'entrenched clauses' in our constitution to prevent certain types of legislation from being amended save subject to special safeguards, such as requiring

a two-thirds majority. This type of provision is not un-
common in other countries. In South Africa, for instance,
the voting rights of the 'coloured' population were protected
by an entrenched clause of this kind. In a leading case[7] the
South African Supreme Court has held that while accepting
the broad Austinian position that, in a Parliamentary
régime, there must be unity of sovereignty, this did not pre-
clude the sovereign body from being differently constituted
for the exercise of different functions, as when a special
majority or a joint-session of both Upper and Lower Houses
is required for particular purposes. For such rules did not
limit sovereignty nor did they divide it. There had to be rules
defining the body invested with sovereign power, and these
rules had the essential function of laying down the form in
which acts of sovereignty were to be exercised and without
which it would not be possible to attribute legal validity to
the activities of the body in question. For instance, if in
England the monarch and the two Houses of Parliament
were to meet together and there and then proclaim a new
law, English lawyers would probably regard this as a nullity
under the existing constitution. This is because there is a
constitutional procedure established for passing English
statutes; in the view of the South African court there was no
reason why such a procedure should not be variable according to the class of matter which was the subject of legislation. It will none the less be apparent how remote is this sort
of judicial approach from the Austinian idea of interpreting
sovereignty in terms of fact rather than law, for everything
turned in this case on the question how the sovereign was
defined by the constitutional rules from which it was derived.

Federal Constitutions

Even more resistant to the Austinian mould is the case of
a Federal constitution where legislative power is distributed
between a central legislature and a number of provincial
legislatures. Austin had already before him the example of
the United States of America, where power under the constitution is distributed between the federal and the state

organs. Where then lies ultimate sovereignty in such a federation? Austin refused to acknowledge that his theory of indivisibility was defeated by so cogent an example, but wrestled to locate an ultimate sovereign which he claimed to find, oddly enough, among the combined electorates of the state legislatures. This may be regarded as the *reductio ad absurdum* of the whole hypothesis and later Austinians have sometimes preferred to treat the ultimate sovereign as the body empowered to amend the constitution. This, however, hardly serves, for the incredibly cumbrous procedure of amendment under the American Constitution does not really set up a legislative body in any reasonable sense of the word, and moreover this procedure has been successfully invoked on only twenty-three occasions in nearly two hundred years. Furthermore, a federal constitution may be, and often is, incapable in certain respects of being amended at all, or not without the consent of a particular body.

Nor is the notion of unlimited sovereignty applicable to a federal constitution. Such a constitution may and frequently does contain overriding limitations, such as a bill of rights, which control and limit subsequent legislation, and the courts may, following the United States pattern, have power to treat legislation as void which infringes these basic norms of the constitution. And it is quite possible for these limitations to be made indefeasible. Austin might declare these restraints to be no more than positive morality, but as the courts and the community itself are likely to treat them not merely as law but as a portion of the legal system entitled to peculiar reverence, the virtue of Austin's classification is obviously seriously open to question.

Constitutional Changes

The problem of constitutional change in the structure of the sovereign also calls for some brief consideration. Suppose for instance that in England the House of Lords were abolished or some differently constituted second Chamber were set up in its place. No one would then doubt that an effective substitution had occurred, so that the legal sovereign would thenceforth be the monarch acting with the House of Commons and the new second Chamber. The House of Lords would thus, even if it still survived as a historical relic for purposes of pageantry, be *functus officio* so far as legislation was concerned. In the same way the present sovereign could presumably go further and transfer its whole sovereignty to some other body. As a matter of legal theory would such a transfer, however expressed, necessarily be final and irrevocable, or would the abdicating sovereign retain some vestige of ultimate authority so that, for instance, it could change its mind the next day and re-assume the power previously surrendered by it?

It must be realized that at this sort of level we are really passing from the realm of legal categories into the field of power politics. But although there comes a stage where it is almost impossible to distinguish between what law and what power politics prescribe this is by no means an endorsement of the Austinian attempt to base law on power itself. For to understand legal systems we need, not a conceptual structure which will enable us to point indisputably to what is legally valid when confronted with revolutionary or remote marginal situations, but rather one which will account for the constitutional patterns of reasonably well-ordered states as well as their legal relations *inter se*. Thus we need a legal theory which will enable us to see how the Parliament Act of 1911, depriving the House of Lords of its financial veto, is a legal norm which fits into the structure of the legal system; how it comes about that Parliament can impose legal fetters on its power to legislate for the Dominions and can even, if necessary, abolish or reconstruct one or more of its composite elements; and how judges can be empowered to invalidate legislation which they hold to be beyond the powers of a federal or state legislature.

When, however, we are considering revolutionary situations such as Parliament transferring all power to another body, whether voluntarily or under compulsion, we are clearly in a realm where power is taking ascendancy over law to a degree where it becomes impossible to disregard the actual factors of power and obedience in determining legal validity itself.[7a] When, for example, the Cromwellian regime succeeded in superseding the monarchy, or when William was called in to replace James II after the latter's expulsion, the Austinian conception of habitual obedience to A rather than B is clearly relevant as explaining how legal authority can pass from one to the other regardless of the legal regulations hitherto in operation. Certainly in this sense an operative legal system necessarily entails a high degree of regular obedience to the existing system, for without this there will be anarchy or confusion rather than a reign of legality. And where revolution or civil war has supervened it may even be necessary in the initial stages, when power and authority is passing from one person or body to another, to interpret legal power in terms of actual obedience to the prevailing power. When however this transitional stage where law and power are largely merged is passed, it is no longer relevant for the purpose of determining what is legally valid to explore the sources of ultimate *de facto* power in the state. For by this time the constitutional rules will again have taken over and the legal system will have resumed its regular course of interpreting its rules on the basis of its own fundamental norms of validity.

Power, Force, and Sanctions

If Austin misconceived the function of power as providing the ultimate source of legal validity, there is perhaps more to be said for his treatment of coercion as the ultimate mark of the legal process. As we have seen, Austin held that law was the command of the sovereign, and this he expounded as meaning that law was a rule laid down by the sovereign to which obedience could be enforced by some penalty prescribed for failure to obey. This penalty, following normal juristic usage, he described as the 'legal sanction' of the rule. We have already, in an earlier chapter,[8] discussed the role of coercion in the organization of a legal system and it is only necessary here to try and clear up a few misunderstandings on points of detail.

In the first place, it is to be borne in mind that a sanction does not necessarily involve the imposition of a penalty in the form of punishment. This is, of course, the special feature of the criminal law and no doubt it is the criminal pattern which is primarily envisaged when a sanctionist approach to law is maintained. Punishment may also be inflicted as a sanction in non-criminal matters, but this is generally for wilful disobedience to a judicial order, for instance a refusal to comply with an injunction restraining a person from doing certain acts, or to comply with a peremptory order in certain legal proceedings to produce relevant documents, and so forth. In such cases, as well as in cases where a person improperly interferes with the administration of justice (e.g. by intimidating a witness to prevent him giving evidence), a court may commit the offender to prison until such time as he is considered to have purged his contempt. In civil matters, however, coercion usually involves not so much the imposition of penalties as the enforcement of the order against the property of the defendant. A defendant who fails to pay a judgment debt may have his goods and chattels seized and sold and the debt paid out of the proceeds, so far as these suffice for the purpose, or he may be made bankrupt and both his assets and his current earnings appropriated for the payment of his creditors. Sanctions in law therefore possess a very wide meaning, referring to any coercive process by which the law seeks to impose its will in the last resort upon an offender or a defaulter who has failed to comply with a legal order or judgment.

There are, however, cases which arise under a legal system where legal rules are imposed but no specific coercive procedure or penalty is provided for non-compliance. There are many instances of this kind in any modern legal system and a few illustrations may be culled from English law. Thus there is a whole group of rules which are permissive in the sense that they lay down the conditions which have to be satisfied if a certain result is to be achieved in law. Much of civil law consists of this type of provision, of which the formalities for making a will, or types of transactions which need to be in writing, may be given as instances. Here the law dows not say that if you fail to have your will duly attested the law will apply coercion in some way; the effect is rather negative, since non-compliance results in any will thus made being treated as a nullity. It will be seen that though the result is one of great importance, it is not directly enforceable by means of a sanction resting on coercion. All the same in a broader sense nullification is a kind of sanction, and when seen in the context of the whole legal system can be shewn to be related to sanctions at least indirectly. For the nullification of a will means that its provisions do not operate as legal norms and hence anyone seeking to rely on the will must fail on this ground. Also any judgment of a court taking account of this nullity will be enforceable in the usual way, e.g. if a donee under the invalid will has refused to hand over the subject-matter of the invalid gift to the lawful successors.

Again, it often happens that in modern law statutory duties are imposed, for example on public bodies, which have no sanctions or penalties attached. Thus the Railways Board is required to carry out certain duties in the organization of a transport system;[9] and the Electricity Commissioners have imposed on them similar duties regarding the supply of electricity.[10] In the same way, although there is provision for actions to be brought against the state, any resulting judgment is not enforceable as would be the case were it obtained against a private citizen.[11] In all such cases the Austinian claims that there is not strictly a legal duty since no sanction can be applied. Yet there is a good deal of unreality in this view, for Parliament has expressly imposed the duties in question or permitted actions to be brought against the state, and all such matters are treated as concerning duties imposed by law. Both the bodies in question and the state if sued will be just as concerned as any other party subject to a legal duty to determine the precise scope of its duty and liability in law. Nor does anyone doubt that if the state is successfully sued it will pay up and do so because of its legal and not merely moral duty to act. There is thus a clear distinction between the state paying on a judgment holding the state legally liable, and the state merely making an *ex gratia* payment where no liability is or can be established.

The answer to this situation seems to be that Austin was mistaken in insisting upon a sanction being annexed to every command of the sovereign for it to constitute a positive legal duty; the core of truth in this approach is that no legal system, in the state of human society and human psychology that has hitherto prevailed and seems likely to continue, can function unless it is ultimately rooted in a background of coercive machinery which can enforce compliance with its rules and decrees. Provided effectiveness is secured in this way, so that the system *as a whole* qualifies as legal, it does not seem necessary in order to determine the legal quality of any particular norm within the system to find that a specific sanction is annexed thereto. It suffices that such a sanctionless duty fits into the whole pattern of norms recognized as possessing legal attributes for it to merit treatment as a specifically legal norm, which can be differentiated from other norms derived from other systems, such as morals, religion, social convention, etiquette, and so forth.

STATE SOVEREIGNTY AND THE INTERNATIONAL SPHERE

We have already seen that there is nothing in legal logic which compels every state to regard its own internal sovereignty as either indivisible or illimitable. Sovereignty can be more appropriately regarded not as an unlimited power to enact any legislation whatsoever as the will or whim of the sovereign may dictate, but rather as a means of expressing in legal terms that a given state is independent in the sense of not being subject to any legal superior. In addition, sovereignty also implies that within that state there is a supreme legislature or legislatures which in their particular spheres acknowledge no superiors and can pass any legislation within the scope laid down by the governing constitution. Some states, such as England, may go further and grant by their constitutions to a sovereign legislative power the freedom to enact any legislation they wish. Equally there is no reason why other constitutions should not, and some in fact do, impose legal fetters on the power even of the supreme legislature itself. In any event supreme legal power, it has to be remembered, is purely theoretical since no legislator that ever lived has been able in practice to pass any law he wished in disregard of the moral values, traditions, sentiments, and prejudices prevailing in the community. What we are dealing with here however are not such *de facto* limitations, which must always operate in every society, but with express limitations imposed by the law itself.

Those jurists who argued for the absolute and unfettered character of national sovereignty found themselves in difficulty when faced with the phenomenon of international law. For if there was such a law, then it must be on a higher level than national law, and must bind and limit even the sovereigns of the national states subject to it. Austin countered this by declaring that international law was really not law at all but no more than positive morality.[12] Followers of Hegel, who regarded state sovereignty as the highest expression of human law, also rejected the legal validity of international law and held it to be always subordinate to 'reasons of state'. Others who desired to affirm the legal status of international law endeavoured to reconcile the subordination of state sovereignty to such a régime as a kind of 'auto-limitation' operating by the consent of the various states, which by long tradition had agreed to be bound by the customary rules of international law, including the rule that treaties must be observed.

If once it is recognized that state sovereignty is capable of internal limitation, two further questions arise for consideration in the external sphere. These are: (1) What is the position of a state such as England, which still regards its own internal sovereignty as unlimited? Suppose, for instance, that Parliament passes an Act which is directly contrary to the rules of international law. (2) Even if a state's sovereignty is capable of internal limitation, how can it be made subject to an external system of law and still retain its independence?

These two questions will be dealt with briefly in turn.

(1) This point is a comparatively simple one, for we have to distinguish between the legal duty within the national system and the international obligation. There is the possibility of a conflict between the two systems, for an English court will recognize that its sole duty is to obey the decrees of Parliament even if these infringe international law. The court will of course strive to put a construction on any English enactment which will not result in a conflict with international law, but if the wording is clear and cannot reasonably lend itself to such a construction the statute will still be enforced regardless of its international impact.[13] In other words there are two possible approaches available to a national court; one is to treat international law as part of its own law and directly binding, in which case it may have to be given an overriding effect abrogating any domestic law in conflict with it; the other is to regard international law as an alien intruder subordinate to the local law though relevant in arriving at a true interpretation of any local law which impinges on international law. English domestic law clearly adopts the second of these alternatives, but there are other states which favour the first.[14] It must not be thought, however, that this concludes the matter, for whatever attitude a domestic court may adopt there may still be a breach of an international obligation for which the state may be answerable in international law. Thus in the illustration just given, the British government will still have to answer for a breach of its international obligations, and any local statute to the contrary, far from providing a defence in the international sphere, may itself constitute an additional breach of international law. We are therefore led to the further question, how a national sovereign state can be subordinated to a system of international legal rules without loss of its independent sovereignty.

(2) International law, though now mustering a number of important international organs and institutions, such as the United Nations, the International Court of Justice, and the International Labour Office, is still a very long way off

constitúting a kind of international super-state set over the various independent national states. Subordination to the norms of international law does not therefore involve the merging of state sovereignty in a higher state entity but rather the recognition of a system of legal rules which are binding on states themselves, which for this purpose are treated as corporate legal persons, just as the state is treated as a person in domestic law for the purpose of suing or being sued in legal proceedings.

Let us take as illustrations of international rules, two different types, namely, customary and treaty rules. It is a customary rule that immunity shall be granted in domestic courts to diplomatic personages. On the other hand the rules governing international copyright and postal arrangements are contained in various conventions subscribed by very large numbers of states adhering to those conventions. A failure by a state to grant diplomatic immunity or to recognize copyright in accordance with the conventions to which it adheres is a breach of international law. This does not mean, as we have already seen, that the rule of international law will be automatically recognized in the courts of the country concerned, though in most instances governments will have taken care to see that their own law is brought into line with their international obligations. Whatever the domestic law, the breach of international law remains. What does this mean?

In domestic law, there is a regular coercive procedure for enforcing the majority though not all, of the duties imposed by the legal system. This is not so in international law, which has not yet attained, if it ever will, the stage of regular adjudication and enforcement of disputes. Even the International Court of Justice has no compulsory jurisdiction and if it had, has no means of enforcing its decisions. Yet there is universal acceptance of the fact that an international legal duty imposes a duty comparable to that of a rule of domestic law, and one differing in quality from a merely moral duty. What a state ought to do morally is quite a different issue from what may be its legal duty. Again a state may be arraigned for breach of legal duty by whatever formal procedure may be available before international organs or tribunals in a manner entirely inapplicable to purely moral lapses, and such an arraignment may be coupled with a claim for legal compensation (not for just an *ex gratia* payment). In support of the legal right of the claimant legal authorities and precedents may be appealed to and discussed in legal terms in ways closely analogous to claims before a domestic court. In other words the whole apparatus of international law, while lacking some of the features of domestic law (including compulsory adjudication and enforcement), possesses many characteristics closely analogous to a national legal system. It must be borne in mind, too, that the very vital difference between the nature of the subjects of the two systems, states on the one hand and individuals on the other, must necessarily entail broad divergencies between their mode of functioning. And as we have already pointed out,[15] there may be compelling reasons in the international sphere for not invoking a regular sanctions procedure; apart from its impracticability in many cases, in the nuclear age it might result in a disastrous war leading to universal destruction.

Moreover, by distinguishing between internal sovereignty and international duty it is quite possible to arrive at a rational understanding of the relation of state sovereignty to external rules of law. Every rule of international law imposes a legal fetter on national states in the international sphere, for this is the very sense and meaning of an international legal community. But within its own internal sphere the national sovereign still retains domestic sovereignty and may legislate or act in disregard of international obligations. But by so doing it cannot alter, abrogate, or lessen the force of these obligations *vis-à-vis* other states, and will have to take whatever consequences its default may entail, having regard to the existing state of international law and the sort of pressures which can be brought upon it in the particular circumstances.

The Treaty of Rome and National Sovereignty

Does adhesion to the Treaty of Rome, which established the European Economic Community,[16] involve an encroachment on the national sovereignty of the states subscribing that treaty? The features of E.E.C. are that it is a permanent arrangement with no provision for withdrawal, and that it has set up various institutions such as the Council and the Commission with power in a wide range of matters, including tariffs, restrictive trade practices, free movement of workers, and establishment of commercial companies, both to make decisions and lay down rules binding on all members of the Community. Moreover there is also a Court of Justice of the Community which is a final Court of Appeal, in matters concerning the treaty, from the courts of the member states. The permanent institutional character of the treaty and its wide scope undoubtedly place it in a very special situation *vis-à-vis* the member states, especially as new legislation laid down by the treaty organs is directly binding on the members and the ultimate interpretation of the treaty and any rules made under it are to be decided, not by the national courts, but by the Community's own Court of Justice.

In theory the national sovereignty of the member states is no more encroached upon by this treaty than by any other, since from the point of view of their national laws the provisions of the treaty could be disregarded with whatever consequence internationally this might provoke under international law. The practical result however is likely to be very different, for the signatory states will regard the treaty as involving very solemn legal obligations and will naturally exert every effort to bring their national law into line with the requirements of the treaty. Accordingly, if Great Britain were to become a member of E.E.C., Parliament would still, *from the point of view of domestic English law*, possess its full sovereignty entirely unimpaired; nevertheless, having passed legislation to enable effect to be given to the treaty within the framework of the English constitution, there is little doubt that such legislation, in its main lines, would remain as an immutable fetter on the English Parliament's future freedom of action. The position would be similar to that of the Statute of Westminster, which created Dominion status and deprived Parliament of its legislative function with respect to the Dominions. And just as the Statute of Westminster has created a new *de facto* situation concerning the powers of Parliament which has not yet finally crystallized into an absolutely clear theory regarding the legal limits upon the sovereignty of the English Parliament, so no doubt it would require many years of consistent constitutional practice before any change in English constitutional theory might be wrought.

Indeed so deeply rooted is the tradition of theoretically unfettered Parliamentary sovereignty in England that it is conceivable that no international arrangement whatever, however permanent and far-reaching, will ever in the foreseeable future shake the doctrine of Parliamentary sovereignty. If this is so then even after the United Kingdom had joined E.E.C. our courts would continue to pay lip-service to the principle that, if Parliament were to pass legislation in direct conflict with the Treaty of Rome, those courts would have no alternative but to uphold the domestic legislation whatever might be the international implications. It is obvious however that such a view, with the passing of the years, might become increasingly academic and unrealistic, a formula uttered year after year by the lawyers without genuine conviction (rather as in the case of Parliament's 'power' to overthrow the Statute of Westminster). A time might eventually come when even the lawyers would recognize that a change had imperceptibly been wrought in the actual law itself and that Parliament could not, even if it wished, and *even as a matter of strict law*, legislate in defiance of such overriding matters as Dominion status, or the E.E.C. Treaty. This possibility then, however shadowy it might appear in this particular instance, must lead us to inquire how the fundamental basis of a legal system comes to be established, and by what means it may be validly upset or amended. It is at this point that something needs to be said about the so-called Pure Theory of Law of Hans Kelsen, which has exercised a considerable influence on modern juristic thought and is particularly relevant to the problem of ultimate validity of the fundamental presuppositions of a legal system.

KELSEN'S PURE THEORY OF LAW

Kelsen's theory, although formally based on neo-Kantian thought rather than upon the empirical and utilitarian foundations of Austinianism, has many features in common with that of Austin. Thus Kelsen calls his theory the 'pure' theory, because he desires to emphasize the positivist position that law is entirely autonomous and self-contained, and that its validity therefore has to be conceived in legal terms and not in terms of morals or of any other extraneous system of norms or values. On the other hand Kelsen has striven, successfully in some respects, to avoid the pitfalls which Austin could not circumvent.

For Kelsen law is concerned not with the facts of human behaviour but with norms, which are rules or standards of conduct forming part of a unified system. That system is really a kind of hierarchy of norms, that is to say, a series of norms laid out at various levels of generality and sub-ordination, the highest norms being the most general and therefore the most abstract. These lay down rules which govern the application of norms on a lower level of generality, and the latter are accordingly increasingly concrete in their form and application. The problem for the lawyer is to determine the conditions of legal validity of any decision or rule within the legal system. If, for instance, a bailiff has levied execution on the property of Smith we need to know whether this act is lawful. For this purpose we have recourse to an order made by, let us say, a county court registrar who has authorized the execution. This order in turn may derive its authority from a judgment of a judge of the High Court. That judgment may involve the application of a statutory order made by a Minister in pursuance of powers given to him by an Act of Parliament. It will be observed that as one moves from the lower to the higher level the legal rules pass from a concrete and specific order to an increasingly abstract and general principle, each stage being dependent for its validity on the norm in the hierarchy of norms which provides the basis for its application.

Like Austin, Kelsen also insists on the need for ultimate coercion to be available in order to confer on the legal system that minimum of effectiveness without which it does not qualify as a legal system at all. But for this purpose it is not necessary for every norm to have a sanction attached to it, since a sanction is not the necessary attribute of each and every legal norm but is merely a description of certain concrete norms at the bottom of the legal hierarchy, which provide a legal basis for force to be applied in particular cases. For Kelsen a sanction is not the threat of force or the actual application of it but simply the final 'concretization' of the series of norms which makes this physical result authorized in the legal sense.[17]

So far, however, we have only traced the hierarchy of norms upwards as far as an Act of Parliament. How does this acquire its authority? Austin, we will recollect, here has recourse to the sovereignty of Parliament derived from habitual obedience to its decrees. Kelsen will have none of this which, he says, confuses fact with law. Parliament's authority must therefore depend upon a higher norm and this norm must be a rule to the effect that the will of Parliament (expressed in a particular form), which may or may not be changeable by Parliament itself, is to prevail. But what does this norm itself rest on? Kelsen's answer is that this norm is the *Grundnorm*, the basic norm or ultimate premiss of the whole system, and that *for legal purposes* we cannot go behind it. It is rather like the idea of the world supported on an elephant, the rules not permitting you to ask what supports the elephant.

The Basic Norm

Kelsen's argument is really that in any normative system

there must come a point beyond which you cannot go because you have come to the outer edge of the whole system and any further inquiry you make is really an extraneous inquiry not within the terms of the system itself. For instance, you can obviously ask the question whether the rule of the constitution conferring Parliament's authority is morally justifiable and so question its validity from the moral viewpoint, but this, says Kelsen, is not a juristic issue at all but an ethical one, and so tells us nothing about the legal validity of the basic norm.

This still leaves open the question how we are to decide what the basic norm is in any particular case. Kelsen tells us that this must be based on the principle of the minimum of effectiveness. The exact scope and logical justification for this principle is not very clear. Kelsen's idea seems to be that the basic norm of a legal system is theoretically a matter of choice, but the choice is normally dictated by the circumstance that there is a consensus of opinion pointing towards a particular solution. In England this would be a rule imposing the sovereignty of Parliament; in the United States, on the other hand, it would be a rule requiring obedience to the norms set out in the written Federal Constitution. Kelsen insists however that there can be only one *Grundnorm*, for otherwise it would be impossible to maintain the unity of the legal systems. Moreover, Kelsen not only rejects Austin's idea of sovereignty as the universal source of law, but holds that sovereignty is no more than an expression for the highest legislative organ in the state, and that there is no reason why the constitution should not allow the powers of that organ to be both divided and limited.

The Basic Norm of International Law

We have so far ignored the international implications of this theory, but Kelsen in fact has much to say upon this. He asserts that each nation can in fact have its own ultimate norm and treat international law as merely valid in so far as its norms are incorporated in those of the individual national system. On the other hand it is equally possible to envisage a monistic system in which the basic norm of every state is a rule imposing obedience to the rules customarily accepted as binding by states *inter se* (a rule which covers treaties, since it is already a customarily established international rule that treaties shall be observed by the parties thereto). Kelsen's view is that this monistic system is not only desirable but is in fact operative, because states do substantially adhere to it to an extent which complies with the principle of the minimum of effectiveness. Moreover, even the need for ultimate coercion is not lacking, since international customary law recognizes the rule of enforcement by self-help, by means of war and reprisals as a last resort, in the case of flagrant breaches of international law. Admittedly this coercive system is hopelessly unsatisfactory compared with an effective national law, but this is due to the primitive and uncentralized state of international law, comparable to the blood-feud stage of national law. This does not deprive it of its legal status, for it remains effective, at least at a minimum level.

Does Kelsen Provide a Solution to the Problems of Sovereignty?

Although Kelsen's approach presents a far more consistent and logical pattern than Austin's it is not without its difficulties. Attention must here be concentrated on the idea of the basic norm. Kelsen's view of the interlocking normative structure of a legal system is undoubtedly an illuminating one, as is the idea that legal validity is something which can only be explained in terms of a higher norm authorizing norms on a lower level. Moreover Kelsen seems rightly to stress the idea that legal validity cannot be reposed (as Austin thought) on purely *de facto* considerations such as obedience, but must be explained in normative terms. Also there seems force in his point that this explanation can only lead to some ultimate presupposition which is the basis of the whole system and which does not lend itself to further justification save on a different plane of inquiry altogether. However Kelsen finds himself in metaphysical perplexities, which, as a positivist, he is anxious to shun, by his insistence

on a single basic norm outside the legal system itself and
chosen on the principle of effectiveness. Kelsen does not really
clarify the status of this peculiar norm and is only able to
assert that it must be unique because of his desire to preserve
the logical consistency of the system. It seems doubtful however whether legal consistency can be equated with logic[18]
and in any event experience shows that legal systems
frequently bristle with irreconcilable internal conflicts.
How, for instance, are we to determine the basic norm of the
constitution of the Soviet Union or of present-day France?
And suppose the House of Lords (as the highest judicial
tribunal in England) were to reject the authority of Parliament to pass a particular enactment? Conflicts are always
possible to a greater or lesser degree under the best laid or
most well-established constitutions, and when they arise
have to be resolved in the light of the political climate that
prevails. This is apparent enough in the present conflict in
the United States over the construction of the constitution
the Supreme Court has attempted to impose, in the non-
segregation cases, upon the Southern States. In fact, therefore, it hardly seems helpful to look for an artificial basic
norm in Kelsen's sense but rather to say that every system
has its own basic norm or norms (in the U.S.A., for instance,
the rules of the Federal Constitution, including the power
to amend them) and that these have to be reconciled
between themselves in such ways as are legally practicable.
So in the international sphere also it is open to doubt
whether we can fit the situation into Kelsen's rigid dichotomy, for the present international situation is far too fluid
and variable to say that every nation accepts or is obliged
to accept once for all a pluralistic or a monistic attitude
towards the validity of international law as an overriding
system.

Kelsen's approach, however, does, it may be suggested,
throw some light on our query as to how the fundamental
basis of a constitution may be established and changes
effected therein even without revolutionary convulsions. At
present in England the basic norm of our legal system is

unquestionably that Parliament is sovereign, but there seems
no reason why, as a result of a long process of customary
acceptance of substantial inroads into this principle, a new
basic norm might not ultimately come into being. Such a
basic norm need not be laid down in any statute but may
itself be customary, like the existing rule of parliamentary
sovereignty. Thus, if this country joined the E.E.C., the view
might ultimately emerge that sovereignty is limited by certain fundamental documents, such as the Rome Treaty, and
is divided between Parliament and other bodies. It can
be said there is nothing to stop this development save the
force of tradition, which can itself, as we shall see when we
come to discuss customary law, be creative of new rules.

Both the natural-law schools and their principal opponents, the positivists, were heavily influenced by an individualist approach to human society. So far as natural law is concerned, this emerges most plainly in the social-contract theory which for so long formed an indispensable link in the structure of natural-law ideology. This view maintained that society was formed by agreement of the individuals who composed it. The actual institution of human society was attributed to an original contract of individuals previously in a state of nature, and it was assumed that the foundations of society rested upon the terms of this contract. The link with natural law was supplied by the hypothesis that the binding character of the social contract itself derived from natural law. Hence natural law formed the basis not only of positive law but of society itself. This theory left scope for much disagreement as to the terms of the initial contract, some, such as Locke, favouring the retention of fundamental natural rights; others, like Hobbes, arguing that absolute sovereignty was transferred to the ruler; and there was a wide gradation of intermediate positions. The essence of all these contentions was that society was nothing more than a collective word for the individuals who composed it, and that the social bond could be fully understood in terms of a binding agreement arrived at by rational individuals seeking to attain objectives deemed to be in their personal interest. It was by no means universally assumed, however, that such an agreement was a historical reality, for most theorists were less concerned to explore historical origins than to formulate the logical presuppositions of human society, law, and government. This theory therefore was rationalist, individualist, and formal in character.

In these respects, though rejecting both natural law and the social contract as fictions, the early positivists were not far removed from the assumptions of their opponents. The utilitarian basis of positivism relied on a rational choice of ends directed to human happiness, and a psychological framework of human nature, whose motive force was conceived as springing solely from the impact of pain or pleasure on the individual organism.[1] Moreover, Austin's development of positivism leant heavily on this psychological approach, especially in his notion of the role of sanctions as involving a threat of the infliction of pain directed to the individual, and thereby inducing that state of obedience which he regarded as the fundamental presupposition of all law.

This rather crude and indeed irrelevant psychologizing has been rejected in no uncertain manner by Kelsen. At the same time Kelsen seeks emphatically to disassociate legal questions from the underlying social problems and relations to which legal norms may be applied. For Kelsen, even more than Austin, legal science is concerned solely with a formal pattern of rules existing in a realm distinct from that of the facts of human problems. He does not deny the existence of such facts but asserts that these are totally separated from law itself and that they are the concern not of the jurist but of the sociologist.

INDIVIDUALISM AND COLLECTIVISM

During the eighteenth and nineteenth centuries individualist thought assumed a more distinctly economic pattern. With the full impact of the industrial revolution and the growth of capitalist enterprise individualism became more than a philosophical or psychological tenet: it developed into a political and economic slogan in the form of *laissez faire*. During much of that period and indeed continuing into the present century, the assumption that law should interfere as little as possible with individual freedom of action, and especially economic action, underlay a good deal of legal

and social speculation. Moreover this speculation was frequently translated into action, most notably in the doctrine
of freedom of contract. Sir Henry Maine spread the dogma
that society had progressed by a movement from status to
contract, and the freedom of the individual to make any
contract he wished was the symbol of a developed and 'open
society'. It was therefore the policy of the law to maintain
this freedom and to strike down any attempt to fetter the
liberty of the individual to choose the obligations (especially
economic) to which he would submit. Hence, to the devotees
of this faith, there seemed nothing incongruous in the
argument that it was wrong for the legislature to limit
the hours or conditions of work in mines or factories, for the
workers were free to accept or reject these conditions and such
liberty of bargaining was of the essence of an advanced society.

But however influential were the forces of *laissez faire*
they were in fact fighting a losing battle against another
philosophy which insisted on the value of social welfare
and the necessity of legislative intervention to create the
indispensable conditions for attaining this. This movement,
paradoxically enough, derived much of its impetus from the
utilitarians, who, though individualists in origin, by their
emphasis on increasing the sum of human happiness provided a philosophy adapted to improving the material welfare
of society as a whole. This philosophy, for all its logical
imperfections, provided an appealing objective for the
progressive-minded Victorians, and seemed to afford a
straightforward justification for social and welfare legislation on a massive scale. For as the nineteenth century proceeded, it became apparent that by blithely leaving the
forces of the economic market to operate, a vast amount of
human misery, poverty, and distress resulted. This therefore
seemed but a poor illustration of the virtues of *laissez faire*,
even though the exponents of that doctrine might urge that
in the long run more harm than good would result by
interfering with the 'natural' law of supply and demand.
But, as Lord Keynes has since remarked, 'in the long run
we are all dead'.

In the course of these widespread social and economic upheavals, which were gradually spreading from the West across the whole surface of the earth and of which the full repercussions have only been experienced in the present century, the voice of the theorists has been far from silent. Indeed it may be ventured that there have been few ages in history where the effect of philosophical speculation and ideology has had a more resounding impact on human affairs.

SOCIETY AS AN EMERGENT ENTITY

Dissatisfaction with the purely individualist and rationalist conception of society was already manifested in the writings of Rousseau, who sought to express the unity of society in his conception of the 'general will', an emergent entity distinct from that of the individual wills of the members of society. A little later Edmund Burke emphasized the traditional and historical roots of the social organism and repudiated the interpetation of a national state in terms of a partnership in a commercial venture. It was, however, the German philosopher Hegel who provided the philosophic groundwork for the pattern of society as a metaphysical entity both distinct from and superior to the individuals who composed it. Hegel's theory was of a highly mystical character, and it is perhaps this which explained much of its influence. Hegel linked his theory to a historicism which envisaged the development of human history as following a preordained pattern. Hegel, like Plato, was an idealist to whom the 'idea' was more real than the world of physical sensations, and for him the 'idea' governing human history was that of 'reason'. The idea of reason was gradually actualizing itself in human history and its highest manifestation was the national state, which represented the embodiment of reason. Such a state was a reality and no mere legal fiction, indeed a far higher reality than that of the citizens comprised in it. These citizens were therefore entirely subordinated to the higher aims of the state, for only in this way could human potentialities be fully exploited.

It will be seen that there is a flavour of Aristotelianism about this theory,[2] and in fairness to Hegel it must be added that he regarded himself as an apostle of freedom, his philosophy being aimed at showing how mankind was developing towards a higher form of political and cultural freedom only attainable by the creation of national states representing the peak of civilization. Hegel, however, was insistent that this type of state was the highest manifestation of human culture and freedom, and far from envisaging any further development in favour of an ultimate international society governed by a régime of law, he regarded the conflict of national states as an essential feature of human progress and freedom.

Although Hegel himself claimed to be a libertarian, his liberty, by democratic standards, was a rather unconvincing one, amounting to little more than freedom to obey the state. On this footing no genuine conflict could be conceived between the state and the individual, for the state was always right. Hegel, like the positivists, denied the existence of natural law, but this was not in order to strike out two autonomous fields for law and morals, but rather to merge the whole of morals into the realm of state law. For him (as for Hobbes in an earlier age[3]) state law itself provided the standard of morality since it embodied the highest development of the idea of reason. No morality, especially no individual morality, could exist outside the framework of the collective morality enshrined in the state and in its law.

It will be evident that such a doctrine has provided a fruitful foundation for many of the totalitarian ideologies which have flourished at the present day. Both Nazism and Fascism subscribed to the idea of the nation-state as an emergent entity embodying the highest reality attainable by man and to which the individual and the dictates of his private conscience and morality were utterly subordinated. These ideologies, however, introduced a new note that was not characteristic of Hegelianism itself. Hegel, mystical though his philosophy may have been, was essentially a rationalist who believed that his organic rationalism achieved a deeper truth than the artificial rationalism of the eighteenth-century Enlightenment. Nazism and Fascism, on the other hand, gathered up in themselves all those forces of irrationalism or anti-reason which came to the fore as the nineteenth century waned and passed over into the tumults of our own age. The dogma of the superman of Nietzsche, the belief in blood and race as against the dead-weight of intellect, promulgated by Wagner, Stewart Houston Chamberlain, and many others, led far beyond the assertion that the law of the state was the highest morality. What emerged was the view that the law itself was no mere matter of legal formulation but rather the intuitive expression of the dictates of the race or the nation itself, and that these dictates were mystically perceived and conveyed by an inspired leader whose intuitions represented the ultimate in truth, law, and morality. It will be seen therefore how the rationalist philosophy of Hegel had ushered in an entirely irrational doctrine steeped in the 'charismatic' flavour of earlier forms of inspired leadership.[4] It is easy to see, too, how under such a régime law would cease to be a system of regularly applied norms and would become at best a set of rules to be treated as no more than guides to the intuitions of the leader, or of those who ruled with his authority, and that all legislation and other legal rules would be subject to overriding considerations such as, for instance, the needs of the German race.[5] Hegel, then, and his irrational off-shoots – not positivism (as has been argued by the natural lawyers[6]) – have provided the philosophical setting for one kind of totalitarianism and its melancholy consequences in human suffering, which have blighted so many of the aspirations of our scientific age. We shall see also that the other main form of totalitarianism, Marxist-Leninism, stems from this same source.

THE ECONOMIC FORCES OF SOCIETY

Hegel endeavoured to give a new turn to the study of logic by his 'dialectic' method. Instead of two contradictory propositions being reconcilable only by deducing that one at least was false he asserted that contradictions could form a thesis and antithesis from which a new synthesis might emerge. This approach he applied to the development of human history in as much as particular 'ideas' in mutual conflict are resolved by a new synthesis. In this way human progress was gradually advancing towards the ultimate realization of the idea of reason. Whatever may be thought of this as an exposition of logic this method is not unfruitful as a means of interpreting certain phases of history, and Karl Marx, who began as a follower of Hegel, turned it to good account. The main change that he introduced was to turn Hegel 'right way up' (as he put it), by asserting that it was not ideas that ruled the world but material forces, especially economic ones, which created not only the social conditions of a particular period but also its basic philosophy or 'ideology' as it is now generally called. Marx described his method as 'dialectical materialism', and in Hegelian style, sought to show how the inherent contradictions in the capitalist system of his day must result in revolutionary upheavals out of which a new socialist society would emerge.

There were really two strands of Marxian thought, both of which have been of great influence in our modern world, but they are not easily reconcilable one with the other. On the one hand, there is the prophetic and historicist side of Marxism, which, like the Hebrew prophets of old, foretells a period of doom and destruction but which looks forward thereafter to a brighter dawn when man will be reborn in a new era of peace and justice. After the revolution, when the class conflict is resolved and the institution of private property is replaced by a communist régime, law and the state, hitherto the main engines of despotism and oppression, will 'wither away'; there will be no need for coercion, since each man will have enough for his needs and universal harmony will prevail. Moreover, this idyllic kingdom upon earth is not pictured as a remote eventuality but as something which history is bound to lead to in the near future as a necessary synthesis of the contradictions in the existing order of society.

On the other hand, the prophetic element in Marx was largely supplemented by an attempt to apply scientific principles to the study of human society. Marx studied closely (though admittedly at second-hand) the features of the existing economic and class system and brought out in a novel fashion the close inter-relationship between the economic ordering of a society and its dominant ideology. In this way he launched a most constructive attack upon the study of the whole field of social studies, for it became increasingly appreciated that society could not be understood without exploring its institutional and economic foundations and assessing their impact upon prevailing ideas. Marx himself is thought by many to have over-emphasized the one-sidedness of this traffic between economic arrangements and ideology, since he contended that the latter was almost wholly dependent on the former. Nowadays it is regarded generally as more acceptable to proceed on the hypothesis that such factors set up currents of mutual influence rather than that one is entirely conditioned by the other. For example, at the present day it is generally accepted that the rise of capitalism was closely inter-connected with Protestant and especially Calvinistic ideology, but that no simple picture of a one-way traffic of influence can suffice to explain this enormously complex segment of human history.[7]

Marx's idea, however biased in its expression, that law was distilled out of the economic order which gave rise to it, and was an institutionalized form of the prevailing ideology whereby the dominant section of society coerced the masses into obedience, shed a new light on the nature of law and its deep roots in the kind of society within which it operated. Moreover this involved in many ways a deeper insight than that of the historical school (also an off-shoot of Hegelianism[8]), for it rested not upon a comfortable belief in the virtues of traditionalism but endeavoured to seek out the real springs of human action, and their translation into existing institutions, by an understanding of the working and necessary social implications of the economic structure of society itself. Marxism therefore can be said to have made a major contribution to the foundation of legal as well as other forms of sociology. It is now necessary to turn to the other, non-Marxist, origins of the sociological approach to law.

THE SCIENCE OF SOCIOLOGY APPLIED TO LAW

The notion that scientific principles could be applied to studies such as law and criminology owed much in the early days to Benthamite utilitarians and was soon reinforced by the French philosopher Comte, who, by broadening the approach to the whole field of social studies, for which he invented the new term 'sociology', gave a great impetus to the belief that man in society was just as capable of being scientifically studied as was any other phenomenon of the natural world.[9] Moreover, the utilitarian preoccupation with the science of legislation gave law a prominent place in these new studies, and as the nineteenth century proceeded a number of leading jurists and sociologists on the Continent, and especially in Germany, began to look to the newly found science as a key to a better understanding of law than had so far emerged from the rather formalist and quasi-logical attitudes of the natural law and positivist schools.

R. VON JHERING

First among the leading names deserving mention in this connexion is Rudolf von Jhering, who exerted a profound influence on the most important sociological jurist of the Anglo-American world, Roscoe Pound. Jhering saw the law not as a formal system of rules but as a prime method of ordering society. Society itself was composed of a mass of competing 'interests', many of them economic but by no means all. An unfettered clash of these interests could only lead to chaos and anarchy. Nor could they all be satisfied, for many were in conflict with one another (for instance, the owner's interest in preserving control of his land might be in competition with the need of the community to run a road across it) and, in any event, there was never enough of everything to go round so as to meet everyone's requirements. Again, some interests might be regarded as of less social value than others, and still further interests might have to be rejected outright as positively anti-social. Hence the law stood as a kind of impartial mediator of all these competing needs and claims, and the real requirement was to relate the legal process to the developing needs of existing society. Hence the lawyer had not merely to grasp the technical principles of his subject but had to bring to it a genuine understanding of the underlying sociological implications of the legal rules with which he operated and how these could be used to resolve and harmonize, rather than provoke or exacerbate, conflict.

WEBER AND EHRLICH

Two other German writers of great distinction explored the sociological aspect of law in much greater depth. One of these, Max Weber, who has already been referred to in regard to the problem of authority,[10] profoundly increased our understanding of the way particular kinds of legal systems reflect an underlying philosophy which is itself both the product and the cause of the society in which it operates. Weber especially emphasized how the modern law of the West had become increasingly institutionalized through the bureaucratization of the modern state. He explained how the acceptance of the law as a rational science was based on certain fundamental and semi-logical postulates, such as that the law is a 'gapless' system of legal principles, and that every concrete judicial decision involves the application of an abstract legal proposition to a concrete situation. There remains a double irony in the fact that soon after Weber's death in 1920, rationalizing law in his own country was totally replaced by a faith in the intuitions of a 'charismatic' leader, though happily this phase is now relegated to history; and that recent sociological jurisprudence has found its main impetus in resisting what it regards as the excessively logical and rationalist approach of the earlier positivist school of thought.

Ehrlich, who was an almost exact contemporary of Weber, made it his main objective to penetrate behind the screen of formal rules, hitherto treated as synonymous with the law itself, to those actual social norms which governed society in all its aspects, and which he described pointedly as 'the living law'. For him every society had an inner order of the associations of human beings which composed it, and this inner order dominated life itself, even though it had not been posited in legal propositions of the positive law. This inner order is really equivalent to what later anthropologists now call the pattern of a culture. The lawyer thus needs to know not merely the positive rules of his system but also the normative inner order of today's living law. This is vital from a number of practical points of view. Lack of correlation between positive and living law may result in a disregard or glossing over of the living law so that mere knowledge of positive rules may give an entirely false or misleading picture of the actual social ordering. For instance, in the commercial world a legal system may nominally impose a web of abstract rules which business men are unable or unwilling to operate, so that business transactions may be found to be governed by a whole series of social and economic norms distinct from or in conflict with the positive legal norms theoretically operative. Again the living law is not static but in a continual process of change, so that the positive law needs to be constantly adapted to it, and this is only possible as a consequence of an empirical study of the inner ordering of the living law as it is at the particular moment. Moreover, the ethical values prevalent in society will be reflected in the living law, so that in so far as law needs to be reconciled with current morality[11] those who are responsible for developing the legal system need to be in close touch with the content of this inner order of society. And this hand on the pulse of society is something required of the legislator enacting fresh statutes and legal reforms; of the judge and legal administrator whose decisions provide precedents for other cases;[12] and of the

T–1

legal profession and all those who by their negotiation and settlement of transactions are instrumental both in developing parts of the living law itself, and in determining what is to be the true scope of the rules of positive law and their correlation with the living law.

ROSCOE POUND AND AMERICAN SOCIOLOGY

Working on the foundations laid by the German sociological jurists, Roscoe Pound introduced a new and distinctively American note to the study of law in its social context. The extraordinary rise of technology in modern times and its impact on man's social and economic life led Pound to explain the legal process as a form of 'social engineering'. At the same time the generally optimistic and forward-looking character of American society, coupled with the extensive attempt to place the study of men in society on a genuinely scientific basis, created a climate of thought where it seemed reasonable to believe that the problems of our society were largely based on ignorance rather than on inherent human defects. With a true understanding of the factors involved, which could only come from first-hand factual investigations scientifically conducted, appropriate solutions would inevitably present themselves.

Pound accepted the view, which is part of the current coin of social anthropologists today, that every coherent society has a pattern of culture which determines its various ideologies. In the broadest sense these entail its particular philosophy of man and the world, but they may be presented on a narrower front in so far as they impinge upon a particular field of human activity. Law, while deeply rooted in the general social complex and its ideology, develops certain fundamental postulates of its own which tend to set the pattern or framework within which the law develops. These postulates are, however, fluid and they change as society changes. The nineteenth century may have seen freedom of contract as one of its basic assumptions, but as Pound himself noted, our own age is now seeing the gradual recognition of new postulates, such as the right to work, and the right to be legally protected against the wear and tear of one's job. A slow ferment is therefore constantly taking place from which the positive legal norms derive their vital force and their future orientation.

Conflicts of Interests

Following Jhering, Pound interpreted the legal process as a form of social control whereby all the conflicting and competing interests in society are scrutinized, compared, and accepted or rejected. The peculiarly prominent role of the judiciary in American law (derived partly from the common-law emphasis on judge-made law through precedents, and more particularly from the constitutional function of the judges, especially of the Supreme Court, to treat legislation as unconstitutional) caused Pound, like most American jurists, to concentrate particularly on the function of the courts as the supreme agent of the law in effecting social control. Much of modern American jurisprudence since Pound has been concerned with facing up to a realistic assessment of the way the courts actually function and their relation to what Ehrlich termed 'the living law'.

Two particular problems exercised Pound's attention: first, how the various interests competing for legal recognition could be classified and correlated; and second, how conflicts between them were resolved by the courts and whether procedures for this purpose hitherto employed, if only implicitly, could be improved. As to the first of these, Pound made the point that interests were not static, since new situations and new developments were constantly creating new needs and claims. For instance, the interest in a man's own privacy – should a newspaper be allowed to reveal sordid details of a private individual's past life, long since forgotten, merely to satisfy a prurient public curiosity? – is a new need of our society which the courts of America, unlike those of the United Kingdom, have gradually recognized. On the second problem, Pound realized that the basic need is to have some system of values by which competing interests can be compared and evaluated and a decision reached as to which is to prevail. Whether a person's interest in publishing information is overridden by the fact that this information reflects on the reputation of another; whether a person's interest in the use of his own property is to be limited by the fact that the exercise of this property right is intended to injure a neighbour, or for some other 'unjust' purpose; whether the interest in public security overrides, and in what circumstances, the interest of the citizen in propagating whatever political creed he may adhere to; all such conflicts call for evaluation if appropriate solutions are to be reached.

The Process of Evaluation

For Pound there are three main ways in which this process is effected by the courts, albeit in many instances unconsciously. The court may simply follow the patterns of the past. The disadvantage of this is that the court will thus, in an age of social change, unduly tie itself to a bygone ideology, as the American courts for long remained wedded to the ideology of *laissez faire* in a collectivist age. Second, the court may attempt, with such aid as contemporary jurists and sociologists may afford, to grasp the fundamental legal postulates of its own age and evaluate disputes in this light. Lastly, the court may simply trust to its own instinct and judge on a rough-and-ready, hit-and-miss basis, relying implicitly on its own understanding of the society in which it operates and its own evaluation of its needs. This last is, no doubt, in practice the commonest approach but it does emphasize the need for courts to be in close contact (and not isolated, as they tend to be) with 'the living law' of their own community. Moreover, as Pound stresses, no amount of positivist insistence that law and morals or policy are distinct can alter the fact that legal decisions are inevitably based on an ideology. It therefore is better to face up to this and make a conscious effort to recognize what are the operative values of one's society and develop the law accordingly, rather than attempt to treat all legal decisions as purely technical exercises in legal logic. Once the law has established a technical rule, such for example as *'caveat emptor'* ('let the buyer beware', i.e. he takes the risk of all defects and so forth) it is so easy to overlook that this simple maxim conceals a whole philosophy of law, the basic postulate of which is economic *laissez faire*. As Professor Northrop has remarked: 'To be sure, there are lawyers, judges, and even law professors who tell us that they have no legal philosophy. In law, as in other things, we shall find that the only difference between a person "without a philosophy" and someone with a philosophy is that the latter knows what his philosophy is, and is, therefore, more able to make clear and justify the premises that are implicit in his statement of the facts of his experience and his judgment about those facts.'[13]

Evaluation of the conflicts inherent in human society in accordance with some accepted or established ideology still leaves open the question how far that ideology itself is susceptible of obtaining some kind of ultimate ethical warrant. It is at this stage that the various types of natural lawyers seek to take over, but as this perennial problem has already been discussed in some detail in previous chapters it is not proposed to add anything further here.

LATER DEVELOPMENTS: LEGAL 'REALISM' IN THE U.S.A.

The sociological approach arose in part at least in reaction to the logical and formalist excesses of legal positivism but it was not long before it developed excesses of its own. On the Continent a so-called 'free-law' school had already emerged rejecting the idea that legal decisions could be based upon rules at all but claiming that they were essentially a matter of policy and choice. Although fettered by a close network of seemingly ineluctable rules the judge was really free to apply them as his caprice, ideology, or sense of social need might direct. In America a strong surge in a similar direction manifested itself after the 1914 war. A number of influences contributed to this development. In the first place, there was, as we have seen, the reliance on social science and technology as a key to resolving the problems of human welfare. Coupled with this was the rise of the philosophy of pragmatism in the United States, a philosophy peculiarly adapted to the American attitude to life. This envisaged the search for truth as a process of continuous experiment to find out what actually worked, and although William James, one of the creators of pragmatism, repudiated what he called the 'bitch-goddess, Success', in fact this doctrine was readily invoked by all those who acknowledged that reverence for practical achievement was the cardinal tenet in the American way of life. Such a philosophy seemed also to provide a ready-made framework for those jurists who argued that law was not a process of deducing correct decisions from established legal principles, but was rather a continuous process or experimental adaptation of decision-making to particular cases in an attempt to arrive at solutions which were correct only in the sense that they actually worked in the social context in which they operated.

Much of the special quality of the approach of the American legal 'realists', as they termed themselves, was imparted by the writings and legal opinions of one of the greatest of modern American jurists, the Supreme Court Justice Oliver Wendell Holmes. Holmes was primarily instrumental in launching one of the dogmas of this school, that what is called 'law' is not a texture of subsisting rules but a mere technique for predicting what decisions courts of law are likely to make in particular cases. Accordingly the lawyer truly worthy of his salt was one who was not merely acquainted with the set of theoretical rules said to be 'binding' on the courts, but who explored all the sociological and psychological factors bearing upon decision-making, and so was able to interpret realistically both how courts function in general and how they are likely to decide in particular cases. No doubt the rules were one of several factors influencing court decisions, but to know these was only a beginning, for these only represented what courts *say*, and what really matters is not words but actions, not what the court *says*, but what it *does*. Moreover, to understand the functioning of law in society it is not sufficient to concentrate attention on the activities of legislators, courts, and other tribunals. The law is a great social fabric constituted by human behaviour in all the mass of transactions which have legal significance, and to this the activities of numerous officials, members of the legal and of other professions, as well as law-creating groups such as the commercial community, are making continuous and important contributions. The traditional emphasis by the lawyers on the rules of law themselves, to the exclusion of all the other factors which give those rules their social reality, is rejected as a narrow professionalism harmful both to the legal profession itself and to the public they should serve.

It will be seen that there are really two aspects to American realism; first, the technique of predicting decision-making, the realists aiming to develop improved methods by which the course of future decisions might be more clearly and readily foreseen; and second, an attempt to achieve a profounder understanding of the functioning of the legal system with a view to rendering it a more effective means of social control and of attaining the aims which society has set itself. These aims are in a state of perpetual flux, like society itself, and it is one of the objectives of legal realists to maintain a delicate perception of the movements in society so as to keep the law in alignment with those movements.

The extreme forms of American realism have encountered a good deal of resistance and indeed ridicule from traditional lawyers, who have sometimes yielded to the belief that the realist attaches less weight to the existence of established rules than to the state of the digestion or the social prejudices of the judge. Certainly, at least some of the more extreme realists have tended to under-estimate the fact that in large areas of legal transactions there are clearly defined rules about whose application and effect there can be little doubt.[14] The realists have tended to concentrate on the areas or points of law which are highly uncertain but it must be admitted that in a modern legal system these are apt to be fairly numerous.

In such spheres no doubt policy decisions do play their part but perhaps less than the realists would always have us believe. More will be said about this in the later chapter on the judicial process, [15] but it should be added here that some realists have chosen to stress not so much the uncertainty of legal rules as the uncertainty of the fact-finding process in any judicial or administrative proceedings. [16] Clearly, it can never be foreseen with certainty what facts may or may not be found to be true and this creates a large element of un-predictability in most legal proceedings, as every practising lawyer knows. Here the realists have concentrated on means of improving legal procedures and techniques, as well as on improving our understanding of the way these actually work.

One curious outcome of these developments in Western legal thought has been to cast doubt upon what the great sociologist Weber held to be the most distinctive feature of Western legal philosophy, namely, the rationalization of the law. Some oriental societies, and in particular the Chinese, have not accepted the idea of law as a means of applying universal rules to particular situations, and have scorned the man who seeks to appeal to rules alone. According to this way of thought the resolution of disputes is a matter of achiev-ing a just harmony by reconciling different view-points in accordance with the requirements of the particular situation. Legal justice is thus a process of mediation or arbitration rather than an adjudication in accordance with fixed rules. [17] It has been sometimes called the justice of 'the cadi under the palm tree'. It is therefore somewhat ironic that modern sociology and the pragmatic philosophy of our technological age should have ushered in a legal approach so antithetical to the tradition of Western civilization. Perhaps this accounts for the fact that realism has proved less persuasive outside the American setting whose rather special features afforded it so much stimulus. [18] Yet it cannot be denied that American realism has acted as a kind of ferment yielding fresh insights after whose impact things can never seem quite the same again. This, perhaps, rather than any specific achievements to which it can point, represents its most effective contribution to the philosophy of law.

THE SCANDINAVIAN REALISTS

Starting a little later than the American movement and probably not uninfluenced by it, a form of realism has developed in the Scandinavian countries which deserves attention. The Scandinavian movement has much in common with the American. It places emphasis on the need to explore the sociological background of legal rules; it explains valid law within a given community as being a prediction of what the courts will probably decide in particular cases; and it postulates the need to investigate the actual way in which the various forms of judicial and administrative process function and insists that this must not be limited to a mere study of the paper rules that ostensibly bind and guide judges and officials. The outlook of the Scandinavians is, however, more philosophical than that of their American counterparts and has led them to explore the foundations of law itself. Some of their findings recall, appropriately enough, Hans Andersen's tale of the king who paraded naked, while his infatuated subjects gazed admiringly on what they continued to describe as his rich and elegant royal robes. Like the royal clothes in the fable, the law turns out, in the view of these writers, to be little more than a figment of the imagination.

One of the leading exponents of this viewpoint, Karl Olivecrona,[19] tells us for instance that the idea that there are rules of law and that these are in a mysterious way 'binding' upon us is a mere fantasy created in our minds by various superstitions and magical beliefs of the past. Law in one sense is really no more than a lot of words written on pieces of paper, and not even this, for what matters is the fact that these words serve to evoke on appropriate occasions all kinds of thoughts, recollections, and notional patterns of conduct, which may influence our actual behaviour. Law is in effect no more than a form of psychology, since it is really a symbolic expression for the fact that the human mind responds in particular ways to certain kinds of social pressures.

Given man's in-built psychological equipment coupled with a certain kind of educational conditioning (and here Olivecrona seems not unmindful of Pavlov's famous experiments) certain patterns of behaviour result. In a given society printed laws emanate from time to time from the activities of a so-called legislative body. This body is in fact a continually fluctuating one and the idea that it has a continuous and collective will is a mere fiction. These laws are read by various persons in the community including lawyers, officials, and judges. By reason of their previous conditioning such persons are psychologically induced to act in certain ways, for instance, to give decisions or orders in particular cases. These orders are carried out by another group of officials who are similarly conditioned to translate what is written on pieces of paper into specific courses of action.

Again, when a revolution occurs, the revolutionaries, if successful, seize the legal machinery which enables them to exert by propaganda psychological pressure upon the citizens. This will cause them (conditioned as they already are) to produce the same responses as hitherto towards the previous constitutional authorities. This will be supported by the same monopoly of force exerted by the former authorities. The psychological basis of law requires the existence of a monopoly of force for it to be effective, but when a régime of law is well established this can be pushed into the background to be invoked only in exceptional cases, for in the majority of instances the psychological conditioning will suffice in itself to produce the appropriate pattern of conduct.

We have already seen, in our earlier discussion of the nature of authority and its relation to law, the considerable role that psychological factors play in enabling law to achieve its social function. [20] But the attempt to reduce law to nothing more than a process of psychological conditioning is part of a wider attack upon the unreality of all legal concepts, and indeed of conceptual thinking itself. Writers such as Olivecrona seem to have attempted to deduce too much from the discovery that concepts such as 'law' do not correspond to some perceptible physical entity. This is no doubt true, for such concepts as law or legal obligation are mental constructs, but this surely does not mean that law, any more than (say) logic, mathematics, or the laws of physical science can be reduced to psychology. Law represents a certain form of language, which, like all other language, is conceptual in its structure, and this language is adapted to convey in certain contexts the normative idea that certain rules are obligatory. This form of language is related, in an exceedingly complex way, to other concepts such as social or moral standards or values prevailing in particular societies or groups, as well as to patterns of conduct actually observed by these. It therefore neither adds anything nor gets rid of anything to say that law or legal obligation is a mere figment to be replaced by psychological conditioning, for as these are not 'things' in a material sense, they cannot be exorcized away by declaring them to be shadows or fictitious entities. They are both a part of our language and a very special part of the human way of life, and the aim of relegating them to 'mere' words or mere psychological reactions seems misguided. Law is neither a mere exercise in linguistics, a mere set of psychological reflexes, nor a mere complex of social patterns. It is a peculiar amalgam of all these, and more, for it symbolizes one of those key concepts or ideas which are central to the social nature of man and without which he would be a very different creature. To describe this and any other part of the conceptual structure of man's being as a mere fiction is to deny an essential feature of man's social heritage.[21]

IDEOLOGY AND LAW

In our own day, when the world-wide spread of Western ideas and technology has brought to light so many ideological conflicts and created many more new ones, it is not difficult to grasp the fact that law, which is after all one of man's main social artifacts, is inevitably deeply embedded in the ideologies of the society in which it operates. It is usual in the era of the 'cold war' to regard the cleavage between Marxist-Leninism and the Western ideology of the 'open society' as the main fissure in the world community, but perhaps even more fundamental than this is the perennial contrast between East and West. This can perhaps be best brought out by considering the case of modern India. In India there is an ancient civilization based on the traditional standards of Hindu culture. The community beliefs derived from the Hindu religion and its law books require adherence to a rigid caste system and the imposition on a large section of the population of an inferior status of 'untouchability'. Much of this still represents what Ehrlich calls the 'living law' of the Hindus. Over and above, and in profound contrast to this, there is the pattern of Western law first introduced by the rulers of British India, and now enshrined in a written constitution which expounds, in language inherited from Locke, the doctrine of individual liberty. This represents, though probably as yet much more superficially, another kind of living law in Indian society. It is obvious therefore that the positive law of India must represent a kind of ferment between these two historically and culturally opposed social forces. In a society with a relatively homogenous cultural tradition it may still be possible for judges to assert that they are not concerned with the policy of the law but merely to state what the law is and to apply it, for here the ideological factors remain concealed and merely implicit for the most part. But in the context of present-day India, it is hardly possible for the judiciary, even if trained in the most rigorous standards of legal positivism, to adopt this detached attitude without, by their very decisions, making it all too apparent how empty a formula this is.[22]

LAW IN THE SOVIET UNION

The ideological conflict between the Communist countries and the West is sometimes referred to as one between East and West, but this is really a misconception. Marxism is itself a product of Western culture closely linked with the scientific materialism derived from the Renaissance, and with the rationalism of the age of the Enlightenment. Moreover, many of the features of Soviet Communism which have developed since the revolution are characteristic of a collectivist age, where the state has assumed large-scale responsibilities in the sphere of industrial control and social welfare. In England we have important state enterprises in the fields of transport and fuel; state corporations run important channels of communication, such as radio and television; there is a system of national health and industrial injury insurance; state pensions are paid to the aged; and so forth. It is true that whereas in Russia the state has become the universal controller and provider, in a limited form of socialism such as has developed in England there is a mixed economy, so that a large field still remains open for private enterprise. Indeed rivalry may exist between commercial and state enterprises, as for instance in the case of independent television and the B.B.C. Even in the private sector, however, there remains scope for a wide measure of governmental control and intervention.

Yet despite all these resemblances, not all of them superficial, it remains true that a deeply contrasting ideology separates the two countries and this is profoundly reflected in the basic assumptions and the institutions of their respective legal systems. For the Marxist the law is merely the means of imposing on the population what the dominant section regards as serving its economic interests, and those who administer the law have no other function than to ensure that this purpose is achieved. The main contribution that Lenin made to the theory of Marx, according to which, after the revolution, law was to wither away with the coming of a classless society, was that a fairly long transitional period would be necessary during which the new socialist state would take over and enforce a new socialist law in the interest of the majority, and so pave the way for ultimate communism.

The actual character of this law has changed a good deal from time to time in the various phases of development which have occurred in the Soviet Union since the revolution. In the early days it was looked upon as a very loosely articulated system, judicial decisions being hardly differentiated from administrative discretion to be exercised as the needs of the socialist society (magisterially interpreted by the heads of the communist party) required. This fluid system has gradually given way, though not without heart-searchings, to a more regular systematization of law resembling in many respects the despised pattern of the bourgeois law of the West. Thus in recent times there have been conspicuous attempts to reform the criminal law by defining more strictly the precise offences of which an accused person can be convicted and strengthening the role of the defence in criminal cases.

Despite these changes, a fundamental distinction remains. In the West, the open society recognizes basic individual freedoms which are maintainable against the state itself, and an independent judiciary exists to uphold and enforce these freedoms. This represents an ultimate value, however far the practice may diverge from the theory. The implications of this ideology of individual liberty for Western law have already been discussed in an earlier chapter.[23] The Marxist ideology on the other hand scouts this approach as a bourgeois illusion and considers that the only freedom which is meaningful is one in which the state controls the whole economic machinery and employs this in accordance with the principles of Marxist-Leninism for the benefit of the people (of which the leaders of the Communist party are the final judges). It is hardly surprising therefore that a very different spirit of living law must infuse the legal systems of countries acknowledging such opposing ideologies.

THE CONTRASTING IDEOLOGIES OF COMMON LAW AND CIVIL LAW

By no means so radically contrasted, but still of considerable significance in the world today, are the cultural differences which underlie on the one hand the legal systems of the countries of Western Europe,[24] and on the other the common-law systems of the United Kingdom, of the Commonwealth, and the United States. For while both of these are deeply rooted in the general culture and philosophy of the West there are considerable factors of differentiation even at the present day. The civil law of the Continent derives, far more directly than the common law, from the Roman law, in its later rationalist form as codified by Justinian, as well as from the rationalizing canon law of the medieval church, itself an off-shoot of post-classical Roman law. Moreover this form of law has grown up largely as the work of learned jurists and reflects a university tradition of logical principles and ideas worked out deductively and systematically in a spirit of rationalism. Hence the ease with which in modern times the civil law has in most countries been codified. Also, although some portions of the Continent yielded to the Reformation, it remains true that the Catholic faith is predominant and that natural-law ideology embedded in or derivative from Catholicism inspires a good deal of Continental legal thought.

The common-law tradition, on the other hand, is primarily Protestant and secularist and is profoundly steeped in the beliefs of English empiricism. Law is thus a matter of political or practical decision to be distinguished from religion and morality, which are best left to the individual conscience. Moreover it is not an inherently logical or systematic body of doctrine to be entrusted to legal scientists and professors but is an essentially pragmatic art to be left to practical lawyers and judges who, as men of the world, will know what to do for the resolving of disputes.

These ideological differences in the two basic types of legal system created in the West are clearly manifested in their mechanisms as well as their substantive rules. The piecemeal creation of law from precedent to precedent in the common law is in vivid contrast with the highly systematized and rational codes of the modern civil law. Contrasts such as these have often been exaggerated and indeed there are strong signs of much more common ground emerging between the two, for instance in the approach to judicial precedent.[25] All the same the cleavage is still very marked and may account to no little extent for some of the doubts and hostility towards the idea of Britain entering the Common Market. For the Treaty of Rome is a document drawn up in accordance with the spirit of the civil-law tradition and establishes institutions, such as the Court of Justice of the European Economic Community, which are framed very much on the Continental pattern of legal thinking. The entry of Britain into the Market would thus involve a good deal of adjustment of common-law ideology to that operative in civil-law countries. This is not the place to speculate whether this would be likely to prove beneficial or the reverse, but there is no reason to assume that the traffic would be purely one-way. Nor should it be overlooked that, for all their differences, Britain and Western Europe both stem from common cultural roots embedded in the soil of more than a thousand years of history.

THE IDEOLOGY OF INTERNATIONAL LAW

In this welter of conflicting ideologies a final word may be said on the prospects of international law in a divided world. We have already discussed the features which that law possesses in common with the national systems as well as those which distinguish it. [26] In particular, it has been pointed out that the element of coercion, whether in the form of the old-fashioned idea of self-help remedies, by war or reprisals, or in the latter-day notion of collective sanctions, seems but ill-adapted to the exigencies and implications of the nuclear age. [27] There is clearly scope here for some radical re-thinking, but this at least can be said, that international law, like any other legal system, will depend for its effectiveness in large measure on the extent to which it corresponds to the underlying 'living law'. In a world containing a variety of conflicting ideologies, some of which are entirely or in important respects diametrically opposed, it is not surprising that international law is likely to be ineffective in many fields, and also to reflect the basic uncertainties and divergencies of outlook of the countries which nevertheless acknowledge its authority.

To this problem there can be no simple solution and purely technical legal machinery can no more exorcize the inherent ideological differences than the brand-new constitution of India can in itself resolve the contradictions of Indian society. All the same, nothing can be gained by denying the quality of law to international law, so long as nations are ready to admit its authority, any more than it would be useful to deny that there is any law in India owing to the ever-present possibility of conflict between the two laws, old and new. Law, as the sociologists have taught us, cannot but be a reflection – however partial and imperfect – of the society in which it operates, and if that society contains inherent contradictions these will be manifested in the fabric of the law itself. Whether and in what manner some kind of Hegelian resolution of these contradictions will ultimately emerge can only be matter for conjecture, but it should not be overlooked that law itself is an important solvent of social conflict and its mere existence can act as a useful emollient if not a cure to the disorders of our times. But without a serious mutual effort to understand the cultural and legal mentalities of other nations little effective progress in international law is either probable or even possible.

We have so far considered law mainly in the context in which it is encountered in a modern state, namely as a system of norms which derives its binding force, directly or indirectly, from some organ of the state invested with legislative authority under the constitution. Many jurists, such as Austin, have been content to confine their attention to legal systems of this character on the ground that the normative systems encountered in earlier or primitive forms of society are so different in character from those of developed communities that they are not deserving of being ranked as law 'properly so-called' or that they are no more than 'primeval substitutes for law'.[1] There is nothing to prevent jurists, any more than other systematizers, from delimiting, defining, or classifying their subject-matter in whatever way they please, and for some purposes it may be desirable or at least convenient to distinguish between normative systems occurring at different phases of human development. There may be good reasons for not wanting to bracket together the obligatory rules found in such diverse societies as those of Australian bushmen, of the Greeks of the Homeric Age, of European feudalism in the Middle Ages, and of modern England or France. To some extent the question of classification is a matter of choice as long as it is borne in mind that the choice is not entirely arbitrary seeing that it must be governed, as in any other classification system, by close attention to the features which the various types possess in common, as well as to those which are dissimilar. In carrying out this process as scientifically as possible, there will enter inevitably some element of value-judgment, for in the last resort we will have to decide on the relative importance of the resemblances and dissimilarities, in the same way as the biologist has to evaluate the comparative structure of different species in order to decide whether a whale is a fish or a mammal, and the physical anthropologist has to settle what characteristics justify him in treating the skeletons of early anthropoids as belonging to a human rather than an ape-like species. Nor are such classifications vitiated by the need to make value-judgments, provided they are related to a close study and analysis of the phenomena from which reasons may emerge for preferring one grouping to another. In the field of legal classification this point has already been considered in relation to international law, where it has been shown that though it by no means corresponds precisely with national law, there are nevertheless good grounds for bracketing the two together as legal phenomena. The differences between the two are not thereby in some magical way made to vanish into thin air; what is recognized is that there are persuasive reasons for treating the term 'law' as wide enough to cover various closely related though not identical types of normative systems.

LAW AND CUSTOM COMPARED

There are many reasons why we may feel disposed to explore closely the interrelation between the legal norms operating in developed societies and the types of norms encountered in earlier or primitive societies. To begin with, the sociological jurists have taught us to see that even in developed communities law exists on more than one level and that to penetrate its mechanisms it is not sufficient to confine our attention exclusively to the sophisticated documentation of legal rules. We must also try to come to grips with the underlying social norms which determine much of its functioning; what has been graphically described by Ehrlich as the 'living law' of a society.[2] Again, the phenomenon of a developed state, with regular organs of law-making, is one which has emerged relatively infrequently in the history of human culture, yet in all human societies, however distant or however primitive, we seem always to find sets of norms regulating the conduct of their members *inter se* and regarded as binding upon them. Furthermore, even in the case of the most developed states of modern times, if we examine their legal systems from the point of view of their historical origins we will be obliged to trace these back to periods when conditions prevailed not dissimilar to those of earlier or more primitive cultures. If then we are to grasp the significance of law as a means of social control, it seems unwise to ignore the way normative rules operate in all different types of societies. For such an inquiry may not only enable us to decide whether there are norms in all known societies which may justifiably be classified as legal but may, by bringing into focus matters more easily visible in a simpler form of society, throw a good deal of light upon the deeply concealed roots of legal processes in more complex social orders.[3]

Custom, Habit, and Convention

The norms operating in less developed societies are frequently referred to as 'customary law'. We will refrain for the moment from using this term, which rather begs at least one of the questions we are engaged in investigating, and adopt the more colourless expression, 'custom'. In the first place, this term must be distinguished from mere habit and from convention. All these phenomena exist in every society and they may be illustrated from our own. A habit is a course of conduct which we regularly, though not necessarily invariably, pursue but without any sense of obligation or compulsion to do so. For instance, I may have the habit of wearing a hat out of doors, or of going to work by one means of transport rather than another. Such habits may become extremely rigid, for it is part of the psychological make-up of human beings that they tend to form habits, and without this tendency life would be so erratic that social order would be impossible. Some individuals are more regular in their habits than others. It was said that people in Königsberg used to set their watches by the time at which the German philosopher Kant was wont to proceed on his afternoon walk. But the point about habits generally is that they are not regarded as *socially* compulsive. I may be so accustomed to take a train to work rather than a bus that I do this automatically and without reflection, yet I do not regard myself as under any social compulsion to do so, and I can change to any other available means of transport without any sense of infringing any kind of norm. It is true that some types of habit, as psycho-analysts have demonstrated, are of an obsessive-compulsive type, but this is a distinct psychological characteristic of certain kinds of neurosis and is not to be confused with the sense of obligation which arises because the individual recognizes that the doing of a certain act is imposed upon him by reason of the existence of a given legal, social, or moral norm.

It is just this socially obligatory element which is characteristic of customary observance. Again, to illustrate from our own society, it is customary for a man to dress in public in a certain way, to eat with a knife and fork, and so forth. These rules are neither absolute nor regarded as equally obligatory by all concerned, for Scotsmen may wear kilts, women may wear trousers, and 'beatniks' may adopt deliberately unconventional clothing or modes of eating, even in a society where customary observances in such matters are fairly accepted and are adhered to. The vital difference, however, between such customs and habits of the kind previously referred to is that those who accept the customs and adhere to them regard themselves as in some way bound or obliged to observe them. The ordinary citizen visiting a restaurant no more considers himself free to pick up his food in his fingers than to assault his neighbour. Although he is unlikely to analyse the reasons for this it seems clear that he regards himself as, in the one case, subject to a binding social norm or rule forbidding certain eating habits in public, as, in the other case, he feels bound by a legal norm or rule forbidding the use of physical violence.

Lying between habit and custom, in the sense explained, are to be found in a given society certain observances which, while not regarded as fully obligatory, may nevertheless be regarded as proper modes of behaviour which people are expected to carry out, though in practice it is recognized they frequently fail to do so, and such omissions are accordingly tolerated. Such usages may be referred to as conventions, and as existing examples may be suggested the acknowledging of letters or of greetings. The weakness of such conventions may be due to the fact that they represent the attenuated survivals of customs of an earlier period, for instance, the now fast disappearing modes of etiquette towards women, such as offering them a seat in a public vehicle. The special feature, then, of conventional behaviour is that while particular individuals may feel themselves bound to observe it, it is not regarded as generally binding, and the individual may largely please himself whether he conforms or not.

It will be observed that whereas both customs and conventions are normative in the sense that they establish rules of conduct for compliance, habits do not refer to or depend on norms, but simply involve regularities of behaviour which are in fact observed. Many, if not most, habits never assume a normative character, but remain on the level of personal idiosyncracy. An individual may lay down norms for himself, as, for instance, in the usually rather fragile 'new-year resolutions'. These, however, have little significance in the field of social regulation, for it is the outward-looking rather than the inward-looking norm that eventually becomes established in customary form. The fact is, however, that habits can and do become converted into customs, though the reasons for this transmutation may not be easy to identify and many factors may cooperate. The tendency towards imitation between human beings may well play some part here, though it has sometimes been exaggerated, especially by Tarde.[4] Much may depend upon whether a practice is established by a member or group of members who enjoy a special authority in a community and whose example is therefore likely to be followed. Again, a practice may gain currency because of its obvious or seeming advantages. Be this as it may, it seems to be a recognized form of human progression that practices which continue to be observed over a period tend, especially if they appear to possess a distinct social function or utility, to be norm-creating. That is to say that the 'done thing' eventually proves to be the thing that *ought* to be, and perhaps ultimately, *must* be done. Customary observance has not necessarily always grown up in this kind of way. Custom may result from deliberate innovations instituted by the ruling class or the example of some authoritative or highly reverenced personage in a community. The headman or chief in a primitive society, for instance, may settle a dispute in a particular way, and although such a society may have no conception of legal precedent, either because of the authority of the chief, or because the ruling seems eminently reasonable, a custom thenceforth may be established which will be regarded as binding in like situations.

CUSTOM IN PRIMITIVE SOCIETY

Custom, it will be realized by now, operates at all levels of society, and it must not be assumed that its character or functioning is identical at widely different levels. It will be as well, however, to begin with the more primitive types of human society, for it is to these that the main attention of modern anthropology has been directed, and widespread research in this field has yielded much information which throws light on the working of custom and its relation to law.

At one time the view commonly held was that in early society it was impossible to differentiate between legal, moral, and religious norms, since these were so closely interwoven into a single texture. Certainly the authoritative source of custom will generally, if not invariably, be attributed to some divine, semi-divine, or supernatural powers, often believed to be the ancestral founders of the tribe itself. To quote an early investigator of Australian totem-clans, when someone asks the reason for certain customs or ceremonies the answer given is 'because our ancestors arranged it thus'.[5] And writers such as Fustel de Coulange[6] and Durkheim[7] have shown the importance of ancestor-worship in moulding social institutions and creating social solidarity. The fact, however, that customary observances may draw upon the religious beliefs of the community and obtain from them a good deal of their binding quality, does not mean, as was supposed by earlier writers such as Sir Henry Maine, that it is not possible to distinguish between religious and secular rules in a primitive society. True it may be that such differentiation is not always practicable, but rules which constitute religious taboos of the community, violation of which will draw upon the offender direct punishment at the hands of the supernatural powers, are often distinguished from rules which regulate the social and economic organization of the community and whose enforcement is in the hands either of some secular authority – the tribe or clan itself, the chieftain, or group of elders – or the next-of-kin of an injured person.

Two other important misconceptions have been gradually dispelled. The first of these was that in early society custom was completely rigid and unchanging, and that primitive man was born into a helpless condition of total conformity to tribal custom. In this view the group rather than the individual was the only unit of the social order. Sir James Frazer tells us in his famous work, *The Golden Bough*, that 'there is more liberty under the most absolute despotism, the most grinding tyranny, than under the apparent freedom of savage life, where the individual's lot is cast from the cradle to the grave in the iron mould of hereditary custom'.[8] Doubtless this sort of approach was a reaction to the romantic notion, disseminated by earlier writers, of the happy and peaceful savage living a life of idyllic bliss in a state of nature governed only by the beneficent control of natural law. Fanciful though this picture was, its successor in the shape of the hidebound primitive, yielding unvarying compliance to tribal custom, and overwhelmed by a sense of fear of the supernatural, was hardly less overdrawn. Some of these clouds have been dispelled by such investigators as Malinowski, who have shown how many of the rules of a primitive society derive not from dark beliefs in and fear of the supernatural, but rather, as indeed in our own society, on the need for reciprocity in social and economic relations. For just as our own society provides a legal and institutional basis for the regulated exchange of various services and commodities, so similar customary rules are to be found in primitive societies in order to provide the means of satisfying their economic and other needs. Moreover, these rules, far from being absolutely inflexible and unchanging, are indeed, bearing in mind the vast differences between the two modes of life and the technological equipment and organization supporting them, in a manner similar to our own legal system, subject to a process of constant adaptation to new situations, old rules being re-interpreted and new rules being from time to time created. [9]

Sanctions and Primitive Custom

This brings us to the second of the major misconceptions among the earlier writers on primitive custom. This was the notion that primitive man was caught up like a fly in a web of inherited custom and that so great was the fear of the forces of religion and magic that violation of custom by an individual offender was virtually unthinkable. From this the conclusion was drawn that no sanctions were really necessary in such a society, for custom was self-enforcing and any occasional violation could be left to the supernatural powers, which would speedily visit death and destruction upon any person or group which disregarded the imperative norms of the tribe. Subsequent investigation of the actual conditions among primitive peoples in many parts of the world has revealed how utterly remote from reality is this model of a primitive social order. For not only is it found that primitive man is just as likely to offend against his customs and, indeed, as Seagle has put it, 'to commit adultery with civilized casualness', [10] but all societies seem to have some form of legally controlled sanctions for punishing breaches of the rules. Malinowski himself underwent some changes of view in regard to the question of sanctions, since at one time he seemed to take a rather too idealized view of the controlling force of 'reciprocity' in the life of the Trobriand Islanders among whom his researches were largely conducted. In the end, however, he came down firmly on the side of those who hold that ultimately the working of primitive, as of developed societies, rests on coercive sanctions, though it may be the feeling or need for reciprocity that accounts for its effective functioning.[11]

The form and indeed the effectiveness which sanctions may take will depend upon how highly the tribal institutions are developed. In a very underdeveloped state of society, as among the Urubus of Brazil, who possess hardly any formal tribal organization and no system of law enforcement, the only sanction, apart from supernatural retribution or the blood-feud, may be that of shaming a defaulter into conformity.[12] Perhaps the simplest form of control is in relation to the blood-feud, where rules are formed, even among so primitive a society as the Eskimos, which enable force to be inflicted without revenge or the blood-feud ensuing, provided the proper procedure is followed. Among such a people as the Trobrianders, use may be made of a primitive 'stop-list'; if a man fails to comply with his economic obligations, for instance by default in making a customary payment, the economic support of the community may be withheld from the defaulter, who will thus be left helpless and alone. Moreover, in more serious cases, socially approved force may be applied, and the ultimate sanction of compulsion and even death may be inflicted when the life of the community is endangered. The main object of sanctions, nevertheless, is not so much to punish the individual offender as to restore the *status quo ante*, that is, to maintain the social order, for the breach is regarded as disturbing social solidarity, which has then to be restored.

In what respects then does primitive custom differ from developed law? We have seen that it constitutes a body of norms distinct from religious ritual and observance, regulating and controlling the social and economic life of the tribe in a manner closely comparable to the functioning of law in a more developed social order. Moreover, many if not all such rules are secular in character and are just as liable to be breached or disregarded as are modern laws. Some kind of enforcement is therefore unavoidable and this generally takes the form of rules which regulate the conditions in which force may be properly applied without incurring the risk of provoking a blood-feud. Very grave violations, which threaten the security of the tribe, may justify death being inflicted either directly or by cutting off the offender from all economic means of sustenance, though is some cases, if religious taboos are involved, it may be left to the supernatural powers to impose the appropriate penalty. There are, of course, many types of primitive society, some much more developed and institutionalized than others. Some of these may possess relatively developed machinery for handling legal disputes, including even a formal court procedure, as for instance among the Barotse.[13] Broadly speaking, however, the vital contrast between primitive custom and developed law is not that the former lacks the substantive features of law, or that it is unsupported by sanctions, but simply that there is an absence of centralized government.

The Absence of Legal Machinery in Primitive Society

This absence of centralization, which, expressed in modern terms, amounts to saying that there is a community but not a state, means that there are no centralized organs either for creating law or for enforcing it. This does not imply that there is therefore nothing but unchanging and eternal and self-enforcing custom. No doubt the more simple the mode of life of the particular society and the more stable it is the less need will be felt for change and the creation of new rules or the modification of old ones. Primitive law (for such, we can now see, it may justly be termed) possesses a flexibility analogous to developed law in its ability to adjust to new conditions. In the absence of regular machinery for formally establishing or creating law, change may still come about in a variety of ways. For instance a council of elders may give a new interpretation of an old rule or even establish an entirely new one. Or again the settlement of a dispute may result in a decision which may be treated (as occurs in modern judicial process) as a precedent for future cases. In neither instance will the new custom or interpretation derive its authority from a formal legislative and constitutional power vested in some person or body; recognition will be given to it because of the reverence felt for the chieftain or the elders, or because these have invoked the spirit of the tribal ancestors or some other supernatural force, or possibly even because the decision or ruling appears to the community as being eminently just and reasonable. It must be borne in mind too, that in a society which has no written records or writing of any kind, the operative custom of the tribe must depend upon the accuracy, reliability, and indeed honesty of the memories of those, especially the chieftains and elders, in whom it is enshrined. Accordingly, the fallibility of human memory alone must account for a good deal of gradual erosion of and accretions to the body of customary law.

The lack of established judicial tribunals to settle disputes and, even in the rare cases where these exist, the absence of centralized machinery for enforcing decisions, mean that primitive law is dependent on rather indiscriminate modes of enforcement, including self-help remedies applied by the next-of-kin of the injured person. All the same in a small and closely-knit society these can prove singularly effective. In considering the views of the modern sociological jurists we have had occasion to refer to Roscoe Pound's hypothesis that every human society possesses its basic legal ideology or 'jural postulates' which form the main, though usually implicit, pre-suppositions of its legal system.[14] This line of thought has been applied by Hoebel[15] to a large variety of primitive societies in varying stages of development, and he has been able to elicit, at least tentatively, the underlying postulates of each one of these, and how they are related to and implemented by the actual rules of customary law observed by these societies.

One or two examples may be given from the many discussed in considerable detail by Hoebel. Among the Eskimos social life is very simple and legal institutions rudimentary, so that there are very few basic premises of their culture which can be translated into jural postulates. Hoebel states that among these are included such postulates as that 'life is hard and the margin of safety small, and unproductive members of society cannot be supported'; and that 'all natural resources are free or common goods, and that it is necessary to keep all instruments of production, such as hunting equipment, in effective use as much of the time as is possible'. As for the first of these postulates, it is shown to provide legal justification for such practices as infanticide, and the killing of the sick and the old, and other forms of socially approved homicide. As to the second postulate, this has a variety of important consequences, including the fact that for the Eskimos land is not treated as being property of any kind, so that any man may hunt wherever he pleases, for the idea of restricting the pursuit of food is repugnant to all Eskimos. Moreover, although game and most articles of personal use are objects of property notions, the Eskimos are strongly hostile to the idea of anybody accumulating too much property for himself and thereby limiting the amount of property that can be effectively used in the community. In one part of Alaska, for instance, prolonged possession of more goods than a man could himself use was regarded as a capital crime, and the goods were subject to communal confiscation.

To take another example, among the Ifugao in Northern Luzon, whose social organization is a good deal more elaborate than that of the Eskimos, one fundamental postulate given is that 'the bilateral kinship group is the primary social and legal unit, consisting of the dead, the living, and the yet unborn'; and that 'an individual's responsibility to his kinship group takes precedence over any self-interest'. This postulate is shown to produce important legal consequences, for instance many types of property are treated more in the nature of a trust than of absolute ownership: a holding in trust for future generations. Again, as the family consists not only of the living but also of the dead and the unborn, and concern for the well-being of the dead exceeds that of those who live now or in the future, family fields may be sold if necessary to buy sacrificial animals to accompany the spirit of a deceased ancestor; they may also be sold to bring about the recovery of a family member who is dangerously ill. It is not possible to provide more details of these and similar matters within the ambit of the present work, but it should be pointed out that Hoebel indicates, with a wealth of examples, the manner in which the postulates of the particular societies with which he deals are related to the actual legal rules and institutions of that society, and the way in which these reflect the physical environment and the cultural circumstances of the societies in question.

Two factors in particular seem to emerge from Hoebel's analysis. One is the way in which each society has a pattern of legal norms directed to maintaining a stable order conforming with its basic postulates. The other is that the success of a society in maintaining such stability will depend upon the degree of integration which it has succeeded in achieving, and this in turn will be reflected in the degree to which its basic ideology commands general assent. Clearly a poorly integrated community, as Hoebel demonstrates in the case of some American-Indian tribes, is likely to have trouble when it comes to enforcing its customary law.

Primitive Law and International Law Compared

Primitive customs can thus be shown to possess many of the distinctive attributes of law while lacking, for the most part, the vital centralized organs of law and government: namely, a legislator, to create new law by regular process; a court, with compulsory jurisdiction to decide disputes; and an executive organ to ensure compliance with the laws. It therefore becomes apparent why many modern writers, such as Kelsen,[16] have argued that international law is closely analogous to primitive law as it constitutes a binding normative system relying for enforcement on self-help remedies, but lacks the centralized organs which are the features of developed law. The main object of such a comparison is not just to establish that international law is really entitled to be classified as law, rather than 'positive morality', as Austin thought,[17] but also to point the way to future developments. For the implication is that just as our modern highly developed and regularly enforced law was only gradually achieved from a primitive social condition with few or no central organs of law enforcement, and the next-of-kin had to do the best they could to secure compensation for their injured brother, so international law may be expected to pass gradually from its more primitive state to one where international organs, legislative, judicial, and executive, will be established. In this way international law may attain the full status of national law, from which it is as yet far removed.

While in some way this may present an encouraging forecast the analogy must not be overdone. For there remain very considerable and inescapable differences between even present-day international law and the law of a primitive society. In the first place, the former is a law between and governing the conduct of national states and not individuals, and those states are for the most part highly developed and technologically equipped communities. Secondly, as has already been indicated, [18] the whole problem of enforcement presents a very different picture when whole nations and not mere individuals (however rich and powerful) have to be coerced. What this suggests, therefore, is that the road for the greater development and integration of international law may prove not only to be a much steeper one than that hitherto taken by national law, but that it must in the nature of things follow a different route. There may well be many valuable lessons to be learnt from the way modern law has developed and a useful role even in the international sphere for legislative, judicial, and even executive organs. There can, however, be no arguing from analogy. Successful achievement will need a very gradual and experimental building-up of international institutions, based both on experience of what is workable, and on a great deal of fundamental rethinking as to the ways in which law can give hope to the aspirations of humanity in our present age in the conditions in which we find ourselves, including the not trifling one that failure to preserve the peace may result in the speedy annihilation of all mankind. [19]

CUSTOMARY LAW IN ARCHAIC AND
FEUDAL SOCIETY

There are many intermediate stages which range between
the entirely customary law of a primitive community and
the sophisticated jurisprudence of a modern state. Many
civilized or semi-civilized states or empires have arisen in
the past whose laws have, to some extent at least, been
embodied in written enactments or codes, as for instance in
the case of ancient Babylon, or the Twelve Tables of the
early Roman Republic, or the priestly code of Deuteronomy.
At such a stage of development it is generally recognized that
there is a legislative power of a somewhat indeterminate
character vested somewhere in the community, whether in
a king, who may be regarded as divine or semi-divine, or
an assembly of the citizens, or some other authoritative
group or class, such as the Roman patricians. The basis of
the law still, however, remains customary, legislation being
regarded as altogether exceptional and resting, if not on
direct divine interposition, as in the case of the Mosaic
Code, then at least upon divine inspiration or the approval
of the gods. [20]

Such legislation, indeed, is often intended not so much to
establish a new set of laws as to codify and clarify the pre-
existing customary law. Class disputes and the tendency in
early times for the ruling or priestly caste to regard the
customary law as a mystery which, whether written or not,
is not to be disclosed to profane eyes, frequently led to up-
risings or disorders, the outcome of which was sometimes that
the customary law was formally published, as in the case of
the Roman Twelve Tables. This law naturally was not a systematic code in the modern sense but enacted a number of
miscellaneous matters of which public knowledge was required
or clarification of the ancient customs was sought. But codes of
this kind did not merely re-enact ancient custom but would
also embrace some innovations. Moreover, once enacted,
an archaic code of this kind would provide the starting-

point for fresh developments, since interpretations of the laws would be called for as new situations arose. In early Rome the priestly officials, the pontiffs, possessed this power of interpretation, though the code itself, once enacted, would generally be regarded as virtually unalterable, like the laws of the Medes and Persians. As society developed in the ancient world, the possibility of legislation, even to the extent of recasting the fundamental laws, became increasingly established. In fifth-century Athens the body of citizens was able to change the law freely, though more traditional-minded Greek states, Sparta in particular, still regarded their laws as unchangeable. Throughout all these stages, nevertheless, much of the law remained customary and unwritten, and this very fact meant that old customs might be forgotten or fall into desuetude or be gradually moulded to conform to a changing social order, or might even be superseded by entirely new customary rules or institutions.

CUSTOMARY LAW IN CHINA

Some highly civilized societies seem never to have developed the notion of rigidly fixed laws, written or customary, inevitably governing the situations for which they have provided. Most conspicuous in this respect is the legal system, if it can be so described, of the Chinese Empire. As has been previously pointed out,[21] the Chinese did not arrive at the idea of a universe governed by fixed physical laws, but regarded the state of the world as a kind of harmony between various tensions or forces. And just as there was no lawgiver to lay down the order of the universe, so there could be no legislator able to provide fixed positive laws or moral codes for humanity. Customary norms undoubtedly prevailed in China as elsewhere, indeed in some respects perhaps more authoritatively, for instance in the case of reverence towards parents and ancestors, and of aid and support to other members of the family. But in the realm of law-disputes, the Chinese apparently never arrived at the idea that these could be resolved by applying pre-determined norms by means of some established judicial process; on the contrary, legal justice consisted of an attempt to harmonize the interests of the parties in accordance with the spirit of universal harmony, of which sufficient intimation had been vouchsafed to human wisdom. Such a society must have combined to an extraordinary degree a social order based upon a deeply rooted structure of legal and social norms together with a high degree of flexibility and uncertainty in all those spheres of social and economic relationship which did not encroach upon that basic structure. Perhaps this accounts on the one hand for the absence of a caste system in Chinese history, as well as for the failure of any organized industrial or commercial system to establish itself there, despite the highly sophisticated quality of Chinese civilization and the technological accomplishments of its people.

MEDIEVAL EUROPE

When we turn to the legal state of medieval Europe we witness a remarkable amalgam of conflicting legal conditions. On the one hand we find that the semi-barbarian kingdoms established on the ruins of the late Roman Empire are governed by a body of customary law, some parts of which are gradually embodied in written codes. These codes for the most part are completely secular and do not rely upon divine origin or inspiration. The slow development of feudalism out of the social and economic disorders of the Dark Ages led to the breakdown of central government, a man's legal status depending upon his tenure of land and his relation to his feudal overlord from whom he held that land. Much of the population were either slaves owned by some feudal lord, or serfs without any legal rights in any part of the land they tilled, but nevertheless tied to that land and to the service of their lord. In this state of affairs the law tended to break up into a vast congeries of local customary laws administered by the feudal lords in their own local courts, and such so-called authority as was retained by the king was extremely weak and virtually unenforceable.

At the same time there were certain forces which tended slowly to offset the anarchic features of feudal Europe. In the first place there was the great institution of the Catholic Church, with the papacy at its head, claiming and often achieving an overall supremacy over the Christian kingdoms of Western Europe. Moreover the canon law of the papacy, related as it was to the earlier Roman law, was a sophisticated written law, and possessed a supreme sovereign legislator in the person of the Pope. While much even of the canon law was doubtless customary in origin and character, none the less it was for the most part incorporated in codes or papal decrees and no one doubted that any part of it could be changed at the will of the Pope himself, as the Vicar of God on earth. Furthermore, even in the sphere of the secular kingdoms, an indeterminate power of legislation was regarded as vested in the king, assisted by his council of the magnates of the realm; he also had an ultimate judicial authority to decide legal disputes and by so doing to declare authoritatively the customs of the realm. It needs no emphasis that decisions of this kind might frequently embody innovations and so assist in adapting customary rules to new social needs. Again, the rise of cities governed by a merchant-class in the later Middle Ages, especially in Northern Italy, created the need for a more developed commercial law and one of more than merely local application. For this purpose recourse was often had to the codification of the late-Roman civil law by Justinian, and this development was greatly fostered by the study of the civil law in the Italian universities, a study which spread to other centres of learning.

All of this made for a very fluid state of legal development in feudal Europe. The idea of customary law, written or unwritten, as peculiarly rigid and unbending, obtains no support from the customs of this period. In the feudal kingdoms the whole of the law was regarded as customary, legislation and judicial decisions being treated as no more than various methods either of declaring old customs or creating new ones.[22] The barons of England in 1236 might declare that 'we do not wish to change the laws of England';

but they did not doubt the power of the king and his barons, if such was their will, to declare new customs. Moreover, the rapidity with which society was changing imparted a great flexibility even to unenacted, unwritten custom. Custom, to be valid and binding, certainly did not need to be immemorial. On the contrary, ten or twenty years usage was regarded as a 'long custom', and forty years made it 'age-old'. [23]

Common Law and Customary Law

In these conditions, a strong monarchy naturally increased the forces of a centralized law and administration, and tended to replace the maze of local feudal customary laws by a royal law administered by the king's judges, who enforced the 'king's peace' throughout the kingdom. One of the results of the Norman Conquest and the establishment of a powerful monarchy in England was to hasten this development a good deal more effectively than on the Continent. In this way a common law for the whole realm was established comparatively easily and local custom was substantially superseded and overrun by the 'common custom of the realm'. [24] The common law, however, was not a customary law in the same sense as the local customs which it replaced, or indeed, the customary laws of earlier or primitive societies, such as have previously been discussed. It was, as it still remains, the product of a sophisticated legal professional tradition and technique; unwritten, in the sense of not being enacted, but contained in innumerable recorded decisions of the judges, whose judgments are the subject of a continuous process of interpretation by means of which legal principles are distilled which can be applied to fresh cases as they arise. Such a law is certainly not created in the way that we have seen norms arising in primitive society and achieving obligatory force by reason of their habitual observance, for these can be said to arise from below, whereas the rulings of the judges, under the common law, are imposed from above.

Yet such a system as the common law, especially in its earlier stages, is something of a bridge between genuinely customary law, and a highly developed codified system of law to be found in many modern states. Judges do not operate in a vacuum but are part of the community in which they function and the legal principles developed and applied by them are bound to reflect to some extent both prevailing sentiments and accepted customs or usages. Nevertheless, the notion of a kind of automatic alignment between judge-made law and community standards and customs cannot be accepted without considerable reservations. For in the first place, judicial law tends to develop a certain autonomy of its own reflecting as it does the many refinements, subtleties, technicalities, and fictions of professional legal opinion rather than the unsophisticated approach that the layman is likely to bring to the rights and wrongs of his daily commerce. And as time goes on, these technicalities are likely to increase and bring the law further and further from the realities of daily life. This situation will become especially marked at a stage of legal development where law reform by legislation is but little resorted to, and the struggles of the common law to break out of some of its own self-created *impasses* so as to adapt the law to fresh needs tend to be accompanied by the use of clumsy and cumbersome fictions which in their turn render the law even more remote from reality. This is sufficiently illustrated by the use of such incredibly involved devices as imaginary lessees or fictitious assignments in order to be able to achieve such simple objectives as the right of an owner to claim possession of his land in a court of law.

In addition to this, it must be remembered that the judges were not so much representative of the community as a whole but were drawn from the rather limited ruling and property-owning class, so that the ideology injected by them into the law strongly reflected the attitude of that class. Thus it is not difficult to see why the law relating to land enjoyed a special sanctity in the old common law; and the harshness of the development and the administration of the criminal law was no less significant in this respect, the hanging of small children being regarded as a lesser evil than any threat to property that their depredations might lead to.

THE ROLE OF CUSTOM IN MODERN LAW

When we turn to the role of custom in a highly developed modern system of law it need occasion no surprise that only a subordinate place, if indeed any, can be found for custom as a source of new legal rules. For this purpose, we plainly have to distinguish between the sociological relationship that the positive law bears to the underlying texture of the life of the community – including its basic values and attitudes – and the way in which social customs may operate as a direct law-creating source. As to the former, enough has been said already in a previous chapter.[25] Here we are concerned only with custom in the latter capacity.

Local Custom

There are three main ways in which custom may operate as a direct law-making source even in the context of a modern state. The first of these is by the recognition and enforcement of local custom. It will be realized that with the establishment of a universal system of law in a given state possessing clearly defined organs of legislation the operation of custom as a direct source of new laws is effectively ousted. Some of the codified civil-law systems of modern times go so far even as to reject local custom altogether as being contrary to the objective of legal unification aimed at by the code. The English common law, while similarly rejecting *general* custom, still allows a very restricted place for the operation of local custom. Proof of a local customary right, however, is subjected to a number of severe legal hurdles which must be surmounted if the custom is to be legally effective. Of these the most extraordinary is that it must be shown to have existed 'from time immemorial', which, quaintly enough, is interpreted as since the year 1189.[26] More easily explicable is the rule that for a custom to be valid it must be found by the court to be not unreasonable. It will be seen that the effect of the first of these tests is to reduce cases of effective local custom to the barest possible minimum, and of the second test, to ensure that the courts retain a considerable measure of control as to whether a custom is to be accorded legal validity. English jurists still engage in the rather sterile debate as to whether a local custom is legally valid in itself or only upon recognition by a court of law. True customary law, of the older type, as we have seen, is obligatory in itself and quite independent of judicial sanction or approval, and indeed may operate even in the absence of any judicial system. In modern English law, however, the fact that the court retains the power to declare that any custom is invalid as being unreasonable shows plainly enough, not only the subordinate role of custom, but also that, whatever the theory, no custom can be regarded as authoritative in itself unless the court has set its judicial seal upon it.

Constitutional Customs

More important than local custom, is the function of custom in determining constitutional practices. This is especially noteworthy in a country such as the United Kingdom which has no formal written constitution. Major features of the British constitution such as the sovereignty of Parliament; much of the procedure of Parliament; some of the rules regulating the monarchy and its constitutional position; and the authority of the courts to develop the law – all these can be regarded as resting on very long-established customary practices which are regarded as unquestionably binding in law. These must be distinguished from mere conventional constitutional rules which, while regarded as in the highest degree obligatory, are none the less lacking in legal authority. Thus the practice that the monarch invariably signs any Bill duly passed by both Houses, or that a Prime Minister resigns if defeated in the Commons on a major issue of confidence are essential features of the constitution, disregard of which is almost beyond contemplation,[27] but neither of these is a legal rule in the sense that it forms part of the hierarchy of legal norms which go to make up the legal system. They must therefore be regarded as binding politically and perhaps morally, but not in law. Further, even as regards those constitutional customary rules which can be regarded as fully established legal norms, it must be conceded that they owe their validity not, as with ordinary customary law, to the adhesion of the community as a whole to these practices, but rather to their acceptance over many generations by the ruling class, including the judges and the legal profession. No doubt the bulk of the population might also be regarded as assenting to, or at least acquiescing in these arrangements, but their role has been mainly a passive one, unlike the active role which adherence to customary practices normally entails.

Mercantile Custom

Third and last comes mercantile custom. In the past the custom of merchants undoubtedly played a crucial role in the development of commercial law. There seems, however, but little scope at the present day for such custom to bring about changes in general mercantile law. In England the last instance seems to have been in 1898, when debentures payable to bearer were held to be negotiable instruments by mercantile custom.[28] There are, none the less, other and far more important means by which the influence of commercial custom may be brought to bear on law. This is through the operation of commercial contracts. Terms may be implied into such contracts either by establishing a trade usage in the strict sense or even by showing that it is reasonably necessary to the commercial efficacy of the contract to assume that it was entered into on the basis of some established practice of the trade. In this way the current of decisions of courts and of commercial arbitrators is able to absorb the effect of changes in business customs and practices, though how readily the courts may be prepared to pay regard to developments in the commercial community may depend largely on the professional traditions of the particular legal system. It is the need for this type of contact between the positive law of legislators and courts and the underlying texture of economic and social practices of the community that was stressed by the sociological jurist, Ehrlich, in his designation of the latter as a form of 'living law',[29] and the fact that commercial contracts constitute so predominant a feature of business relationships sufficiently testifies to the importance of aligning positive mercantile law with the fundamental assumptions upon which different classes of business transactions are based. It is perhaps due to a failure on the part of judges, lacking first-hand acquaintance with the world of commerce, to correlate the two realistically, that the trend away from the courts in the direction of commercial arbitration has manifested itself so conspicuously in recent years.

'Standard-Form' Contracts

Yet another vital way in which the commercial community is able to impose, in quasi-legislative fashion, its own practices and requirements in many types of transaction is by means of 'standard-form' contracts. This type of contract, consisting of a printed form in standardized terms, has become an increasingly familiar phenomenon in the modern legal world. Notionally the party invited to sign such a contract is free to choose whether to do so or not, but the choice of 'take it or leave it', is often a very unreal one for the person who can only exercise his right of refusal at the expense of foregoing supplies or services which can be secured in no other way. Contracts of this kind have therefore to a large extent exposed the hollowness of the old-fashioned concept of freedom of contract, already heavily encroached upon in many particular classes of contract, such as hire-purchase agreements, by legislative provisions designed to protect the imprudent consumer.

Some standard-form contracts which are drawn up by independent or professional bodies may be aimed at consolidating or establishing the best or fairest practices and rules recognized in the particular field of activity – for instance, the standard building contract of the Royal Institute of British Architects – and such contracts may be said in some sense to embody the best commercial or professional usage as hallowed by the practice of the most reputable practitioners in the trade.[30] The bulk of standard contracts, however, are devised rather to consolidate and confirm those rules and usages which are best fitted to protect the interests of particular industries or suppliers, rather than to strike a balance between the needs and practices of all concerned including the humble consumer. The extent to which such contracts, far from giving effect to the usages and needs of the community, confer one-sided benefits on those who possess the power and the resources to impose their will on the consumers has posed many new and complex problems which are still far from being adequately resolved. Most countries have introduced in recent times a good deal of piecemeal legislation aimed at restraining some of the more flagrant and wide-spread abuses which have occurred.

CUSTOM IN INTERNATIONAL LAW

Lastly, a few words may be added as to the function of custom in modern international law. Theoretically, as we have seen,[31] international law is based upon the established and gradually developing customs prevailing between civilized states, including the general customary rule that treaties are to be regarded as legally obligatory. In a sense therefore, international law is a form of customary law, and shares with earlier forms of customary law a lack of definition as to the means by which practices and usages are transmuted into legally binding customs. It is therefore hardly surprising, in the absence of any universally accepted authoritative organs for declaring or deciding what is the established customary rule of law, that many vital principles and precepts of international law are the subject of sharp controversy, the contestants for the most part mustering the evidence and arguments which are conceived as advancing the position of the state or group of states they desire to support. At the same time the crucial differences between international and early customary law must not be overlooked. International law, for all its weaknesses and ineffectiveness, is not a law directed at individuals as such, least of all primitive tribesmen, but is a law governing the relations of developed or semi-developed states, and its prevailing rules have therefore to be sifted in a highly sophisticated manner: by a study of historical example and precedent; by the legal interpretation of treaties, state papers, and other relevant documents; by reference to decisions of international tribunals (so far as these exist) and to the resolutions and opinions of international bodies and their organs; as well as to informed juristic writings and opinions. Hence the curious amalgam of undeveloped legal machinery and refined subtlety of interpretation which is the feature of international law at the present day.

CUSTOM AND THE HISTORICAL SCHOOL

The excessive rationalism of the Enlightenment during the eighteenth century resulted in a reaction which is generally referred to as the Romantic Movement. Beginning as an artistic and literary movement in favour of feeling and imagination it speedily developed a mystic sense of the organic growth of human institutions and the mysterious invisible forces which move society. Already in Burke we find a brilliant and rhetorical expression of the idea that the nation-state is no mere rationalist construction of freely-consenting citizens but is a historical entity deeply rooted in tradition and possessing an organic unity and value over and above the petty strivings of the individuals who comprise it at any given stage in its development.

It was in Germany that this organic idea of law and the state found its most fertile soil. The German philosopher Hegel, in language which was not conspicuous for its intelligibility but was perhaps all the more effective on that account, propounded his doctrine of the State as a living organism, an end-in-itself, and the highest embodiment of human reason. This State was the product of inexorable historical forces in the grip of a World-Spirit whose ultimate attainment, oddly enough, was the Kingdom of Prussia, under whose aegis Hegel was engaged in spreading this new gospel. The melancholy part that this historicist philosophy has played in the modern cults of nationalist totalitarianism is sufficiently well-known to require no further elaboration here;[32] we cannot however ignore the important German historical school of law, which drew heavily, though not unreservedly, upon the background of Hegelianism.

The greatest figure in this school was Savigny, a German jurist of eminence who flourished in the first half of the last century. For him law was not a deliberately created product of some artificially contrived legislator, but was a slow organic distillation of the spirit of the particular People (*Volksgeist*) among which it operated. But the only law which can unqualifiedly claim to be of this order is customary law, and it was to this form of law that Savigny and his followers therefore pinned their faith. Such a law must be understood as the product of a long and continuing historical process and its validity depended on the fact that its traditional character was rooted in the popular consciousness and was thus a true national law in accordance with the spirit of the people. Hence legislation was viewed with great suspicion as an arbitrary interference with the gradual development of historically based customary norms, and codification – very much in the air since the classic Code Napoléon of 1804 introduced order into the chaos of French law of the *ancien régime* – was especially despised.

Undoubtedly the historical approach contributed an important insight to modern legal thinking, by grasping the valuable truth that law is not just an abstract set of rules imposed on society but is an integral part of that society deeply rooted in the social and economic order in which it functions and embodying traditional value-systems which confer meaning and purpose upon the given society. There are therefore affinities between the historical view, the later Marxist doctrine of law (itself an offspring of Hegelianism[33]), and modern sociological jurisprudence. At the same time there remains this vital line of demarcation that whereas the historical approach is essentially backward-looking, seeking historical precedents and explanations for law as it has developed in modern society, both of the latter are forward-looking, being concerned not with the historical background of law either as an explanation or a justification for existing rules, but rather with the moulding of the law to enable it to tackle new social problems as these arise. It is for this reason that Mr Justice Holmes attacked the historical attitude in his much quoted dictum that 'it is revolting to have no better reason for a rule than that it was so laid down in the time of Henry IV.'[34]

The 'Volksgeist'

Moreover a cardinal weakness in the German version of the historical school was its emphasis on the highly dubious conception of the 'People' as an identifiable entity, a collective entity resembling the 'general will' of Rousseau – another supreme romanticist – and possessing a mysterious collective consciousness whose product is not merely language, art, and literature, but all national institutions, including that of law. The German word *Volk* is itself suspiciously ambiguous in this respect, being capable of reference not only to a people but to a nation, a race, or a racial group. Although differing cultures and cultural artifacts have undoubtedly been developed by or associated with particular groups of mankind it is no more possible in law than in any other sphere of culture to identify a legal system with an isolated national or racial group. Perhaps the nearest example of this in the modern Western world is the development of the 'native' common law of England, but it would be impossible to classify the nature and composition of the 'People' who created this law, and it was certainly not a product of the collective consciousness of the people as a whole but was very largely developed by a small group of professional lawyers.[35] This difficulty was indeed foreseen by Savigny who claimed that the development of customary law at the professional level was achieved effectively because the judge and jurist were acting as the organs of popular consciousness. But the complexity and technicality of law in a modern society means that courts and judges have to assume a creative role which is far from being that of inert instruments of the legal consciousness of the people, assuming such a collective state of mind could be shown to exist. Furthermore the common law has now been carried throughout most of the Commonwealth, where with various adaptations, it is applied to an immense diversity of national and racial groups. So too, the modern civil law, derived from the law of the later Roman Empire, is widely diffused over Europe and many other parts of the world, and has been successfully adapted to the needs of a welter of national groups from Turkey to Japan, as well as to some of the newly created African states which have emerged from the dissolution of the French colonial empire.

The English Historical School

In England, where the old common law seemed to provide as good a modern prototype as the historicists were likely to discover in the modern legal world, the historical school made important advances. This was largely due to the pioneering efforts of Sir Henry Maine, who substituted for the mysticism of the *Volksgeist* the evolutionist hypothesis of the Darwinians. Borrowing from Herbert Spencer the idea of a movement from a rigid status society to a freedom-loving society whose relations could be voluntarily established on the basis of contract, he showed the need of a progressive society to adapt its law to new social requirements. Maine stressed both the continuity of historical development from an age of primitive or archaic customary law right down to the complex systems of the modern age, and the ways in which early law was gradually adapted to a constantly changing society, through such machinery as elaborate legal fictions and the paring away of its rigidities and harshness by the principles of equity[36]. His approach was also truly historical in as much as he insisted that earlier ages could only be understood in their own terms and their own historical context. At the same time, contrary to Savigny, he urged that only legislation and codification could be effective to solve the complex legal problems of the modern state. Maine therefore handed on to such great legal scholars as Maitland and Pollock the attitude that though history might increase our understanding of the past and of the present state of the law, and though we cannot ignore the extent to which that present state is historically conditioned, history must not be used as a strait-jacket to impose traditional attitudes upon the needs of a new age.

THE SEPARATION OF POWERS

In his classical exposition of the English constitution, the French writer Montesquieu laid stress on the doctrine of the separation of powers. According to this doctrine a constitution comprised three different sorts of legal powers, namely, legislative, executive, and judicial, and any constitution worthy of the name would ensure that each of these powers was vested in a different body or person. The role of the legislature was to enact new laws; of the executive to enforce and administer the laws as well as to determine policy within the framework of those laws; and of the judiciary, simply to interpret the laws established by the legislative power. This neat classification had some considerable influence on the form of constitution subsequently adopted by the newly created United States of America after the Declaration of Independence. In particular the separation of the executive from the legislature was effected by precluding the President and his ministers from belonging to Congress or from participating directly in its business, a system entirely contrary to the English system, where the government is an integral part of the legislature and is in effective control by reason of its parliamentary majority.

THE INDEPENDENCE OF THE JUDICIARY

The notion that the third arm of the constitution, the judiciary, should be entirely separate from both the legislative and the executive powers, seemed, however, to be based on more solid foundations than the somewhat arbitrary division between the legislature and the executive. Two principles could in this instance be invoked, each of which might be regarded as entitled to a good deal of weight. In the first place there is the question of the independence of the judiciary. If the laws are to be fairly interpreted and impartially applied it is obviously important that the judiciary should enjoy an independent status and be free from the political pressures engendered by association with either the executive or even the legislature itself, dominated as the latter is likely to be by the divisions of party politics. As against this it may be said that since judges have to be appointed by someone, this means in practice nomination either by the government or some member of the government, as for instance by the Lord Chancellor or the Prime Minister in England, or by a Minister of Justice in many other countries. How then, it may be asked, can independence be preserved if appointments are in their very inception made by politicians? Experience has shown that there are ways of overcoming these difficulties, though any such methods may not invariably prove successful. One very important factor is the development of a strong tradition in favour of ignoring political considerations when making judicial appointments. Such a tradition has in fact gradually developed in England though its consolidation may be regarded as fairly recent, and the earlier strong links between the law and politics is still reflected in such features as the dual role of the Lord Chancellor as politician and as head of the judiciary, and the claim of the Law Officers to certain types of judicial preferment. In the United States, where the President appoints to the federal judiciary but only with the approval of the Senate, the influence of political considerations has been less easy to escape, especially having regard to the importance of this patronage in the American party system, and the quasi-political role that the Supreme Court and the federal judiciary have inherited as guardians and interpreters of the Constitution. Moreover, in many of the States of the Union judges are not appointed but are elected, just like any other politicians.

Yet if difficulty is experienced in avoiding some political element creeping into judicial preferment, a very powerful weapon in support of the independence of the judiciary has been found in the rule, established in England as a result of the constitutional struggles of the seventeenth century, that judges should hold office for life or until retirement, and should not be removable by executive action. This has proved to be one of the vital means of preserving judicial independence in the common-law world, from which it has spread to many other countries. In some countries also attempts have been made to take politics out of judicial appointments and promotions by requiring, for instance, the concurrence of the judiciary or of bodies representing the bar or the legal profession in any particular nomination. Such experiments are interesting and important and may prove to be of genuine value but it remains to point out that all such experiments are likely to prove still-born in the absence of a firmly established belief in the essential need to preserve judicial independence. For without this governing ethos the concurrence of the various bodies in question is likely itself to proceed on political lines. Certainly the requirement of Senate approval in the United States for Presidential nominations to the federal judiciary has had the effect of injecting a powerful political element into many such appointments.

The question of promotion is almost as important as that of initial appointments in regard to judicial independence. For if the judiciary has to look for its future prospects to the politicians they may be unwilling to incur executive displeasure and so mar the chances of later promotion, even although they are secure in their posts. In England this difficulty has been largely overcome by avoiding too hierarchical a pattern in regard to the higher judiciary. A certain uniformity of status has been retained in regard to all the higher judiciary from the High Court level to the House of Lords, particularly by keeping salaries on almost the same level throughout and by avoiding any form of promotion on the basis of seniority. This system has been greatly aided by the historical antecedents of the English judiciary and its exceptionally strong traditions and long-established status.

So strong indeed have these factors proved that wherever the common law has spread, even in countries such as India, with an entirely different racial and social pattern, and with profoundly differing cultural antecedents, the strongly independent status of the common-law judge has tended to establish itself. A striking example is also provided by the Union of South Africa. There the dominant Roman-Dutch legal system has been overlaid with a judiciary of the common-law type, and one which has to a notable extent proved its calibre of independence, despite the almost intolerable political and racial strains to which it has been subjected since the Nationalist Party with its relentless policy of racial apartheid secured office after the last war.

DO THE JUDGES 'MAKE' THE LAW?

The separation of judicial from other forms of constitutional power may thus be said to rest heavily on the need for preserving judicial independence. There was, however, another principle which undoubtedly weighed with Montesquieu in proposing the rigid demarcation between judicial and legislative power. This was the belief that the judicial role is really not properly legislative at all but consists merely in stating what the existing law actually is, and in interpreting authoritatively doubtful points as they arise. This attitude towards the judicial function was in harmony with the traditional approach of the common law, which insisted that the judges had no power whatever to make law but simply 'declared' it as it had always been. Such an attitude stemmed from two closely related views of the nature of law which derived from a long-past order of society. On the one hand there was the view of law as a kind of sacred mystery in the hands of a priesthood, a mystery not to be revealed to profane eyes. This view, particularly associated, as we have seen,[1] with an aristocratic order of society, was not altogether alien to the older common law. The judges, as the exponents of an unwritten law, and as representatives of the royal fount of justice, were regarded in a peculiar sense as the 'depositaries or living oracles of the law', in Blackstone's phrase. That law was, almost in a mystical way, treated as deposited in the bosoms of the judges and so discoverable by them alone and revealed piecemeal to the profane only to the extent which seemed good to the judges, and then in such hierophantic language as was intelligible only to the initiated. If this is something of an exaggeration, there still remains the second and related view of the early common law as a body of customary rules established for the whole realm and of which the royal judges were no more than the especially qualified exponents rather than the creators.

We have already discussed how far this customary theory of the common law was removed from reality. To a large extent that law was a body of rules fabricated by the judges themselves over the centuries, though strongly linked in certain respects, as law of any kind inevitably is, with the economic and social patterns of the society which gave rise to it.[2] At the end of the eighteenth century it had become manifest to anyone with eyes to see that the idea of judges doing no more than declare the law was a hollow pretence, and this idea was roundly stigmatized by both Bentham and Austin as a childish fiction. Bentham insisted that the common law was 'judge-made' law, or as he somewhat disrespectfully called it, the 'product of Judge and Co.', by which he meant that it was derived from the state of legal professional opinion of which the judiciary was only an element, albeit, in England at any rate, the most important element. Austin, too, accepted this view and had some difficulty in reconciling it with his theory which derived all law from the command of a sovereign legislator. This he did by appealing to the principle that what the sovereign permitted, by not interfering with or repealing judicial decisions, it must be taken implicitly to have commanded, but unfortunately this was to substitute one fiction for another, as indeed Austin virtually admitted. So much is revealed from the following passage gleaned from Austin's own writings:

In this country where the rules of judge-made law hold a place of almost paramount importance in our legal system it can hardly be said that Parliament is the author of those rules . . . In truth Parliament has no effective power of preventing their being made and to alter them is a task which often baffles the patience and skill of those who can best command parliamentary support.[3]

Yet Bentham and Austin were by no means in agreement as to the merits of this type of law-making. Bentham believed in the virtues of rational codification and thought that by this means judicial legislation could be avoided. His hostility to the uncertainties created by judicial law-making is shown by his comparing it to the way a man makes law for his dog, namely, to wait until it does something of which he disapproves and then to beat it and thereby teach it that what it did was wrong. Austin, on the other hand, not only recognized the inevitability of judicial law-making even under a codified system, but expressed approval of it as an essential means of bringing the law into line with the needs of a modern community. In fact Austin deplored the timid, narrow, and piecemeal manner in which English judges had actually legislated and their mode of doing so under cover of vague and indeterminate phrases.[4]

Despite this frank approval by Austin himself of judicial legislation if directed to proper goals, to be identified in accordance with the doctrine of utility, it must be admitted that another aspect of Austin's approach gave further strength to the assumption that it is no concern of the judges to make law but only to say what it is. For Austin, by insisting on the cardinal tenet of legal positivism that we must differentiate between the law as it is and the law as it ought to be,[5] provided the essential ammunition for maintaining a restricted judicial role. The judges, it could be and was (and indeed still is) said, are not concerned with what the law ought to be but merely with what it actually is. This proposition is perfectly or at least arguably sound, as we have seen,[6] if it is taken to mean that the judge, once he has ascertained the relevant rule of law, is not entitled to refuse to apply it or to change it because it meets with his disapproval. But where it ceases to be sound is if it gives rise to the assumption that there is a clearly established rule applicable to every possible situation and that the judge merely has to search for this rule and, having found it, to apply it mechanically to the case before him. Moreover, even if it was conceded, as conceded it must be, that the law bristles with uncertainties and obscurities, and that even where a clear rule exists it may still be exceedingly difficult to decide how it is to apply to particular cases, the view could still be maintained that these difficulties could be solved by a close analysis of the rules themselves and their interpretation and exposition in accordance with the rules of logic and the principles of semantics. It followed, therefore, that the power of judicial law-making differed fundamentally from the true legislative function, under which policy decisions could be made in favour of new laws. For it was limited, broadly speaking, to working out the logical implications of legal rules and could not generally go beyond these or, in the case of the construction of statutory enactments, beyond the semantic structure of those enactments. Moreover, so important was it for the judiciary to avoid involving itself in policy decisions, that in cases of uncertainty where choices had inevitably to be made, these should be made rather on grounds of logical consistency than on some manifestly 'extra-legal' basis such as social purpose, morality, justice, or expediency.

THE LIMITS OF JUDICIAL LAW-MAKING

This approach, although not without its influence, even at the present day, has never been effectively adhered to for the simple reason that it is not only unrealistic and impracticable but is based upon a fallacy. The role which value-judgments play in the texture and in the development of the law has already been discussed,[7] and it only needs here to be reiterated that choices involving values form an essential feature of a good deal of decision-making. Judges, like other human beings, cannot divorce themselves from the pattern of values which is implicit in the society or the group to which they belong, and no amount of consciously applied impartiality or judicial lack of passion will succeed in eliminating the influence of factors of this kind. If, for example, we consider how in modern times various fields of law have been gradually moulded by judicial legislation in an effort to adapt them to the needs felt in a new type of industrial and welfare-minded society we can perceive how the law can move from decision to decision in a slow and piecemeal progression towards giving effect to a changed pattern of values.

Development of the Law of Negligence

This sort of development may be illustrated from the rise of our modern law of negligence. This has grown out of legal principles laid down before the Industrial Revolution when there was little sense of any social obligation to make reparation for harm casually and unintentionally inflicted, save in cases of special undertakings or relationships, such as arose when a surgeon performed an operation negligently or a carrier was negligent in driving his vehicle. Gradually, over the last century or so, this body of special duties has been replaced by a broad acceptance of the principle that there should be a duty to make reparation whenever injury is inflicted owing to negligence. In a society such as ours, there is a constant exposure to risk of injury due to the vast extension of the use of machinery in every aspect of daily life, and accordingly there has developed a strong feeling that human welfare requires, so far as practicable, a distribution of the impact of that risk to prevent it falling exclusively on those who are unfortunate enough to suffer injury. Indeed, in a number of instances the courts have also established a legal obligation to compensate the victim of injury even where there has been no fault or negligence on the part of the defendant. This principle has been applied not only to the escape of dangerous things, such as noxious substances or explosions resulting from the accumulation of such substances or the carrying out of dangerous operations, but more important, to the whole field of vicarious liability. An employer is now held liable for the negligent acts of his servant even though the employer himself may have been entirely blameless.

This extension of the law serves to demonstrate not only the way in which new policies may be gradually injected into the substance of the law but also the limits within which such a process may operate. The rise of the welfare state contains the implicit assumption that many of the social and economic risks from the ordinary wear and tear of existence should be as widely distributed as possible and not allowed to fall only on the unfortunate. The idea of an earlier and sterner age of individualism (where misfortune was almost equated with the culpability of the sufferer who was therefore no more than an object of charity to be relieved from destitution but without any legal claim whatever to relief) has been replaced by a partial attempt to provide a legal claim to a reasonable subsistence in relation to many of the main contingencies of human life. Such provision has been made in the case of sickness, industrial injuries, old age, and the death of a breadwinner leaving dependants behind him. Yet it is obvious that however favourably courts of law may desire to react towards this general change in human attitudes it is not for them but for the legislature to introduce far-reaching schemes of social insurance in order to secure the citizens against undeserved misfortune.

Moreover, even in the context of those fields of law where courts have scope to adjust the law to new situations, their ambit of operation remains rather limited. If we take one of the main activities of our present-day courts, which is to try actions for damage arising out of negligent driving of motor-vehicles on the highway, it has to be borne in mind that this whole branch of law has only been rendered tolerable in modern times by legislative intervention imposing compulsory insurance against third-party risks on all drivers. For in the absence of such insurance much of the compensation recoverable in actions of this sort could not be paid. In addition there remains the grave lacuna in the existing law that such liability requires proof of negligence, and so depends upon an assessment of the facts in each case so far as they can be ascertained, the decision frequently turning on an opinion as to the interpretation of these facts which might well differ substantially from one judge to another. It may be argued that what is needed here is some kind of social insurance against the misfortunes of road accidents comparable to that which operates already in the field of industrial injuries. Indeed, a case could be made out against the whole idea of actions for damages amounting in some instances to vast sums which can only be met by large corporations or an insurance company. Social insurance can and should provide a reasonable subsistence in all cases; compensation for serious injuries or loss of earning-capacity might arguably be left as a field for private insurance, as it is to some considerable extent already. The argument that possible liability to heavy damages is an important deterrent against careless driving on the roads is hardly convincing, since people who are not deterred by the thought of suffering death or serious injury owing to bad driving are unlikely to be influenced by the financial risk incurred by their conduct. It may also be said that it is the function of the criminal law rather than of the civil law to act as a deterrent, for, apart from anything else, punishment can be made to fit the crime, whereas in the civil law of tort, the actual damage suffered, for which compensation may be payable, bears no relation whatever to the degree of culpability.

Be this as it may, one thing is perfectly clear and that is that it does not lie within the power or the function of courts of law to evaluate all these considerations and to decide whether or not to replace a code of liability based on compensation for injury suffered by negligence by a system of social insurance. Nor indeed is it desirable that courts should be invested with any such function for they are not equipped to evaluate large schemes of social reform in the course of deciding day-to-day litigation between particular parties. Nevertheless there is scope for introducing important changes in the law by means of judicial decisions, as we have already seen in the case of the broad extension of the law of negligence and of vicarious liability. The courts could, if they had been so minded, have carried the law a good deal further. For instance, by deciding that motor-cars were dangerous things which imposed strict liability on their users without proof of negligence, or by laying down that it was not for an injured person to establish that the driver was negligent, but rather that the onus lay on the driver to establish that he was driving properly and taking all due care. Whether such changes in the law would be desirable is clearly open to argument; our aim here is merely to point out that there are many ways in which the courts are free to make certain choices of an important character, choices which are likely to be much affected by the view the judges entertain as to the social purposes of the law and how these purposes may best be achieved.

At the present day our law of negligence is in an uncertain state of development as to how far it ought to provide compensation for merely financial loss as opposed to physical injury. Suppose, for example, that a valuer gives a valuation of certain property knowing that it is going to be used by someone as a basis for deciding whether to invest his money or not. The valuation is carried out so negligently that it substantially exaggerates the value of the property and the investor as a result loses his money. In a leading case[8] it was held that in the absence of a contract between the valuer and the investor no action will lie, though Lord Justice Denning, in a dissenting judgment, strongly castigated timorous judicial attitudes which stood in the way of what he regarded as a socially desirable development of the law within the scope of judicial law-making. Another aspect of this decision involved the question whether in any event the law of negligence extended to cover statements, whether oral or written, as opposed to actual conduct resulting in injury. Here again it will be seen that the judiciary is faced with a definite possibility of choice between holding that liability does or does not extend to negligent words as opposed to other conduct. On what basis can it choose between these? Of course, as we shall see, in a system which accepts the rule of binding precedent a previous decision of a higher court may be decisive. This, however, amounts to no more than saying that in this instance there is in fact no choice.

Where there is no such precedent, or the previous decided cases are of doubtful scope and interpretation, the court has to decide one way or the other.[9] By what process can it arrive at such a decision? This brings us back to the question whether logic or logical consistency can in some way resolve the issue without the need for embarking upon any policy considerations whatsoever. As we have already ventured the opinion that this idea is based upon a fallacy, it remains to say something more on the general nature of legal reasoning in order to attempt to justify this opinion.

THE NATURE OF LEGAL REASONING

Let us begin by taking the case of the court faced with the problem just discussed, namely, that there is an acknowledged rule that a person is liable to compensate anyone for personal injuries resulting from his negligent acts, but that doubt exists as to whether this liability covers either the use of negligent words, written or spoken, or mere financial loss without any physical injury having resulted. How is a court to set about tackling problems of this kind? In what way is its mode of reasoning peculiar to itself? To what extent does its reasoning resemble the way in which we all reason in our everyday affairs?

In the first place it is apparent that mere logic or logical consistency cannot in itself provide a definite solution to this kind of problem. There is nothing in logic which compels us to infer that because a rule imposes liability for negligent *acts* this rule must therefore extend to negligent *statements*; or that a rule creating liability for negligence causing physical injury must necessarily extend to pecuniary damage without any such injury. At the most we can say that legal, like everyday reasoning, leans heavily on argument by analogy. The human mind feels a natural disposition towards treating like cases alike, and this tendency, as we have seen, plays an important role in the functioning of the principles of justice.[10] What constitute like cases, however, though in some instances fairly easy to resolve, may in others give rise to considerable doubt. In relation to liability for negligent acts, there is little difficulty in accepting the fact that the rule applies to driving a vehicle of any kind or setting any machine in motion. The fact that these are 'acts' for this purpose seems obvious and virtually beyond dispute to everyone. But what of *omissions*, that is *failures* to act? Are these to be classified as acts for this purpose? For instance, I see someone proceeding up a steep path which I know to be dangerous, but I fail to warn him of the danger. Or I am a strong swimmer and see a small child drowning in a pool of water but do nothing to save it. This marginal type of problem cannot be resolved simply by examining the logical or semantic implications of the word 'act', or even by attempting to assess whether there is any decisive analogy between negligently driving a car or negligently failing to rescue a drowning child. For neither logic nor semantics can dictate what inference we should draw or how we are to apply words to doubtful cases, and mere analogy gives us little assistance in cases which are so far apart that their obvious similarity does not make an immediate impact upon all minds alike.[11]

Does this mean that in all those numerous instances of doubt and uncertainty which arise in the application of legal rules, courts really have a completely free choice in the matter and arrive at merely arbitrary decisions? Anyone who studies the elaborately reasoned judgments of English courts must be surprised if not shocked to hear these carefully considered conclusions stigmatized as arbitrary. These are certainly no more, and indeed usually, a good deal less arbitrary than the decisions which we take in other non-legal affairs of daily life. If we are considering whom we should appoint to a particular job, or where we should go for our summer holidays, we may put a number of names on pieces of paper and draw one out of a hat in order to give us an answer. Such a procedure would undoubtedly be regarded as arbitrary in the full sense, since our choice is simply left to random selection. In practice, we are more likely to examine the range of choices which are reasonably available and attempt to weigh the merits and demerits of each possible choice against the others in the light of such facts and previous experience as we may possess, as well as being guided by the aims or purposes we desire to achieve. And although in the end a definite choice has to be made and, in a sense, we remain free after every argument has been canvassed to accept any candidate or to make for any resort on the globe, in practice a procedure of this kind is the reverse of arbitrary, involving as it does a rational scrutiny of alternatives and leading frequently to a fairly clear-cut decision in favour of one course rather than any other.[12]

Broadly speaking then, the way in which lawyers reason out their cases follows a pattern similar to that of everyday life, and this is hardly surprising, for law is a practical science dealing with everyday problems and is expressed and argued in ordinary language. True it is that lawyers, like other professional or specialist groups, tend to create within that language a certain esoteric jargon of their own. This creation of a specialist jargon is a necessary tool of any science which is to attain a greater degree of precision and definition than is needful in ordinary life, though it can also produce harmful consequences, especially in a sphere which is concerned with everyday problems. For the danger is that certain unreal and merely terminological solutions may be developed in relation to situations which call for other factors to be taken into account. We shall later see some illustrations of this when we come to examine in more detail the influence of conceptual thinking on legal problems.[13]

The lawyer brings to bear upon the solution of his problems a specialist terminology which frequently enables him to give more precise scrutiny to the process of differentiation and choice which operates in decision-making generally. But the lawyer also commands other and equally valuable aids in arriving at decisions. He possesses an elaborate procedure governed by strict rules whereby the issues in a case can be closely defined, and irrelevant matter excluded, and all the relevant arguments for and against a particular decision can be ranged in an orderly fashion, and all the differing viewpoints presented, if necessary or desired, by legal representatives skilled in the art of assembling arguments and presenting them in their most persuasive form.

Analogies and Value-Judgments

Moreover, when it comes to decisions on points of law, there exists in most legal systems a very large apparatus of previously decided and recorded cases with the reasoning for those decisions systematically set out in the courts' records. These cases may not always provide a ready-made answer to the problem that the court is now faced with, but they frequently provide clues or guiding-lines as to what considerations need to be taken into account and the types of solution which are available.

In examining these earlier decisions lawyers will pay close regard to the analogies that they may or may not present to the case with which the court is now concerned. And in inviting the court to weigh these analogies those arguing the case on behalf of the different parties will seek to work out the implications of treating like cases alike if these analogies are accepted or rejected. The object of such advocacy may be, for instance, to show that if a certain analogy is accepted it will lead to unfortunate consequences in other cases not easily or rationally distinguishable from the present case. Thus in the *Candler* case already referred to,[14] much play was made with the point that a decision in favour of the plaintiff might have the effect of imposing liability on a cartographer who makes a mistake in one of his marine charts for the loss of an ocean liner whose navigator has relied on such a chart. This argument appeared to carry some weight in the ultimate majority decision in that case. It must be borne in mind, however, that whether one considers it desirable to make the cartographer liable or not is a value-judgment which depends upon an assessment of social purposes and ethical standards. It is for this reason that no amount of rationalized presentation of so-called logical argument can eliminate the need for choices to be made which may and often do depend largely upon such valuations, whether conscious and deliberate or not.

Courts often seek to minimize or conceal the element of conscious choice involving value-judgments in their decision-making. The reason for this is not a desire for mystification or an attempt to pretend that the law is a completely rational and certain science capable of solving all problems by sheer logical inference. What is felt fairly strongly by most legal professions brought up in the traditions of Western rationalism is that there are and should be very definite limits to the extent to which judges and courts should be treated as free to change the law, either directly or indirectly, under the guise of developing or re-defining it. The availability in Western countries of regularly constituted legislatures makes the division between law-making and judicial interpretation seem both intelligible and justifiable, and the exercise of judicial restraint is thought to be conducive to the preservation of the independence of the judiciary. Consequently, even when courts are patently making new law by their decisions they tend to shun too open an avowal of what they are doing, lest they be accused of usurping the functions of the legislature. Hence a tendency on the part of courts to play down the element of conscious choice in their decisions, and to expose their reasoning in the form of logical deductions from well-established rules. All the same the inexorable way in which judicial law has changed and developed from generation to generation reveals that this is to a large extent a façade of continuity. Still, it also contains an important truth, namely that by its very nature, dealing as it does with sporadic litigation as it arises, judge-made law is necessarily a very gradual and piecemeal process and that it operates not by sweeping reforms but, in Holmes's phrase, 'interstitially', that is by making small insertions here and there, from time to time, in the vast and intricate fabric of the legal system.

The Effect of 'Public Policy'

So abiding is the reluctance of judges to concede that their function is in any way tainted with policy decisions – since it is their duty to say what the law is and not what it ought to be – that the layman may be surprised to encounter the occasional use of the concept of 'public policy' in common-law cases, or of its approximate equivalent,[15] 'morals and public order', in decisions of civil-law judges. Yet the very caution with which these concepts are employed, especially in common-law jurisdictions, sufficiently demonstrates the deep-felt disinclination to parade judicial law-making powers. In England, for example, this idea of public policy is mainly used as a very limited means of relieving the court of the duty to enforce contracts which are formally valid but which strongly offend the court's sense of morality or justice, while not involving any actual illegality. The doctrine has been applied to agreements involving sexual immorality as well as to a number of other types of case, perhaps the most important being agreements in undue restraint of trade, e.g. a clause in a contract of employment which imposes an excessive restraint on the employee after his employment has ceased.

Public policy was described by an early nineteenth-century judge as 'a very unruly horse which may carry its rider he knows not where',[16] and this dictum, together with the more recent warning that it is 'a very unstable and dangerous foundation on which to build until made safe by decision',[17] is regularly repeated in most of the modern cases where this doctrine is invoked. Moreover, in some of the cases there are judicial expressions of opinion that the categories of public policy are now forever closed and that the court cannot, if it would, create a new head of public policy. It is not proposed here to examine further this rather sterile controversy, which clearly impinges on the question how far the existing categories are susceptible of exact definition. For like other forms of judicial law-making the scope of these categories cannot, as we have seen, be resolved by purely logical or semantic demonstration. What does emerge plainly enough is the judicial attitude of hostility towards any suggestion that this comparatively minor field of policy can be used as a means of enlarging, to any significant extent, the judicial function.

Of course it may be validly pointed out that in a sense

whenever a court creates a new rule or lays down a new application of an old one, this decision, so far as it rests upon a value-judgment as to what social need or justice demands, is really an exposition of the court's assessment of the requirements of public policy. It remains a testimony to the strong sense of restraint which motivates most courts that this doctrine is extremely rarely invoked in such cases, and then mainly in cases where the public and social element is very strong, as for example in matrimonial cases.

THE BINDING FORCE OF PRECEDENT

We have so far assumed that courts will inevitably refer to and pay regard to past decisions, but without any implication that they are necessarily bound to follow such decisions. It is here that we encounter a distinctive feature of the common-law system, namely, that, in certain instances, previous decisions are actually binding on courts which subsequently have to deal with similar cases. This is in sharp contrast with the civil-law systems of the Continent which do not treat case-law as actually binding in later cases. Something here needs to be said about the reasons for this difference of approach; the actual mode of operation of the two systems; and their respective merits and demerits.

The Common-Law Approach

The reasons for the difference of approach are largely historical. The English common-law system grew up as a closely-knit professional tradition within the Inns of Court, whose members were the repositories of all the legal learning the profession could command. From the earliest days the royal judges were regarded as the true founts and expositors of legal principle and their recorded judgments in decided cases have always enjoyed a peculiar sanctity and authority. At first a clear distinction was not drawn between judgments which were binding and others which were merely persuasive, but gradually the doctrine was developed, especially as a more scientific mode of reporting cases developed in the eighteenth and early nineteenth centuries, that in certain circumstances decisions were to be regarded as absolutely binding in subsequent cases. Moreover, this long-standing tradition of treating judicial opinions as authoritative pronouncements of the law has coloured the whole attitude of common-law courts and lawyers towards the development of legal science. Accordingly, in common-law countries the exposition and development of legal principle is regarded as peculiarly within the province of the higher courts and this process is aided by the comparative detail and elaboration of judgments on points of law as reported in common-law jurisdictions. Thus the practice has developed, when new points arise, for the court to give a full exposition of the law including a careful review of the earlier relevant judicial decisions, explaining, distinguishing, or applying such decisions to the instant case. And even mere judicial opinions, whether casually expressed as *obiter dicta* or more carefully considered, are given a high degree of persuasive authority under the English system. On the other hand, the exposition of the law by learned writers in treatises or periodicals is accorded far less attention, and indeed until recently was virtually ignored by the courts save in the case of a few authoritative books rendered sacrosanct by their antiquity and the high status of their authors. Admittedly in more recent years there are signs of some winds of change blowing through the system, particularly owing to the development in modern times of a learned tradition of legal study in the universities of the common-law world. This has led to a great improvement in the scientific character of common-law textbooks and treatises and the growth of an extensive legal literature in learned legal periodicals. In this way a definite if limited contribution has been made to the scientific presentation and development of the law by extra-judicial sources, though this tendency has proceeded much further in the United States, with its great and flourishing law-schools, than in England, or in the Commonwealth generally.

The Civil-Law Approach

On the Continent, by contrast, the law developed from Roman-law foundations by way of a learned and university-derived tradition. Although the pronouncements of some tribunals of high authority might be regarded as especially weighty – for instance those of the old Parlement de Paris under the French monarchy – by and large the exposition and development of legal principle was regarded as the province of learned legal professors and writers rather than of the courts, which had the task not so much of expounding or developing the law, as of applying it to particular cases. It is only in relatively modern times that the regular reporting of decided cases has been introduced into Continental civil-law systems, and even to this day the judgments of Continental courts tend to be brief, with little exposition or review of the previous authorities, though this applies more to those countries which follow the French rather than the German pattern. Moreover, in all Continental countries single decisions of courts, save for the very highest of these, do not enjoy the sort of reverence which a judicial pronouncement arouses *eo ipso* in a common-law jurisdiction. And even in the modern system, the legal profession still looks to the learned commentaries and treatises upon the law for the scientific exposition of legal principle, and these therefore continue to enjoy an exceptionally authoritative status even *vis-à-vis* the actual decisions of the courts. Here again, however, there are certain signs of change, and the tendency in most, if not all civil-law countries is for more and more cases to be reported and for increasing weight to be given to judicial decisions as authoritative expressions of the legal principles to be applied in other cases.

The Status of the Judges

It should be added that much of the authority enjoyed by common-law precedent has stemmed from the high status, independence, and substantial salaries accorded to the judiciary in common-law countries. This again contrasts with the markedly lower standing the judges enjoy, earning relatively very modest salaries even at the highest level, in civil-law countries, which inevitably tends to depress the authoritative status of their pronouncements even when delivered *ex cathedra*. Admittedly the exceptionally high status of the judiciary in England is far more easily maintained by reason of the very small number of the higher judiciary, whereas in civil-law countries the judges are much more numerous. This exceptional situation is rendered possible by the large amount of judicial business conducted in England by lay benches of magistrates or by special tribunals. In the United States, on the other hand, owing to the size of the country and its separate jurisdiction in every State of the Union in addition to the federal jurisdiction, the judiciary is very numerous and accordingly does not attain the same standing uniformly throughout its ranks, even at the higher levels. This, as well as the enormous bulk of American reported cases, no doubt accounts to a large extent for the diminished reverence granted to judicial decisions as such, and the growing influence of learned treatises and other scientific expositions and commentaries upon the development of American law.

How the Common-Law System Functions

A few words must now be said about the actual working of the system of precedent. In England a fairly rigid system has developed with the consolidation of the hierarchy of the courts in the course of the nineteenth century. Broadly speaking the main operative rules are these. A decision of a higher court is binding on all lower courts in the hierarchy. In addition the Court of Appeal treats its own decisions as strictly binding on itself. Thus a decision of the Court of Appeal can only be overruled by the House of Lords. The House of Lords itself, though the supreme tribunal in the land, also held (until 1966, when it changed its mind) that it was bound by its own earlier decisions. Apart from this, any judicial pronouncement by any of the higher courts (even of a single High Court judge sitting at first instance) is regarded as deserving of the closest consideration and will only be departed from after careful scrutiny of the reasons given for it, and then with hesitation. A similarly strict attitude towards precedent prevails in other Commonwealth countries, even in those, such as South Africa, which have not received the common law as such – though in this latter instance the highest court has always imputed to itself the power to overrule its earlier decisions. In the United States the attitude to precedent is more flexible, though the decisions of higher courts are generally regarded as binding on those lower down in the hierarchy. On the other hand the Supreme Court claims the right, which it frequently exercises, to review its earlier decisions and to depart from these if they appear to the later court to be wrong or inappropriate to the new conditions with which the law has to deal.

The 'Ratio Decidendi' of a Case

The fact that common-law courts, in certain circumstances, regard previous precedents as binding makes it obligatory for them to consider what particular element of an earlier decision is binding, so that this can be distinguished from other elements which may be merely persuasive. The portion of the decision which is binding is sometimes referred to as the *ratio decidendi*, i.e. the reason for the decision. The underlying idea is that every case which applies the law to a given set of facts is animated by a legal principle which is necessary to the decision arrived at, and it is this principle which forms the binding element in the case. For instance, suppose a court has to decide for the first time whether the posting of a letter amounts to a valid acceptance of an offer so as to create a binding contract in law even though the letter was lost in the post and so never reached its addressee. The court upholds the validity of the contract by treating the posting as an acceptance. This decision involves the proposition of law that an offer can be effectively accepted by posting a letter of acceptance and this proposition is *necessary* to the decision since without it the court could not have upheld the contract. Hence it must be regarded as forming the *ratio decidendi* of the case.

This does not necessarily mean that the *ratio* is to be found always in the statement of the rule appearing in the judgment of the court as applying to the particular case. For it is a further established principle that cases are only binding in relation to other cases which are precisely similar. In other cases which are not precisely similar the court will have a choice as to whether or not to extend the analogy to other circumstances not exactly corresponding to those previously adjudicated upon, on the lines already discussed earlier in this chapter.[18] Accordingly a subsequent court may find, upon scrutinizing the earlier judgment, that the governing principle was incorrectly or too broadly or too narrowly stated, and may itself have to elucidate what the governing *ratio* of the earlier case actually was. This process may be rendered particularly complex and difficult where the previous case was an appellate one with three or more separate judgments, each one stating in differing terms what is conceived to be the governing legal principle.

Moreover, much may depend upon the attitude of the later court to the earlier decision. The later court may take a favourable view of the principle embodied in the earlier case and be ready to apply it very broadly to any analogous situations. This is what happened after the majority decision of the House of Lords in 1932[19] laid down the duty of a manufacturer of goods to take reasonable care to ensure that the goods were not in a condition likely to do harm to potential consumers. This case so plainly involved a sensible rule that it has been treated as possessing the widest application. It has, therefore, speedily been set up as expressing the essence of the law of negligence in imposing a general duty of care where physical injury to others can be reasonably anticipated from the conduct of any person. On the other hand, if the result of a binding decision is later viewed with disfavour, subsequent courts may strive to confine it very strictly to 'its own facts' and so, by making subtle distinctions (what the layman and indeed many lawyers may regard as 'hair-splitting') give the earlier case a very limited field of operation or virtually distinguish it out of existence. In this way, for instance, very heavy inroads were made upon two established but unpopular doctrines of the old common law, namely, the rules that in a negligence claim any degree of negligence by the defendant himself which contributed to the accident would defeat the whole of his claim, and that a master is not liable to his servant for injuries caused by the negligence of a fellow-servant. Nevertheless, these two doctrines still maintained an uneasy if diminished role for many decades before Parliament finally abolished them both a few years ago.

The 'Realist' Viewpoint

Reference has already been made to the view of the American realists that what matters in law is not so much what courts *say*, as what they *do*.[20] This approach attains some plausibility when one studies the way courts will wriggle and hedge in order to avoid what they regard as the more unfortunate implications of earlier decisions. And though this process is certainly more easily illustrated from the American law reports than from the English, examples are not difficult to come by in English cases. Nor does the more absolute rule of binding precedent in England eliminate this process, since courts always retain the power of distinguishing one case from another, and law cases, like nature itself, rarely seem to repeat themselves in identical terms. Moreover, even in the case of binding precedents the courts recognize a reserve doctrine that the earlier case may have overlooked some point contained in a statute or another binding precedent, so that the original decision was given to that extent *per incuriam* and therefore is still subject to review.[21] A whole body of rules and fine distinctions has been erected upon this foundation and so provides the courts with further escape routes in some cases where the main road appears to be solidly barricaded.

How Does the Civil-Law System Function?

Turning now to the working of the precedent system in civil-law countries,[22] it still generally remains the theoretical principle that individual decisions are not in themselves binding, but only a line of decisions which places a principle beyond controversy. Moreover the large number of courts and judges in Continental countries would in any event render the strictly hierarchical attitude of the common law entirely unworkable, a feature which has also transformed the American attitude to precedent, despite its common law origins. Yet too much must not be made of these theoretical distinctions, for strong tendencies are at work in civil-law systems towards treating judicial precedents, if not as absolutely binding, then at least as containing authoritative opinions which other courts, especially lower courts, will be slow to depart from. This has also been coupled with a marked disposition to treat single decisions of the highest court, such as the Cour de Cassation in France, as completely binding on all other tribunals. What, however, civil systems are not prepared to accept is that appellate courts should be precluded from reviewing their own earlier decisions.

Criticism of the Common-Law Doctrine

This last point leads us to consider what merit is to be discerned in the strict rule of precedent evolved by the common law. The main argument in its favour is that it confers certainty on the law, but even without the assaults of the realists, we may recognize that such certainty is somewhat illusory, in view of the ability of courts to 'distinguish' the rulings of their predecessors. The case against binding precedent rests mainly on the undesirability of higher courts, especially the highest, such as the House of Lords, being rigidly bound to adhere to its own earlier decisions, however mistaken or undesirable these may now appear to be. It is indeed very doubtful how far the slight additional certainty attained by retention of a bad precedent – slight, because even House of Lords cases can be virtually distinguished

into oblivion[23] – can compensate for the harm done by per-
petuating a thoroughly objectionable but established rule.
Nor does the history of law reform in this country suggest
that the availability of reform by Act of Parliament is always
an effective substitute. It took Parliament practically a
century to introduce the very simple changes entailed by
abolishing the two much maligned doctrines (referred to
above) of contributory negligence and common employment.

CODES AND STATUTORY INTERPRETATION

One conspicuous contrast between common-law systems and
those of the civil law is that the latter, in modern times, have
leaned heavily upon a rationalized codification of the basic
principles of the law, whereas the common law still regards
codification as alien to its traditions of piecemeal and empirical development. The civil law started from the Roman
law codification of Justinian and its university tradition has
always favoured systematic rationalization. In modern
times the main impulse sprang from a desire for legal unification and the elimination of local variations in legal institutions and rules within the same country. Napoleon set the
pattern with his famous Civil Code of 1804 and since then
most civil-law countries have either based their own codification on the French model or upon the more elaborate
German code finally promulgated at the end of the nineteenth century.

Some sporadic efforts at codifying specific topics have
been made in England but these have been mostly confined
to a few branches of commercial law and the movement
largely spent itself by the early years of this century. Common
lawyers usually assail any attempt at codification by arguing
either that the time is not yet ripe, or that such a process is
unduly rigid and will impede that empirical growth which
is regarded as part of the spirit of the common law. The first
of these arguments is difficult to take very seriously. If the
law is not ripe for development after six centuries of growth
it is unlikely ever to attain that state. Experience of

Continental codification also belies the suggestion that courts are hamstrung by the provisions of the code from developing the law and adapting it to new social needs. It is not without significance, for instance, that French courts have developed a doctrine of the abuse of rights without any express provision to that effect in the code, while English courts have been debarred from doing so by a decision of the House of Lords given in 1892.[24] Of course much depends here on the form of drafting of the civil-law codes, which, in accordance with Continental practice, are expressed in very broad principles without any attempt to work out all the details in advance. This leaves full scope to the courts to develop the appropriate applications of the principles in relation to individual cases as these arise. The English tradition of very detailed legislation, on the other hand, might well create more serious obstacles if followed in relation to any general codification. There remains, however, always the possibility of amending a code by legislative enactment, as in the case of any other legislation.

A code being a form of legislation, much will depend on the way the courts approach the general problem of legal interpretation. A vast amount of judicial time is now occupied by the interpretation of the endless stream of parliamentary or subordinate legislation. English courts theoretically attempt to give effect to the intention of the legislature but this is often fictitious, since a new point may never have been present to the minds of the legislators when the statute was passed. Moreover, any attempt to arrive at that intention by examining parliamentary debates or preliminary reports or papers ushering in the legislation is strictly taboo by English, though not by American, practice. English courts fasten primarily on the actual words used in the enactment and study these in the context in which they appear and so endeavour to extract a literal meaning from these words. This meaning is the one which it is then assumed that the words bear, unless this results in an absurdity. Here again, English courts are by no means so restricted as they sometimes declare themselves to be, for they will often modify the apparent literal meaning in favour of a more socially just or rational interpretation in the light of what they regard as the ultimate purpose of the statute. This more sociological approach to statutory construction has won increasing favour and is frequently applied in modern English law, though sometimes earning sharp rebuke as a usurpation of the legislative function if stated in too overtly frank terms.[25]

Both on the Continent and in the United States the impact of the sociological school has been more strongly felt and the purpose of modern legislation is gleaned where possible from any available preliminary legislative material or *travaux préparatoires*, such as ministerial or committee reports or debates. Whether, if England were ever to join the Common Market, some retreat might be made from the traditional attitudes on these matters, remains in the realm of speculation. Perhaps a fresh spark might then re-ignite the long extinct ardour for codifying some parts of English law.[26] But any such enterprise is unlikely to be successful unless accompanied by considerable modification in the traditional approach towards the rules of binding precedent and of statutory construction generally.

Human language, whatever may have been the situation among prehistoric mankind, does not consist solely or even to any great extent in applying particular names to particular physical objects. Its outstanding achievement is rather the creation of a large number of general concepts which provide the essential tools of human reflection, communication, and decision.[1] It is only necessary to consider the complexity and unworkability of a language requiring a separate 'name' for every specific 'thing' (concrete or abstract) to which we might wish to refer, to make us realize the enormous benefits obtained by the possession of words denoting not just individuals, but also classes, such as person, cat, dog, wealth, or weather. Such generalized terms or class descriptions are all abstract in the sense that they do not refer to any specific cognizable object, at any rate unless we accept the Platonic view that they refer to some actual ideal entity which in fact exists on a higher plane of existence than the individual objects of the class in question. Yet apart from Platonic idealism, which is not a fashionable cult at the present day, class terms differ in so far as the individual members of the class may be physical entities or phenomena on the one hand, or mere abstractions, such as a desire, a belief, or a group. (We can point to a person who by his speech or behaviour is expressing a desire or a belief, but we cannot point to an actual desire or belief.)

Concepts, then, whether generic or specific, seem to exist as ideas in the human mind rather than as concrete entities. This notion has, however, since at least the days of the ancient Greek philosophers, aroused dissatisfaction or hostility among some thinkers. On the one hand, there is a strong tendency to try and 'objectify' everything which is capable of being the subject of human thought and language. This approach may lead to the 're-ification' of all abstract conceptions either on the pattern of Plato's 'ideas', or by presupposing that everything which we can refer to meaningfully in speech must have some sort of referent in fact, though what kind may be a matter of acute controversy. Words are thus conceived as a means of naming or 'sticking labels' upon objects, though admittedly many of the objects are of a peculiar kind, such as unicorns, or the present king of France, or Mr Pickwick. The temptation to treat abstractions as real entities has been and remains particularly strong in the field of legal and political concepts where such concepts are highly-charged with various emotional overtones, as in the case of the law, the state, justice, and so forth. We may, of course, speak of 'the vigilance of the law', 'the omniscient state', or 'blindfold justice', as mere figures of speech, with a full realization that this is no more than a rhetorical flourish and not accompanied by any belief in an actual subsisting entity. For others, however, this sort of language may be no mere form of speech but the embodiment of a living reality. So far may this line of thought be carried that an abstract conception may be treated not only as a real entity but as a super-personality, more real and more sublime than any actual perceived physical entity or person. This disposition may be found in the way some religions have deified such abstract conceptions as justice, the city, or the state, and to this day many fervent monarchists will regard the 'idea' of the monarchy as in some sense more real than any individual incumbent of the throne. Such an approach attained its culmination (and, some will say, its *reductio ad absurdum*) in the Hegelian conception of the state as the highest reality on earth, a sort of deified super-person more real than all its constituent members and embodying the highest ethical and religious values of humanity.

IS LAW A KIND OF GAME?

The tendency to personify or re-ify abstract concepts and the dangers and absurdities which this process has created, especially in the realm of legal and political theory, has led, on the other hand, to an attempt to reject all the concepts of human thought – or at any rate those whose members do not correspond to physical entities – as mere metaphysical fictions which have no more real existence than that of a unicorn or of Mr Pickwick. This seems a hard saying when one comes to deal with such a field of human activity as legal science, for it seems to suggest that the subject-matter of law is nothing more than a huge game in which counters rather than real money are employed and in which the rules refer not to concrete realities but to mere figments of the imagination. Yet we know too that in another sense law is certainly no mere game but is very closely related to actual human social life, that it enters into our daily calculations, and that for all of us it possesses a genuine reality and no mere fictitious existence. How then is this paradox to be resolved?

Surely not by falling into the opposite trap of trying to treat all the concepts or 'counters' with which the law operates, such as the state, rights, duties, contracts, torts, liability, negligence, persons, and corporations, as if they were real 'entities' in the sense of corresponding to some identifiable though intangible objects. Nor does it assist much to talk of such entities existing only 'in the mind', for this can equally be said of unicorns or of Mr Pickwick. What we need to see here is that in certain respects a system of law does resemble very closely a kind of game and that this is not necessarily a denigration of the nature of law. At the same time we need also to grasp the ways in which a legal system differs from a game. By doing so we may then obtain a firmer understanding of the role of conceptual thought in an abstract frame of reference, such as a legal system, which is nevertheless correlated to actual behaviour and phenomena in the real world of human social life.

Certainly the law, in no derogatory sense, does resemble a kind of game. The characteristic of a game is a self-contained system of rules which provide a framework of reference and meaning for certain types of contest which can be fought out to a result within that framework. Any such game employs a number of general concepts, or notions, which are conventional in the sense that their meaning and function are arbitrarily defined by the rules of the game, but which can operate perfectly meaningfully within their particular linguistic framework. The pawn or the knight in chess is not just the name of a particularly shaped piece of wood standing on a chequered board, but is a general concept whose meaning is given by a study of the rules of chess. Does a pawn 'exist' in a sense other than an actual piece of wood of a certain shape? Or is it a mere fiction in the mind of a chess-player? Surely it can be said that the confusion here is to apply the language of existence to something to which it is not readily applicable. A pawn does not exist in the sense of being a tangible entity, but it is a meaningful concept which functions intelligibly within the context of a game of chess. Nor is it in the ordinary sense of the word a 'fiction'. Mr Pickwick is a fiction because he is not a real person, but for the purposes of the novel in which he appears, we are prepared to treat him as if he were an actual live human being. This is why we dub him as fictitious even though he may seem more real than our actual neighbours. In the case of the pawn in chess, however, we do not pretend that the pawn in our game is really a flesh-and-blood object that we encounter in real life. For here there is no contrast between reality and pretence and the language of fiction is totally inappropriate. We know that chess is a game and that the pieces only operate within that game. This does not imply, however, that the concepts of chess are therefore meaningless superfluities, so that chess can be reduced to no more than people sitting opposite each other and moving the pieces about in particular patterns. For the meaning and purpose of these activities is contained in the system of rules. Chess can no more be reduced to human behaviour and psychological reactions than can a legal system. The one, like the other, is a normative system within whose framework, linguistic though it may be, human behaviour is rendered intelligible.[2]

Law and Reality

Still, as we have indicated, if law, like language itself, bears many features in common with the rules of a game, this is not to say that it is indistinguishable from this sort of activity, even if, in Stephen Potter's sense, 'gamesmanship' applies in law as much as in any other kind of sport. Without attempting to enumerate all the differences here, some of the more obvious can be mentioned. The scope of law entails a vastly more complex system than that of any game, having regard to its ramifications over the whole social life of the community. Then again law has a creative disposition to develop and change in a constant process of flux whether by new legislation or by the gradual adaptation of customary judicial or administrative rules in the many ways we have already discussed. It is true that certain established games or sports, such as cricket, football, tennis, golf, or chess, have their internationally accepted laws or rules and even, in many instances, recognized law-making bodies which can amend the old rules or make new ones. This however bears little relation to the constant day-to-day process of law-making and law-adaptation on the largest scale within the framework of a developed legal system. There is also the element of coercion which law has at its permanent disposal. In a game sanctions may and usually do exist in the form of disqualification, suspension, and even the imposition of fines. Such sanctions can be very powerful and normally operate in well-regulated sports with the same precision and effectiveness as legal sanctions. But they could only be physically enforced in the last resort by invoking police powers or other modes of redress, through the machinery of the legal system.[2a]

For all this we have still not mentioned the distinction between a game and a legal system which is the most significant for the present purpose. This distinction is that the rules of a game, such as chess, and the moves made within those rules, are not in any way related to real life but occur solely within their own self-contained context. Law on the other hand, if it is a game, is one which operates not with self-contained counters or pieces but with rules and concepts which are related either directly or symbolically to matters and transactions which have occurred, are occurring, or are likely to occur in actual life. For instance, if we take the rules of the criminal law relating to such matters as murder and theft, it is quite true that these are in themselves legal concepts which only have meaning in the context of legal rules which go to form a legal system. We can only understand what is meant by murder by acquainting ourselves with the legal constituents of this offence and how these operate in the legal system, just as a 'foul' in football, together with its appropriate penalty, is made meaningful only by the rules of that particular game. Here, however, we perceive a significant distinction, for whereas the 'foul' in football refers only to conduct taking place within the game of football itself, the rules regarding murder relate to conduct in ordinary life and have to do with forms of killing and intentional states of mind which actually occur in the ordinary course of things. Indeed to deter such conduct and to punish its occurrence is the very purpose of the legal rules, so that these rules are given meaning not just by their own internal structure but by their relation to actual situations. We may, if we like, following Shakespeare's line that 'all the world's a stage, and all the men and women merely players', treat the whole of life itself as a game, but even here the analogy breaks down, for the 'game of life' is not in any event one regulated solely by legal rules. It has endless other aspects upon which legal rules as such do not impinge, aspects which are sometimes within the field of other normative systems such as morals, religion, or social convention, or which may be completely 'normless', as, for example, where conduct is based on emotion, feeling, or mere impulse.

The law is therefore concerned to classify and regulate types of transactions which occur in real life. It is a feature of social life that people desire to make promises or give undertakings to others with the intention that these should be fulfilled. The law steps in, and having given a more precise formulation to those promises which it will treat as effectual, adds to these the element of legal validity, with all the consequences which this may entail within the legal system. Again, people in the course of daily life are wont to do acts which may result in inflicting physical or financial injury on others. Such acts may range from relatively crude and direct acts such as physical assaults to comparatively indirect and refined forms of causing harm, such as failing to keep property in a proper and safe condition, or depriving another person of his property by the use of fraud or by wrongfully disposing of it. Once more we see the law stepping in, and by defining and determining the rules governing civil responsibility it builds a complex of rules into which these classes of activities may be fitted and controlled.

It must not be thought, however, that the law is concerned merely with the task of translating everyday occurrences into legal terms. The inter-relationship of law and fact is of a much more complex character than this. For, in the first place, the scope, meaning, and definition of everyday transactions will usually, if not invariably, be lacking in the precision required to enable law to deal with these in a systematic and regular way. We need, for instance, not merely to know that in a general way people make promises intending to keep them but to define as precisely as possible what is meant by a promise; what sort of promises should qualify for legal recognition and which not; what circumstances may render promises inoperative, such as mistake and misrepresentation, and so forth. The law then needs to build up a great apparatus of manageable concepts which provide a workable framework for giving effect to agreements and promises, and it is this complex of concepts and rules that is contained within the law of contract. Again, people know in a general way what they mean when they talk about killing and they can distinguish easily enough between accidental and intentional killing. The law, on the other hand, needs to conceptualize these and other related ideas much more precisely before it can operate a system of criminal law in a rational and systematic way. It needs to define very precisely the exact classes of acts that are unlawful; the precise states of mind which need to be established to render these acts criminally punishable as murder; the sorts of defences which may be available to an accused person, including insanity or other mental defects; and what may be the effect of particular defences as either exonerating the accused completely or merely diminishing the gravity of the offence and so on.

THE CREATIVE ELEMENT IN LEGAL CONCEPTS

Moreover, there is another aspect of legal conceptualism which is very important, especially for modern law. A good many fundamental legal concepts are to a large extent legal creations in their own right with a vitality of their own, which may set off a chain of social and economic reactions much more far-reaching than the initial social impulses which have assisted at the birth of those concepts. Something here might be said about the origins of some of the most fundamental of all legal concepts, such as rights and duties, property and ownership. For it might well be argued that concepts such as these first grow out of the development of rules defining, for instance, in what circumstances in early society a man could claim to exclude others from using certain land or goods (or indeed human beings), or could enjoy these things (or persons) solely for his own or his family's use, and be entitled to protect them by physical violence, if necessary, without such violence resulting in a blood-feud. Without, however, embarking on controversial problems of legal history and anthropology, attention may be concentrated on other and more recently developed legal conceptions. As an example the English institution of the trust may be taken. This was undoubtedly inspired in the Middle Ages by the desire of the English Chancellors to give legal protection in cases where persons had conveyed property to others on the understanding that the latter would use the property in certain ways (for example, for charitable purposes) or hold it for the benefit not of themselves but of third parties. To some extent therefore this amounted to a legal reaction to certain kinds of felt social needs, but at the same time the law of trusts which developed out of this situation was something of vastly greater scope and significance, and which to this very day has had an immense influence on the social and economic arrangements prevailing in this country and in other common-law countries which derived it from England at a later date. In this connexion it is only necessary to cite the enormous influence of settlements of property by way of trust on family life among the propertied classes; the effect of the trust as a vital factor in moulding our modern tax law; and the way in which unincorporated clubs and associations have been able to flourish free of governmental intervention or control by use of the trust instrument.[3]

Other instances come easily enough to hand. Striking among them is the commercial company with limited liability. Here, again, this arose out of certain needs which came to be acutely felt by the commercial community in this country in the first half of the last century, so that the company can be regarded as owing its inception to a felt economic need. But the response of the lawyers in creating this novel and unique concept of the limited liability company has led to the development of a vast new legal world dominated by the conception of a company distinct from its shareholders. It may be said almost without any exaggeration that this legal creation has largely brought into being, or at any rate alone made possible in its existing form, the whole fabric of modern commerce and industry, with its tremendous complex of inter-locking and inter-related companies, without which all the developments, for better or worse, of modern capitalism would have been inconceivable.

Yet other examples may be found in the concepts of patent rights, copyright, and trade marks. Certainly these also arose to meet social and economic needs. The inventor, the author, and the manufacturer have all, fairly enough, claimed protection for their different products, but the legal creativeness which in response to these claims has devised novel forms of property, such as patents and copyright, has once again given rise to whole new fields of human activity which have had an immense influence on modern social and economic life. Moreover, these legal concepts have grown into huge and ramifying fields of law containing masses of refined and subtle rules which seem to proliferate, once a fruitful legal concept is given birth, 'thick as leaves in Vallombrosa'. In this connexion we need only to mention the complexity of the idea of 'originality' as worked out in countless cases in the law of patents, and the variety of ways in which the law allows the bundle of rights constituted by copyright in a work to be divided up and parcelled out to many different owners. Thus the publishing rights in volume form of a novel may belong to one person, the serial rights to another, the film rights to a third, the television rights to a fourth, and so on; and all of these rights can be granted for limited terms to others, as well as there being almost limitless scope for the granting, by each of these part-owners of the copyright, of licences to do certain acts in relation to the work (e.g. to perform it in public), and for those licensees to grant sub-licences, and so forth. Indeed it may be said that out of an idea the law makes a world.

DANGERS OF A RIGID CONCEPTUALISM

Yet in this very fertility there lurk certain dangers of which the lawyer himself is perhaps not always sufficiently aware. It is said that in the realm of literary creation the author finds that having breathed life into his characters these develop a kind of impetus of their own which carries the author himself along by the very force of his creation. Something of this kind may and does occur in the field of legal creativity also. When lawyers have breathed meaning and purpose into their legal concepts and found these to be good, these concepts tend to develop a life of their own which may carry them on into many and unexpected paths by their own vitality and by what are felt to be the laws of their own inherent logic. We have already referred to this tendency in connexion with some of the excesses of the so-called analytical approach to law.[4] It is unnecessary to repeat what was there said, and it will suffice here to emphasize two main points.

First, to try and jettison the whole idea that legal principles may be developed by systematic and rational analysis is in effect to throw the baby out with the bath water. It is true, as has already been emphasized, that logic as such will not solve legal problems,[5] but this is very far from asserting that principles cannot be systematically explored, analysed, and developed along rational lines consistent with legal modes of reasoning (bearing in mind that these are only a more intense and systematized form of ordinary human reasoning). For to reject this kind of approach is really to suggest that rational systematization in regard to human affairs is impossible and ruled out *ab initio*, for if law cannot attain such a system then what other apparatus could? Of course to assert the value or usefulness of this approach is not to establish its practicability. The usefulness of rationalized systematization seems beyond question so far as law is concerned, since one of its vital aims is to bring into the social and economic life of man a tolerable measure of security and predictability. It will be recalled too that the legal sociologist, Max Weber, put at the very forefront of Western legal science, as an integral part of modern Western social and legal development, the attainment of legal rationality.[6] And as to the practicability of attaining this, the very existence and functioning of modern legal systems, despite their imperfections, sufficiently testify that this aim, if not wholly attainable in an ideal sense, is far from illusory. Systematic analysis in accordance with established modes of legal reasoning and procedures may not attain anything like full certainty or precision, but it does yield a high measure of rational systematization and predictability in a great many cases, without which a legal system is hardly worthy of the name.

This leads us, however, to our second point, which is to present the other and darker side of the picture. It has already been remarked that legal concepts, like other symbols of man's creativity, are apt to possess a vitality of their own which may end by leading their authors instead of being led by them. Concepts, it may be said, are excellent servants, but not always good masters. Once the meaning and scope of important concepts are crystallized within a legal system, especially in one which like the common law adheres to a strict system of precedent, this may result in courts deciding new cases on what they conceive to be the logical nature and requirements of particular legal concepts. This may result in a sort of hardening of the arteries of the body of the law; an undue rigidity and inability to adapt to new social situations; and a tendency to adopt the attitude that the courts have no alternative but to work out the strict logical implications of the rules, and that it is best to leave it to the legislature if hardships or other undesirable social consequences ensue. We have already seen that this involves some misconception and an unnecessary restriction upon the proper scope of the judicial process, and it is only necessary here to add one or two illustrations of the way in which this attitude may hamstring the judicial development of the law.

Some Examples of 'Legal Logic'

Thus, in the field of contract law, English law has long been dominated by the notion that the essential nature of a contract, as an agreement between parties to create fresh rights and duties *inter se*, inevitably rules out the possibility of conferring enforceable benefits on third persons, who are not parties to the contract. This has imposed a severe and socially unacceptable limitation on the modern law of contract, not found in civil-law systems.[7] Again, English law has largely committed itself to the doctrine that no contract is complete without valuable consideration,[8] so that a promise without consideration must inevitably be unenforceable and without legal effect. It is noteworthy, as an exercise in the operation of legal logic, that while still adhering to this approach, a remarkable inroad has been made in it in recent years, due almost entirely to the legal acumen and energy of one judge, Mr Justice (now Lord)

Denning. This inroad is to the effect that a promise made without consideration, but acted upon by another party, may be effective in law as a defence to a claim which would otherwise be maintainable in the absence of the promise.[9] At the same time the honour of legal logic is preserved by still refusing to allow anyone to sue upon an unsupported promise, as against using it by way of defence.[10] To the non-lawyer the result may appear neither artistic, nor logical, nor particularly socially defensible, but the example provides a striking illustration both of the rigidities of conceptualism and of the ways in which courts can, at times, be astute enough, if the will-power is there, to outflank these self-created hurdles.

The field of property law provides numerous instances of concepts proving to be masters rather than servants. The difference between a merely personal right and a proprietary one, good against all the world, lies at the root of much legal analysis, such as the distinction between an easement conferring a proprietary right of way across another person's land, and a mere personal licence. From this position it was thought to follow as a matter of legal logic that a mere licence, being non-proprietary, could always be revoked, though possibly at the cost of an action for damages if the licence was contractual. However, once again legal ingenuity got to work upon this simple dichotomy and the position is now considerably transformed by recognition of the fact that in certain circumstances an injunction might be obtained to restrain a threatened and premature withdrawal of the licence.[11] In the same way, in the sphere of copyright law, the rigid conceptual distinction between an assignment of property in the form of copyright and a mere licence giving only a personal right against the assignor himself has to some extent been overcome in the case of an exclusive licence, though it has taken a recent statute to put an exclusive licensee in a position substantially comparable to that of an assignee of the copyright itself.[12] Again, difficulty in our modern law has been created by trying to treat all forms of unfair competition as invasions of property rights, so that the question to be asked in each case is what right of property in the plaintiff has been infringed. This type of reasoning is peculiarly inapposite in relation to many situations in the modern commercial world, for instance where an advertiser without permission imitates the voice or appearance of a well-known actor in order to push the sale of a product. To ask, as is sometimes done in this type of case,[13] whether a man can have a 'property' in his own voice or appearance would seem to be a singularly sterile exercise in conceptualism.

One last instance may be cited here in the realm of civil liability. English law has insisted, in its law of negligence, on establishing in each case that the defendant owed a duty of care to the particular plaintiff. Does this mean that the plaintiff must have been an actual living person at the date when the negligent harm was inflicted? Suppose that a pregnant woman is involved in a road accident and that the unborn baby is subsequently born deformed as a result. Can an action be brought for damages on behalf of the deformed baby? Or suppose, to take an example of a strongly topical flavour, that, as a result of exposure of a person to nuclear radiation, offspring not yet conceived is ultimately born suffering from congenital defects. The answer to this type of question is far from easy, and no clear or settled solutions have yet emerged in English law. But to base the solution on the 'logical' character of the duty of care, which stipulates that no duty can be owed to a person not in being at the date of the accident,[14] is hardly a socially satisfactory way of arriving at a decision which involves choices dependent on many factors, social, moral, and economic.

LEGAL CONCEPTS AS 'INCOMPLETE SYMBOLS'

Enough has been said here to indicate in a general way the manner in which legal concepts function. The purpose of the ensuing chapter is to select one or two of the leading concepts in modern law, to indicate the way in which these function, and to discuss, very briefly, a few of the problems they have given rise to. One last word still needs to be said as to the nature of these concepts which are so central to the structure of a legal system.

We have already endeavoured to dispose of the argument that these are mere fictitious entities or metaphysical figments of the legal imagination. But another more subtle and perceptive attack has been made upon this legal stronghold. What is said is this. Take the conception of legal ownership. This is regarded as a kind of legal right a person has in relation to certain property. But really there is no right as such at all. All that ownership amounts to is a shorthand expression for the whole congeries of rules within the legal system which go to make up the various forms of legal enforcement and protection which an owner may enjoy or be able to claim in relation to that property. In other words, by a kind of analytical reduction it is suggested that the concept of ownership can be spirited away and we are left with the only genuine reality, which is a tangled complex of legal rules governing a whole multitude of possible relationships. [15]

Now, that there is an element of truth in this viewpoint cannot be denied, for in so far as ownership is a legal concept this must imply that it is a focal point or symbolic expression of a bundle of legal rules. But does this therefore entail that ownership itself is really nothing more than that bundle of rules? Those who take this view generally admit that there is an overwhelming practical need to use such concepts as ownership to describe this complex of rules but insist that it is mere illusion to suppose that there is something else, some kind of ultimate residuary core, which is ownership itself, over and above the rules for which it serves as a shorthand description.

In so far as this view is aimed at rejecting the idea that ownership is a kind of metaphysical entity with an inherent life and nature of its own we may regard it as fully justifiable. But we must still observe that this view also ignores or minimizes two other essential aspects of such a concept as ownership. First, as we have seen, the law is not just a static collection of ascertainable rules by means of which we can at any given moment analyse all the legal implications and relationships which a given concept may entail. On the contrary, the law is a great complex of rules, precepts, standards, and principles in a process of continuous though slow-moving flux. Among the central features of this complex are certain key-concepts, not rigidly fixed in character nor finally determined in number – for new concepts may emerge, such as the right to privacy. No doubt these concepts can at any given moment be reduced to a large extent to a pattern of rules and principles, but still there is always a certain area of indefiniteness, a sphere within which the concept may be put to fresh and not altogether predictable uses and applications. For this purpose the concept has a certain symbolic function within the law as the focal point for a certain type of attitude or approach, and its significance therefore goes beyond any particular pattern of rules ascertainable at any given moment. Moreover this symbolic ganglion in the legal system is not and never can be a fully grown and finally developed organ. It may be compared, perhaps, to what modern logicians have referred to as an 'incomplete symbol'[16] and in this incompleteness lies its fundamental utility as a tool of legal development.

In the second place – and this is perhaps only an aspect of the previous point – the analytical reductionist scheme seems also to make light of the normative function that legal, like moral, concepts perform in the pattern of their respective systems. An essential concept, such as ownership, has a unifying function as pointing to a pattern of approved behaviour. This acts not only as a psychological stimulus to conform to the whole code of legal and moral precepts which the very idea of property conjures up in the mind of man in society, but also functions as a symbol of the purpose of the law itself as a means of preserving peace and good order in the community and some measure of security, upon which all human planning for the future must ultimately repose.

I

PERSONS, INCLUDING CORPORATIONS

It may seem strange at first sight that the idea of a 'person' should rank as a legal concept. Yet if it is remembered that legal concepts are generally related to phenomena of real life, while applying to these a degree of precision as well as many distinctive features required for legal purposes, then the apparent oddity of treating persons as legal concepts may dissolve away.

Of course the notion of individuality that we associate with the human being as a person gives rise to many difficulties of a philosophical character, though seemingly simple enough to the plain man. The lawyer, perhaps wisely, tends to avoid or evade the philosophical depths in favour of the plain man's general view, while attempting to refine that view so as to provide solutions for problems not envisaged by the ordinary person. Thus the lawyer needs to have decisions upon the moment when a human being can be said to come into existence; the means of establishing the identity of an individual in the course of his life; and the fixing of the moment of death. Such matters by no means exhaust the range of problems, as will be realized by considering the legal implications of such phenomena as changes of sex, Siamese twins, and so forth. Attention here will, however, be concentrated mainly on the human being coming into existence.

Human Personality

Suppose for instance that the law lays down, as in this country, that the intentional killing of a human being constitutes the crime of murder. Is an unborn baby a person in being for this purpose? And if not, is the child considered to be born only when it is fully extruded alive from the mother; when it has been heard to cry; or when the umbilical cord has been severed; or at what stage? Lawyers need to provide answers to questions of this character, and arbitrary though these may be in a certain sense, important questions of social policy may be involved, such for instance as the attitude towards abortion or towards a mother who destroys her newly-born infant. Nor is this type of problem confined to the criminal law. In the law of property questions of title may well turn upon whether a person has had living offspring, so that the fixing of the moment of birth may be all-important for such a purpose. And we have already referred to the troublesome question whether there may be a liability to pay damages for negligence in respect of injury inflicted upon a child unborn when the damage causing the injury was sustained.[1]

'Group Personality'

Of far greater complexity in modern law, however, is the attribution of personality not just to the individual human being but to groups or associations. It is a familiar feature of social life that human beings tend to unite together in groups, some permanent and some merely transient or ephemeral. Such groups may come into being either for limited or specific purposes, as in the case of a commercial company or a social club, or for purposes of the widest and most general scope, as is clearly the case of the national territorial state, even if we do not go so far as Burke in regarding this as 'a partnership in all science; a partnership in all art; a partnership in every virtue, and in all perfection'.[2]

In common parlance it is usual to personify many such groups: to treat them as persons in their own right possessing continuity and a separate identity from the particular individuals who may compose them at any given moment. Thus we talk of dying 'for our country'; of the policy 'of the company'; of the opinion 'of the club'; or the militancy 'of the trade unions'. Moreover, whatever the sociological or psychological sub-structure of this phenomenon may be, it seems clear that in many instances this is more than the language of metaphor, since the group can and does stand for a continuing set of attitudes, policies, or values which possess a degree of permanence and self-sufficiency not completely identifiable with the existing members.

Some jurists, and in particular the eminent German lawyer, Otto von Gierke, have urged that this emergent personality of groups must be recognized by the law as a real entity, just as real as the individual human personality; any group is therefore entitled to be treated as a separate person in the same way as a human being with all the implications that this may entail, of which more will be said later on. This approach was doubtless encouraged by the Hegelian doctrine of the state as a supra-real person, representing a higher reality than the citizens comprising it,[3] but Gierke himself and many of his followers aimed rather at preserving the autonomy of groups within the state. What their argument really amounts to is that any group within the state, be it a church, an educational or charitable foundation, a profit-making company, a professional association, a trade union, or even a mere social club, once it has so organized itself as to make manifest its separate identity as an institution distinct from its members, is entitled to claim legal recognition of its personality without the need for any official grant or concession of legal personality. This runs counter to the general approach of most legal systems which holds that group or 'corporate' personality can only come into existence by express grant or certification by the state, for corporate personality is regarded as a legal privilege and only the state can therefore create a corporation.

Two difficulties, however, face the supporters of the realist theory[4] of group personality. First, even if it be accepted that the emergent personality of groups is a sociological reality of a kind (as indeed the great French sociologist Durkheim insisted was the case), it still remains true that this social personality is by no means identical with the psychosomatic personality of the individual human being. At the most there may be a sufficient analogy between the two to justify the use of the same word personality, but it can only lead to confusion to treat group personality as a kind of emergent entity precisely comparable with the physical entity of a human being. Accordingly, though the argument that 'like should be treated as like'[5] may possess some general cogency, there is no exact correspondence between a group on the one hand and an individual person on the other which leads irresistibly to the conclusion that both must be accorded identical treatment. For legal purposes it may be that one human being is much the same as another and so all should be treated equally, though even this argument has never been fully accepted, and indeed, as we have seen, has only begun to earn something like effective recognition in modern times.[6] Groups on the other hand differ enormously in size, character, composition, and purpose, so that it by no means follows either as a matter of logic, sociology, or even common sense that all should be accorded similar recognition on the doubtful analogy of the individual human person.

In the second place, the fact that in the case of the individual legal personality is attributed to a recognizable and distinct human entity makes the problem of ascertaining who possesses such personality comparatively simple, save in the sort of marginal cases already discussed. In the case of a group, however, there is no such identifiable entity to be discovered and therefore some test would have to be established to enable the law to say or at least to accept that a particular group personality had come into existence. Moreover, even if, which is far from being the case, sociology had some assured and agreed way of deciding this question, it does not follow that this would necessarily be either adequate or suitable for legal purposes. For just as the law may find it necessary or desirable to apply its own criteria of insanity even if these do not coincide with psychiatric classifications of the insane, so too the law, if only in the interests of precision, will need to formulate its own specific criteria of group existence. This means in effect that some organ of the state will in any event have the task of applying those criteria in order to decide whether a group possesses legal personality or not. The difference then lies in this, that instead of the need for a preliminary certificate of incorporation, the group would be enabled to establish its personality by showing subsequently that it satisfied the appropriate legal criteria.

Modes of Incorporation

Most modern legal systems of the Western democratic pattern have rendered this distinction of little significance by enabling new corporations to be created by very simple, expeditious, and cheap methods. In English law it is an extremely easy and inexpensive proceeding to create under the Companies Act a new company which possesses a distinct legal personality of its own. Still there is nothing in English law which obligès every group to incorporate itself in this way, and in fact the English social scene is crowded with unincorporated groups or associations which from preference, apathy, or ignorance have neither applied for nor obtained corporate status. Social clubs are the most common example, but there are many others such as churches, trade and professional associations, sporting clubs, learned societies, and so forth. Apart from the facilities of the Companies Act, English corporations may be created by a royal charter or under some special Act of Parliament but only bodies of a rather special kind are incorporated in this way. As to those associations which eschew incorporation, English law, adopting a rigidly conceptual classification, declines to treat these for legal purposes as other than a collective name for the individual members themselves. This means that any legal transaction has to be regarded as being entered into by or with all the members themselves or in some cases with some of them only, such as an executive committee.

Consequences of Incorporation

Before enlarging on the difficulties of this situation something should be said as to the legal consequences of the incorporation of a group. Briefly the law treats a corporation as a legal person separate from the members and this means that, except for those acts which are obviously inapplicable – a corporation clearly cannot marry – the corporation may in its own name and on its own account engage in all the ordinary transactions of the law. Thus it may own property; it may enter into contracts; it may appoint and be represented by agents; it may sue and be sued in the courts or in other tribunals; its liabilities are its own and distinct from those of its members, who cannot be sued in respect of the corporate debts. Moreover a corporation can even be prosecuted for any offence which is punishable by fine, and in such a case the fine will be payable out of the corporate assets.

The contrast therefore with an unincorporated association is striking. An association cannot own property in its own name, it cannot contract, it cannot sue or be sued, and it has no debts or liabilities distinct from those of its members. In English law, the inability of such a body to own property in its own name has largely been overcome by the instrument of the trust. By this means property can be vested in trustees on behalf of the existing members and thus for legal and practical purposes the premises of a club and its common funds may be kept distinct from the separate property of the individual members. Other legal difficulties, however, have not proved so easy to resolve – and in particular the procedural difficulty of enabling an unincorporated club or association to sue or be sued in the courts in respect of club rights, obligations, or liabilities. Here then is a striking example of how an analytical approach to the law may result in socially undesirable consequences, for the refusal of English law to recognize the legal 'suability' of a club because it lacks legal personality involves a logical inference from the nature of that concept which may seem a good deal less than compelling to the legal sociologist. From this point of view, even if we reject the theoretical arguments of those who urge the 'real' nature of group personality, there still remains a strong case for conferring on the courts the power to treat an unincorporated body as possessing at least some of the attributes of legal personality where this body has conducted its affairs as a group, and where hardship would result by a refusal to acknowledge some degree of separate legal entity. In this way, for instance, a tradesman who supplies goods or services to 'a club', without investigating – as he could hardly be expected to do – the precise legal status of such a body, might be authorized by the court to sue the club in its own name and recover judgment against its common funds. There seems to be much in favour of adopting such a solution rather than maintaining the rigours of 'legal logic' despite the injustice which it may produce.[7]

Some attempts have been made in English law to break down the rigid line of demarcation between corporations and unincorporated bodies. This can only be achieved by Act of Parliament.[7a] Thus a partnership, which in English law is treated as unincorporated, possesses the statutory power to sue and be sued in the partnership name. Again trade unions, though not incorporated, are, when registered under the Trade Union Acts, given some of the powers and characteristics of corporate bodies. This intermediate status, which is sometimes referred to as that of a 'quasi-corporation', has recently been held, in a leading case in the House of Lords, to entitle a member of a registered union to sue the union itself and recover damages from its funds, for having wrongfully excluded him from his membership in breach of the contract of membership which he had entered into with the union.[8] In the same way a registered union could also have been sued for damages in tort[9] but for an Act of Parliament of 1906 which has exempted trade unions from any such liability.[10]

The Separateness of Corporate Personality

The sheet-anchor of the modern law of incorporated companies is the well-known decision of the House of Lords in *Salomon* v. *Salomon Ltd.* [11] In that case Mr Salomon owned virtually all the shares in a so-called one-man company. He lent money to the company when it was perfectly solvent in return for the security of 'debentures', a kind of mortgage on the assets of a company which confers priority upon the claim of the debenture-holder over other creditors. Later on the company became insolvent and Mr Salomon claimed to be paid his debt in full in priority to the other creditors. It was held that as the company was an entirely separate entity from Salomon (even though the latter was sole share-holder therein and in complete control of the company's operations) he was entitled to be paid in full, just as in the case of any other completely independent debenture-holder.

The development of the commercial company as a distinct legal entity, with the liability of shareholders limited to any unpaid calls on their shareholding, has had an immense influence on the social and economic structure of our indus-trial society. For not only has it provided the machinery for raising vast sums for capital investment but it has also pro-vided the means, by a complex congeries of interlocking companies, controlled generally by one or more so-called 'holding' companies (owning the controlling shareholding in the subsidiary companies), for the construction of industrial and commercial enterprises on a scale hitherto undreamt of. The ramifications of this process have been enormous in the legal systems of modern commercial countries. To take but one example, the question of the 'domicile' of a corporation from the point of view of the tax laws of the countries within which a company and its subsidiaries may operate is of crucial importance, and has resulted in a spate of case-law in every country in the Western world. Space, however, will only permit us here to touch upon one general problem of interest to legal theory, a problem of a peculiarly perplexing kind.

The so-called rule in *Salomon's* case[12] has been likened to a kind of corporate veil or curtain drawn between the company and its members, the shareholders.[13] Yet is this to be an altogether impenetrable 'iron curtain' to be rigidly main-tained at all costs or can it be drawn aside in certain instances, and, if so, when? This type of problem is apt to present itself particularly in the case either of the so-called 'one-man' company under the control of a sole shareholder, or of a

subsidiary company whose shares are owned wholly or substantially by another controlling company. The problem
thus resolves itself into whether the court will be ready in
certain circumstances to pierce the corporate veil and treat
the company as no more than another name for those who
control its fortunes.

Broadly speaking, English courts have shown a marked
reluctance to recognize any exceptions or qualifications to
the *Salomon* principle.[14] That decision can plainly be
regarded as based on the policy that it is in the general
interests of a commercial society that inroads should not be
made upon the inviolate character of the separate corporate
entity. Thus it has been held in the case of a wholly owned
subsidiary company of the Transport Commission that
services provided by the former could not be regarded as in
effect provided by the Commission for the purposes of the
transport licensing laws;[15] and that a business run by a
company, all of whose shares were owned by one person,
could not be said to be carried on by that person so as to
entitle him to a renewal of the lease of the business premises
under the Landlord and Tenant Act, 1954.[16] Decisions, the
other way are not wanting, however. Thus in order to
determine whether a registered English company possessed
'enemy character' in wartime the court had regard to where
the seat of control lay.[17] And the residence of a controlling
company may be decisive in fixing the tax liability of a
wholly-owned subsidiary company.[18] Moreover, where a
transport licensing authority is satisfied that a subsidiary
is so much under the control of another company that they
together form one commercial unit, the authority can disregard the separate personality of the subsidiary so as to
prevent the controlling company using it to get an advantage
that company is not entitled to.[19] Again, where, prior to
completion of a sale of land, the seller re-sold to a company
within his sole control so as to try and prevent the buyer from
getting an order from the court that the seller should transfer
the land, the court nevertheless granted specific performance
of the contract of sale against the company.[20]

These examples provide excellent illustrations of the way legal principles and concepts establish a broad framework setting out the general line of approach which the court will be disposed to adopt without necessarily depriving it of all freedom of manoeuvre in particular cases. From the present point of view, nevertheless, the importance of the conceptual approach lies in this, that the court starts off with a strong disposition to move in a particular direction, as for instance, to maintain the separate nature of the corporate entity. This means inevitably that exceptions will be accepted only sparingly and then usually without admitting that the cases are exceptional but rather seeking to justify them on some separate ground, so as to leave the fabric of legal logic intact. Thus the court will say that 'enemy character' raises quite a different issue from that of legal personality, or that a wholly-owned subsidiary company is nothing but a 'cloak' or a 'sham'. This sort of explanation does not, however, altogether conceal the fact that the court is really finding special reasons for not adhering to too rigidly consistent a doctrine.

That there are advantages in adhering to a conceptual framework of this sort is plain, for without it the law would lack coherence and consistency. The danger only arises when the court ceases to recognize that it still retains some freedom of action within this framework and that it is a question of policy how far such freedom is exercised or not. Experience shows that there is in all legal systems a constant tension between a rigid conceptualism and a freer and more flexible philosophy of adjustment to new social needs, and it is this sort of tension that imparts to the law much of its vitality.

II

RIGHTS AND DUTIES

As soon as a legal system arrives at the stage of development when it can yield to juristic analysis it will be found that the concepts of rights and duties form a pivotal point in the structure of the legal machinery by which the system is enabled to perform its social functions. The very idea of a legal norm seems to carry with it the corollary that those to whom it is directed are in some sense 'bound' by it or subjected to some kind of 'obligation'. (This term itself contains the Latin word meaning 'binding'.) It is this idea of being bound to act (or not to act) in a certain way that is expressed in the terminology of duty, though as we have already seen, duties imposed by law have to be carefully distinguished from duties derived from other normative sources, such as morals, religion, or social convention. It remains, however, a sociological fact of some importance that law and morality employ the same terminology of duty and obligation and that in so doing they have regard not merely to the external aspect of both law and morals in imposing rules *ab extra* upon those who are for one reason or another subject to them, but also to the vital internal aspect, in as much as such persons feel themselves in a very real sense to be bound by these duties. The importance of this from the point of view of legal duties is that the citizen should feel himself committed to compliance, not merely in a formal manner because he is within the jurisdiction of the law, nor solely because he fears that a breach of his duty will bring punishment upon himself, but because the rule of law itself is a vital part of the social morality of his community.

The link between legal and moral duty is further underlined by the use of the terminology of 'rights'. The word 'right' has both a moral connotation and an emotional overtone which carry with them a strong sense of justification going beyond any merely formal authorization, under a technical system of legal rules. This point is perhaps more strongly brought out in those European languages where the very word for law (*Recht, droit, diritto*) stands also for moral right. The fact that within the framework of a legal system a person claims that he has a 'right' to do or refrain from doing something, to exert control over some property or to exclude others from it, to call for the services of another person, or to claim that something be handed over or payment made to him, carries with it a feeling of justification and entitlement which exerts moral as well as legal weight in the minds of those concerned. Thus the very terminology and conceptual framework of the law contrives to arouse in people's minds a strong sense of moral right and obligation as a result of which the task of the legal order in directing and channelling human behaviour is conspicuously facilitated. Whether or not this aspect of the legal order is essential from the analytical aspect, it clearly remains a sociological factor of the first order.

The Connexion Between Rights and Duties

Some jurists have argued that not only is the machinery of rights and duties a necessary feature of a legal system but that these two concepts are themselves logically inter-connected in an essential way. Rights and duties are said to be 'correlatives', that is to say that they are simply opposite ends of a legal relationship, and that this bilateral relation must invariably exist. If Jones owes Robinson a sum of money, then we say that Robinson has a right to payment of that sum from Jones, while Jones is under a duty to pay it to Robinson. They are therefore opposite sides of the same medal. Others, however, such as Kelsen, have pointed out that the conjunction of right and duty, though common enough, is not a necessary one, for there may be duties which are imposed without conferring any rights, as for example in the case of many public and social-welfare duties. This applies to much (if not to all) of criminal and administrative law. There may be a duty not to publish obscene literature, or to make a tax return to the appropriate authority, but such duties do not create corresponding rights in favour of other persons. Attempts to meet this point by asserting that rights exist in all such cases in favour of the state or of some organ of the state lead to a highly artificial result, for we would hardly wish to say that the state has a 'right' that its citizens should not publish obscene matter; and as for the state's power to invoke the process of the law to suppress such publication (which may be regarded as analogous to

Robinson's right to invoke legal procedure to recover his debt owed to him by Jones), this may be more in the nature of a duty than a right. Moreover, if every duty has a right associated with it this seems to lead to the odd conclusion that the condemned criminal has a 'right' to be hanged. For these reasons Kelsen and others have suggested that duty is really the fundamental concept of a legal system, and that a right is something which may or may not be attached to it according to whether that system is willing to confer upon some individual the power to decide whether to set the legal machinery in motion to enforce the fulfilment of the duty. Such an apparatus of individual rights is thus regarded as a distinctive feature of a society based on the institution of private property where legal claims normally take the form of an assertion of some proprietary interest or something capable of being evaluated in money's worth.

Primary and Remedial Rights

This view of legal rights as a power to enforce the law, however, seems to ignore or obliterate another distinction often made by jurists, namely that between primary and remedial or sanctioning rights. This distinction to some extent corresponds with the contrast between substantive and procedural or adjective law. Substantive law is regarded as laying down all the various rights and duties which the law treats as governing people in all their legal relationships and existing prior to any actual breach of duty. Procedural law on the other hand comes into play only when a breach of duty has occurred and the injured party seeks by legal proceedings to obtain some remedy or relief. At this stage then the injured party's rights can be expressed rather in terms of the claims he may have upon the court to a particular kind of order, for instance, he may be entitled to damages or an injunction.

Thus in the case of a property owner, the owner is treated as being entitled in law to do many classes of acts in regard to the property, such as using or disposing of it, and all other persons are held to be under a duty to refrain from doing any acts which would infringe the owner's rights. Again, a person driving a motor-car along the highway is under a duty to take reasonable care for the safety of other road users, but so long as he does take such care or until an accident occurs none of those users has any right or claim that he can enforce by legal process. In other words the law creates a huge apparatus of rights and duties which may properly be regarded as primary, in as much as they are directed at controlling the behaviour of people in general by delimiting and demarcating those classes of acts which they must do or refrain from doing in the course of their daily lives. There seems every reason, of common sense, utility, and legal practice, for describing these basic relationships in terms of rights and duties and as distinct from, though closely connected with, the subsequent remedial rights and duties of a procedural character which arise only after infringement has occurred and which may result in the injured or aggrieved person setting the law in motion in order to vindicate his claim.

The division between primary and remedial rights and duties also tends to be blurred by the extreme sanctionist view of law according to which nothing can rank as a legal duty unless it is capable of actual enforcement, by which is meant some order of a court imposing a sanction or penalty upon the defendant. This however represents an untenable position, not only because many duties are *de facto* unenforceable (e.g. because the defendant has disappeared, or is without means) but also because there are numerous instances where the law distinguishes between a substantive and a merely procedural bar to obtaining enforcement of a legal right. Instances of the latter are statute-barred debts, certain contracts required to be evidenced in writing, or a claim against a person enjoying diplomatic privilege. In such cases it makes perfect sense for the law to treat the primary duty as subsisting though subject for the time being to a procedural impediment. So, for instance, if the defendant ceases to be a member of the diplomatic service he thereupon loses his immunity from suit and proceedings can then be launched in respect of the subsisting claim. A further point is that courts frequently give judgment in the form of a declaration as to the legal rights and duties of the parties even though no other relief may be available in the particular circumstances. A court may declare that a person is or is not qualified to be a member of a trade union,[21] or that a person has been improperly deprived of his right to pursue a particular job or occupation,[22] even though no other remedy, such as damages or an injunction, could or would be granted in the particular case.

Hohfeld's Analysis of Rights and Duties

Legal analysis however, does not stop short at differentiating between substantive and procedural rights. An important contribution to modern legal theory has here been made by the American jurist, Hohfeld, who demonstrated that the traditional legal pattern of rights and duties conceals a number of different situations which need to be carefully distinguished for the purposes of legal analysis. Hohfeld pointed out that existing legal terminology already contains most if not all of the requisite terms to enable this differentiation to be effected but that this terminology needed to be deployed in a more exact and systematic way.

Put briefly, Hohfeld splits up the traditional 'right–duty' pattern into four distinct pairs of correlatives. These are right–duty; liberty–'no-right'; power–liability; and immunity–disability. It will be seen that only the term 'no-right' is a neologism, since legal language has not hitherto devised a term to fit this precise concept.

Hohfeld's proposal is that the 'right–duty' correlatives should be confined to the situation where one person is entitled by legal process to compel another person to act in a certain way, for example where Jones can enforce payment of a debt from Robinson. Many so-called legal 'rights', however, do not correspond to this simple situation. For instance, a landowner may have the right to walk on his own land, or any person may have a right to make a will controlling the succession to his estate. In neither of these situations is there any corresponding duty imposed on anyone else in the sense that such a person can be forced by the possessor of the right to act in any particular way. In the former situation what corresponds to the owner's right to walk on his own land is the legal consequence that everyone else has 'no-right' to interfere with the exercise of the owner's privilege. Hence the dichotomy, 'liberty–no-right', is applied as the legal expression of this situation. And as to the position of the person entitled to dispose by will of his property upon his decease, this in substance represents a legal power to produce a change in the legal relationships of other persons, who are therefore 'liable' to have their legal relations changed in this way. Accordingly Hohfeld describes this as a 'power–liability' relationship. Finally, the fourth pair of correlatives is aimed at covering the situation where a person enjoys freedom from having a given legal relationship altered by the act of another person. For instance, in making a statement in the course of a parliamentary debate the speaker enjoys absolute privilege from suit however defamatory the statement might be. This position therefore involves an 'immunity' from legal action with a corresponding 'disability' on the part of the person defamed, since he is legally disabled from bringing proceedings.

Two Hypothetical Examples

The main argument in favour of this revised terminology is that it assists in clarifying legal analysis and avoids confusion between different legal situations which may have different legal consequences. Let us consider two hypothetical examples for this purpose.

(1) *An Irrevocable Licence:* In the first example Smith buys a theatre ticket for a reserved seat at a performance at Brown's theatre. If, as a matter of law, Brown is not able to exclude Smith from taking his seat, this would amount to the grant of what is called in law 'an irrevocable licence'. Smith in this case has a liberty to enter and take his seat and Brown has 'no-right' to interfere with this freedom of Smith. Suppose, however, that before the performance is due Brown

wrongfully purports to withdraw Smith's permission to enter. The law may well say in this case that though Brown has acted wrongfully, Smith cannot legally compel Brown to let him in, so that Smith's only remedy is to sue for damages for breach of contract. This means therefore that Smith has no liberty to enter but only a right to sue for damages.

Let us next suppose that Smith has actually entered the theatre and taken his seat but that during the performance for some entirely unwarranted reason Brown tells him to go, and upon Smith's quite proper refusal, he is forcibly ejected. Clearly Smith can in this case also sue for damages for breach of contract. But can he also claim damages for the tort of assault, and thereby perhaps recover much higher damages? Here the law may well say that Smith has a right not to be assaulted by Brown and that Brown was therefore under a positive duty not to carry out or authorize any assault upon him. It is true that Smith was only on the premises with the licence of Brown but, as Brown had 'no-right' to withdraw that licence, Brown cannot, by wrongfully purporting to withdraw the licence, treat Smith as if he were a trespasser, unlawfully upon the premises. Accordingly it could be held that Brown has, by ordering Smith to be forcibly ejected, committed an infringement of Smith's right not to be assaulted, which is quite distinct from his liberty to use his ticket for the purpose of seeing the performance and amounts to a breach of duty for which damages are recoverable separately from any liability for breach of contract due to the premature revocation of Smith's ticket.

The above, it may be added, represents broadly speaking the result achieved in English law,[23] but in arriving at this result considerable difficulty was experienced because it was felt that Smith's only 'right' was to sue for breach of contract if his ticket was improperly revoked. It might therefore be contended that a precise analytical terminology which enables a line to be drawn between Smith's licence or 'liberty' to see the performance and his separate 'right' not to be assaulted, rather than following the traditional course of describing the parties' relationship at all stages as representing rights with correlative duties, assists in clarifying the several issues raised in a case of this kind.

(2) *The Right of Compulsory Purchase:* Another, and briefer, example may be given to show how vitally the legal relationships between parties may differ at different stages of a legal transaction or under varying conditions. If all of these are then subsumed under a uniform classification of rights and duties confusion can readily creep in, leading to faulty analysis and possibly even unjust adjudications. The example is that of a power of compulsory purchase exercisable in regard to privately owned land on behalf of some government authority. The normal procedure here is that the authority initiates the purchase by serving what is called a 'notice to treat'. In a case, therefore, to which this procedure is applicable an authority, prior to service of the proper notice, has a 'power' of compulsory purchase in relation to the particular piece of land and the owner is under a 'liability', as being exposed to the possible exercise of this power. If then the power is actually exercised and is followed by the other formalities (which can be ignored for the present purpose) the authority will then obtain a 'right' to the transfer of the land and the owner will be under a 'duty' to proceed with the transfer. On the other hand if the owner can establish that the authority's legal powers do not extend to this particular land, then the owner can be said to enjoy 'immunity' from this procedure and the authority is under a correlative 'disability' in regard to this transaction.

The reversal of traditional habits tends to encounter stronger resistance in this country than in the United States, so that the arguments in favour of introducing a more precise analytical terminology on the Hohfeld pattern have produced little response among English lawyers. Some headway has nevertheless been achieved in America. The most noteworthy achievement in this respect has undoubtedly been the adoption of the new terminology in the various *Restatements* of branches of the law compiled by the American Law Institute. These *Restatements*, although lacking authority in the formal sense discussed above [24] are extremely influential and cited with great frequency in American courts, and therefore can be assumed to exert a continuing influence not only as to the substantive rules contained in them, but also in regard to their analytical form and pattern.

Sociologically minded lawyers may urge that the fundamental element with which rights and duties are concerned is the recognition and classification of the human 'interests' which those concepts are designed to protect. [25] It may be said, for instance, that mere formal analysis can tell us nothing which enables us to identify or recognize interests which compete for protection and in particular cannot afford any criterion by which new interests (such as the so-called 'right to privacy') [26] may achieve recognition. No doubt there is some force in this contention, but what must never be overlooked is that sociological factors, however important, have for legal purposes to be expressed and presented in a conceptual framework without which they cannot be given significance as elements in a legal system. This conceptual framework has the three-fold function of allowing expression to be given to the existing rules of law; of providing machinery which affords scope for the rational development of those rules or for the creation of new rules; and of affording a means of directing or channelling human behaviour by creating the feeling in people's minds that they are or are not justified in doing or refraining from doing certain things or making certain claims. The importance therefore of the conceptual aspect of legal rules is not diminished by referring to this as mere legal formalism. For it is out of the interaction of the formal structure of legal thought and language with the sociological facts of human activities that meaning is imparted to the living body of the law.

III

OWNERSHIP, PROPERTY, AND POSSESSION

So much of legal systems has been taken up with the protection of property that it is hardly surprising to find the concept of ownership enjoying a key position among the diverse rights afforded legal recognition. Yet even the most refined and subtle legal analysis has failed to yield any clearly established criteria by which ownership may be identified, though much has been done to clear away certain confusions and misconceptions.

Ownership and Property

In the first place, it is necessary to distinguish between the right of ownership itself and the subject-matter of that right. Here the use of the word 'property' has introduced some confusion. For a piece of land, a book, or a motor-car, are treated by layman and lawyer as forms of property both in the sense of being physical objects which are capable of ownership, and also as part of the patrimony of particular owners and therefore as a collection of rights to those particular things. It is necessary to realize, however, that although 'property' is often used in this loose way to refer either to the thing itself or to the rights in that thing, the concept of ownership itself is quite distinct from any tangible things to which it may relate, for it is no more than the expression of a legal relationship resulting from a set of legal norms. This point becomes manifest when it is realized that there are many types of 'property' in modern law which have no tangible subject-matter at all to which they can be related. Examples are patent rights and copyright, which merely represent the right of a first inventor or author to manufacture his invention or publish his work (the ownership in any actual product of such manufacture or publication is of course an entirely separate matter). Again, a share certificate in a company may be regarded as involving ownership of the piece of paper involved, but in fact the important rights it transfers from a pecuniary point of view relate to entirely intangible matters such as the potentiality of receiving a share of profits by way of dividend from time to time and, in an ultimate sense, a share in the potential break-up value of the company's assets less its liabilities. All the same it must never be forgotten that ownership in a physical thing, such as land or goods, is just as 'intangible' as ownership of a patent, since both are merely types of legal rights whatever may be their respective subject-matter.

Ownership of 'Rights'

Equally confusing is the use of the concept of ownership as applied to all or any other type of rights. Thus of any right, whether one of ownership in the proprietary sense or not, it may be said that that right is 'owned' by a particular person, or transferred from one person to another. For instance a contractual claim to a debt or a licence to publish a book granted by the copyright owner, may be said to be owned by the creditor or licensee and may possibly be transferred by them to other owners. This is not to suggest that all so-called legal rights can be transferred to others, for some are obviously by their nature non-transferable, such as a right to one's own reputation, and often rights, either on grounds of public policy or for other reasons, may not be capable of transfer, as for instance in the case of a right to claim damages in tort (such as a claim for damages for causing personal injuries as a result of negligence). Ignoring the case of non-transferable rights, to which the conception of ownership is not generally applied, [27] it remains true that rights generally can be and frequently are treated as themselves capable of being owned. What this terminology implies, however, is no more than that rights are exercisable by certain persons and that such persons may accordingly be described as owners of those rights. [28] The reference to an owner in this general sense tells us nothing as to the nature of the particular right owned and must not be confused with that particular species of proprietary right which is described as 'ownership' in the sense now being discussed. Indeed the muddle which arises by using the term 'owner' in this dual sense is revealed plainly enough when it is pointed out that, if applied universally, we would have to speak of the owner of a proprietary right as the 'owner' of the 'right of ownership'. This absurdity is in fact avoided, but the difficulty remains that in English there is no convenient word which can be found to describe the person who is entitled to exercise any particular right. Sometimes the words 'holder' or 'possessor' are employed, but linguistic usage frequently imposes 'owner' as the more natural designation.

If then we put aside the confusions which arise by attempting to treat ownership as if it were nothing but an intangible right to a tangible thing, or as a description of the relation of a person to any right whatsoever which he can exercise, we are left with the problem of trying to isolate the specific criteria of that class of proprietary rights which are more properly designated as forms of ownership.

Is Ownership an Absolute Right to 'a Thing'?

One approach to this problem has been to treat ownership as involving an absolute right to some thing which may be either tangible or intangible. Two objections to this immediately present themselves. First, the idea of an intangible thing as the subject-matter of ownership is merely an attempt to avoid the difficulty created by such instances as ownership of patents or copyright. In fact, however, as we have seen, there is here no identifiable subject-matter in such cases other than the legal rights themselves and therefore this definition amounts to saying no more than that there is an absolute right to legal rights, which is a pleonasm for 'absolute legal rights'. Second, the notion of absoluteness is introduced to indicate the unlimited character of the owner's right (he can do anything he likes with the thing).[29] This criterion fails for two obvious reasons, namely, because ownership may be virtually completely divested of the elements of enjoyment and control and still remain ownership, and, further, because there is no such thing in law as an unlimited right, for the law will inevitably impose restraints on the use or disposal of property. In earlier systems the main restraint may have been the fetters imposed by the criminal law, but in modern times the huge development of the public-law aspect of property has confined within very narrow limits the potential freedoms of the property-owner. To give but one instance, the extent to which a land-owner is limited as regards his mode of use, control, and present or future disposition of the land, by a heavy overlay of town-planning and building regulations and possible powers of compulsory acquisition of the land by various authorities, sufficiently emphasizes that ownership is not so much a general liberty of a man to do what he likes with his own, but is much more in the nature of some kind of residual right which remains after all other relevant rights and restraints have been duly discounted.

Rights 'in rem'

Yet another approach to ownership is to have regard not so much to the content of the right itself but rather to its ambit. This is brought out in the traditional terminology (still much used by lawyers) which distinguishes between rights *in rem* and rights *in personam*. The idea underlying this distinction is that certain rights are only exercisable against a particular person or closely defined group of persons, whereas other rights are available against everyone. A contractual debt or a claim for damages in tort can only be pursued against the debtor himself or the wrongdoer, whereas a proprietary right, such as ownership, is available against the whole world. This is certainly a distinction of considerable value but it does not serve by itself as an effective means of defining ownership. For, on the one hand, there are some rights which would not qualify as proprietary rights in law but which are nevertheless enforceable against everyone, including the true owner. One example is that of an exclusive licence granted by a copyright owner.[30] Again, on the other hand, even rights of ownership may not be universally enforceable, as for instance in the case of the wrongful sale of another person's goods by a 'mercantile agent'[31], or a sale 'in market overt'.[32] Particularly troublesome from this point of view is the fact that in English law there have for centuries been two distinct kinds of owners, known as legal and equitable owners, the latter arising under what is called 'a trust'. The institution of a trust, which is a key feature of modern property law in all common-law jurisdictions, enables the legal title to property to be vested in a trustee or trustees, but on such terms that they hold the property on behalf of a beneficiary who owns the beneficial interest and is in effect the real owner. Yet under this arrangement the trustees have full legal ownership and the equitable title of the beneficiary is capable of being defeated if the property is sold by the trustees to a purchaser who gives valuable consideration for it and who buys in good faith without knowledge of the existence of the trust.

The fact is that ownership, although one of the most important concepts known to the law, cannot be reduced to one simple central idea. Indeed so widespread are its legal implications and so complex its refinements in modern law that it can only be fully understood by analysing all the interrelated legal rules which make up the law of property of a given legal system.[33] This, however, should not be taken to mean that certain classifications of that inchoate mass of rules may not yield a better grasp of the underlying conception of ownership itself.

Ownership as 'a Bundle' of Rights

For this purpose it may be said that ownership is not a single category of legal 'right' but is a complex bundle of rights whose precise character will vary from legal system to legal system. Broadly speaking, this bundle of rights divides into two categories or aspects, one concerned with what may be termed the 'root of title', and the other, 'beneficial' ownership. Of the two, the first may be said to be the more fundamental. The notion here is that a certain right, which has a specific (but not necessarily a material) subject-matter, and which is capable of being treated as a pecuniary interest or of pecuniary value, and is further capable of being exercised against the public as a whole, may be regarded as owned by the person who can lay claim to the ultimate core of title to that 'thing' or subject-matter. If every possible right of this kind were subject to a system of registration then the original owner could be regarded as the first-named person on the register, and the present owner as the person who now stands on the register as having acquired the title from or through that person by some lawful means of acquisition, such as sale, gift, inheritance and so forth. As, however, no legal system could possibly in practice work a universal register of this kind (though registration of title to land and certain other kinds of property, such as company shareholdings, has been widely established in modern times), the law has to have recourse to some other means of tracing a root of title. It is for this reason that the idea of possession plays such an important role in property law, for legal systems tend to regard possession as good evidence of lawful title.[34] Hence the doctrine '*possession vaut titre*' or, in popular parlance, 'possession is nine points of the law.' Still, possession cannot, like registration, be regarded as conclusive evidence of a good title, but must always be relative to the circumstances in which it was acquired. For this reason the lawyer distinguishes between actual or physical possession and the 'right to possess'. If for instance a person is in possession of property and another person physically wrests it from him, the latter may thus acquire actual possession but the right to possess may still adhere in the former, who may be entitled to reclaim the property in a court of law on the basis of his prior possession.

Beneficial Ownership

The notion of beneficial ownership, on the other hand, is tied up with the various ways in which an owner may exercise certain legal powers or 'liberties' in relation to its subject-matter. These include a wide range of activities such as using or disposing of the property, or excluding others from its use, or even of destroying the physical thing itself.

Such powers, central though they may be to the popular conception of ownership, can normally be separated from the root of title to the thing, so that the legal owner may be virtually divested of any beneficial interest whatever. This is the situation of a trustee who holds property on trust for some beneficiary with an absolute equitable interest therein, as it is equally of a landowner who grants a 999 years building lease to a lessee at a 'peppercorn' ground rent. It is indeed rather a distinctive feature of common-law systems to facilitate the splitting up of the beneficial aspect of legal ownership in this way and this has conferred much flexibility, though inevitably also much complexity, upon the English law of property. The so-called 'strict settlement' under which the ownership in land is divided between a succession of life tenants and other future interests has played a large role in the historical formation of English society, though its retention at the present day may owe more to tax considerations than to the former anxiety to preserve land under family control. The civil-law systems, on the other hand, have tended to follow the Roman-law pattern of treating ownership as less readily divisible. The modern civil law knows nothing of the English trust as such and treats a lease not as a form of ownership but as a kind of contractual right. Where, however, the civil law has proved conspicuously more flexible in its approach to the concept of ownership is in its readiness to recognize a variety of possible types of shared rights of husband and wife in the matrimonial property as against the rather rigid common-law view that the property of each spouse is virtually separate for all purposes.[35] But this is too large and specialized a topic to embark upon here.[36]

Conclusion: Some Problems
for the Future

*The Law, like the traveller, must be ready for the morrow. It must have a
principle of growth.* (Mr Justice Cardozo.)

We began this inquiry with a question, and this concluding
chapter does not in fact contain a conclusion, but poses a
series of questions as to some of the problems which the idea
of law may have to adjust to in the imminent future. Save for
those sporadic voices who say that law has produced little
but evil consequences for mankind and who would prefer to
see it disappear altogether from the human scene, the foregoing discussion may have served to review some of the ways
in which the idea of law has proved to be one of the truly
fundamental civilizing factors in the development of human
society. The conceptual systems within which man has interpreted the world and the place of human society therein
constitute an essential feature of his culture, and help to
differentiate him from the higher animals. The particular
ways in which man may look upon the world and the place
of human society in that world will be reflected in all the different types of conceptual system: his religion, his scheme of
morals, his ideas as to the scope and purpose of law will all,
in various ways, mirror his basic outlook and fundamental
assumptions; and in addition we must expect to find a subtle
and complex interplay between all the different aspects and
manifestations of man's culture.

Moreover, just as no universal agreement as to the nature,
meaning, and purpose of religion or social morality can be
discerned, in view of the tremendous variations in cultural
and technological development and outlook among different
peoples and in different periods, so it is hardly surprising

that no universally acceptable pattern of the idea of law emerges from a study of human society at all its varying stages of development. Each society will inevitably see its law, just as it will see its God, in its own image, and even within the same society there will be a constant process of flux and development, though not necessarily along the line of social progress, as our Victorian predecessors believed so firmly. As the particular society changes so the image that it has created or cherished of its legal framework will also tend to be re-formulated, though generally at a slower speed. The idea of law is notoriously a conservative one, and in a progressive and rapidly developing society such as a social democracy, the re-formulation of this idea tends to lag behind the actual movements that are gradually emerging in society itself.

Yet the enormous importance of the idea of law as a factor in human culture only serves to emphasize how great is the duty upon those who are concerned with its exposition, as well as with its application in practice, to strive continuously to refurbish that image, to keep it bright, and to subject it to constant re-analysis so as to keep it in touch with the social realities of the period. This is not to say that the jurist is concerned solely to look to the future, for after all one of the cardinal elements of law is to provide a solid foundation for society and this can only be done by giving ample weight to the values and traditions represented in that society in its past history, at any rate in so far as those values and institutions are relevant to the needs of the present. A subtle transformation of past conceptions in the light of existing needs has represented an important function of the lawyer in maintaining social continuity. But important though this aspect of law may be, it requires no special emphasis, for the simple reason that such an approach is an almost inevitable feature of the inherent conservatism and traditionalism of lawyers and legal thinking generally.

It is in this context then that an attempt will be made in this concluding chapter to indicate briefly, in the light of the foregoing inquiry, what are likely to be some of the more general problems which can be expected to loom large on the legal horizon in the immediate future of mankind, fraught as it is both with high hopes and unprecedented perils.

DEMOCRACY AND THE RULE OF LAW

Reference has already been made to the immense complexity of the problem of trying to formulate and work out the detailed interpretation of those fundamental values of a democratic society which are capable both of being expressed in terms of legal norms, and of lending themselves to enforcement by regular legal machinery. The growth in modern times of written constitutions and entrenched Bills of Rights, has led to a very profound belief in the need for giving legal effect to systems of democratic values. The old idea, associated with the régime of *laissez faire*, that save for a certain number of essential penal prohibitions, the economic and social life of mankind should be left to resolve itself without recourse to legal regulation, has been virtually abandoned in favour of the idea that law should provide the essential guarantees for all those freedoms which are looked upon as vital to the 'good life' in a social democracy. So far has this process gone, that doubts may reasonably be entertained whether modern society has not allowed itself to be carried away with a certain degree of enthusiasm, in yielding to the belief that man may be educated and his social progress assured by legislation alone. Certainly, as the Greeks were well aware, legislation may prove a very important educative factor, but this is far from saying that the mere passing of legislation can effect overnight a fundamental change of ideology, or provide a magic wand by which the prejudices or built-in emotional attitudes of a given society can be instantly waived aside. On the contrary, as the experience of the American federal executive and judiciary has painfully revealed, in the great struggle over segregation, an immense gap may emerge when the formal legal decisions even of supreme courts come up against the stubborn re-

sistance of unyielding human ideology, which is solidly in-
grained in the 'folk-culture' of the society in question.

Yet surely this does not mean that the law must abdicate
in the face of such powerful social resistance. Law in itself
exerts a kind of moral authority, and there can be no doubt
that the persistent pressures of legal norms, even if inade-
quately enforced, or even if openly and deliberately evaded,
can still serve as a vital ferment in gradually creating a
climate of opinion where important advances in implementing democratic values can be realized.

THE DANGERS OF MONOPOLY

But there is more involved here than the mere question of
adequate legal enforcement. In the complex web of our
social and economic structure, which tends to place the vital
organs of expression and public opinion in the hands of a
few individuals or of the public authorities themselves,
there is constant need to ensure that the essence of democratic
values is not eroded at its very source. Is it really practicable
to create a climate of genuinely free opinion and discussion
within a framework of control retained by a tiny minority
of powerful individuals or groups? As Lord Radcliffe has
recently remarked, 'Censors will be very powerful but will
not even be identified as censors',[1] for what may be permitted
to emerge in these various organs of opinion may depend
upon what the owners and publishers of newspapers and
the producers of broadcast programmes consider as suitable
for the public eye or ear. Hence, in the future, the idea of
law must not confine itself to grappling with the technical
problem of giving effect to human values through legal
machinery, but must take thought as to what means may be
devised for ensuring that the stream of free thought does not
dry up at its source, by virtue of monopoly control.

MINORITY OPINIONS

Yet another aspect of democratic values is that the very

establishing of a canon of values, which everyone is expected to accept, contains within it certain inherent dangers which are in themselves inimical to democracy. For those very values, especially when they have been authoritatively interpreted by legislative and judicial bodies, and have come to be accepted by the educational and institutional authorities of the state, may easily be erected into a kind of dogmatic system not dissimilar in some ways, however different in scope and content, from a form of dogmatic theology. The tendency in our present mass age to produce a high measure of conformism might easily lead to a situation where minority opinion and attacks upon or criticisms of the established 'theology' of the age may be so severely frowned upon that independent thought and constructive criticism may be repressed. A genuine social democracy, as John Stuart Mill so cogently argued a century ago, must ensure that minority groups are not utterly overborne by the weight of majority opinion. Of course this raises in an acute way the problem of how the state is to deal with those sections of minority opinion which deliberately aim at subverting the essential democratic values of society, for instance by inciting prejudice against particular groups of citizens on account of their race or colour. No easy answer seems to be available for this type of problem,[2] which will require all the idealism of the moralist coupled with the acute discernment of the best legal brains if it is to be adequately resolved in our future society.

LAW AND THE NEEDS OF SOCIETY

While law was looked upon as having hardly any greater role than preserving the security of life and property in the state, and enabling people to rely upon their solemn engagements in the confident belief that these would be enforced if necessary by process of law, it was natural enough to regard the science of law as something entirely self-contained and autonomous, which therefore needed to concern itself little, if at all, with other departments of human knowledge. The modern welfare state, on the other hand, presents a very different picture, where some form of legal regulation has infiltrated into almost every conceivable aspect of man's social and economic affairs. Yet the lawyer is still entitled to claim a certain measure of autonomy, in the sense that the highly technical processes of a modern legal system call for a special degree of legal experience and of legal training and insight, which can only be possessed and effectively deployed by a highly skilled legal profession, including the judiciary. Lawyers, for instance, possess unique experience in and qualifications for the drafting of documents, the evaluation of evidence, and the conducting of proceedings and inquiries in a way which is calculated to arrive at rational conclusions based on a careful and impartial sifting and evaluation both of evidence and of arguments.

LAW AND THE SOCIAL SCIENCES

At the same time a modern legal system makes impact at innumerable points with the everyday concerns of ordinary people or of special groups of people, and it is far from being the case, as some lawyers fondly imagine, that legal training and experience alone are sure guides to the real character of the social and economic problems with which the law has to make contact and for which it has to afford solutions. The mere fact that prosecutors and judges are constantly concerned with criminal trials does not give them a unique or necessarily a specially valuable insight into the character of delinquency or the minds of criminals; indeed it may be said that continuously concentrating on one aspect of the life of accused persons, namely, their behaviour and demeanour during a trial, and the statement of their past misdeeds with which the court may be supplied from police records, may well tend to create a very one-sided picture which can be highly misleading. Again, matrimonial cases are concerned with matters which are of enormous importance both to the community and to the individuals who are involved in particular disputes before the courts, but here again the legal profession, and the judges and magistrates who deal with these matters, have little opportunity for exploring the deeper implications of such disputes and their consequences for society as a whole. In such matters then, there is a large field for impartial and scientifically conducted inquiry into the basic facts and the true nature of the problems with which the law is attempting to wrestle. Such social sciences as criminology, psychiatry, and sociology are no doubt in their infancy, and therefore unable to afford positive answers and solutions to every inquiry which might be raised. Still, sufficient advances have already been made to show that these fields of study can make important contributions to the understanding and working of the legal system and to its improvement for the future.

THE LAW AND INDUSTRIAL RELATIONS

It would not serve any useful purpose here to attempt a catalogue of the sort of problems on which law might make useful contact with investigations in the field of other disciplines. One or two however do deserve a brief mention. In the field of industry and labour law, it is clear that any attempt by the law to regulate such matters as the restrictive practices which are employed both by industry and by trade unions is likely to prove singularly unconstructive if the inquiries and evidence of economists and sociologists are disregarded. It is significant that the recently established Restrictive Practices Court in England has marked a new departure in this type of matter, by having a tribunal presided over by a judge but assisted by a number of experienced laymen; by affording ample scope for evidence to be put before the tribunal by expert economists; and by not tying the consideration of such evidence to the highly technical rules which govern the giving of evidence in normal legal trials.

The settlement of disputes either arising within unions themselves, or between unions and employers, calls for much careful exploration into the economic foundations of the types of disputes that are apt to arise, as well as a searching investigation into the various types of procedure which might be employed for resolving them. The comparative study of different types of procedure used in various countries, and the degree to which these afford effective machinery, might prove of very great value in a country such as England where the approach to these problems is still somewhat bedevilled by a restricted idea of law, according to which industrial disputes are not justiciable issues in the full sense, but involve matters of policy which can best be left to negotiation or voluntary arbitration. The fact that many other developed countries, such as Australia, Sweden, and Germany, find it perfectly possible to regulate these disputes by judicial or quasi-judicial machinery, and are satisfied that objective criteria exist by which they may be adequately resolved, is surely a sufficient indication that a good deal of rethinking is called for in England on matters of this kind.

THE REFORM OF LEGAL PROCEDURE

Nor, even in matters which may be said to fall decisively within the sphere of the legal profession itself – namely, such questions as the form which various types of trial may take; the use of juries; the introduction of different types of evidence and its evaluation – does it necessarily follow that the lawyers are justified in regarding these as matters to be determined solely by lawyers in the light of their legal experience and insight. There seems no reason at all why such matters should not lend themselves to a good deal of informed fact-finding, in the shape of inquiries conducted by sociologists or possibly combined teams of sociologists and lawyers. It is therefore to be hoped that no part of the legal system will be regarded as so sacrosanct that it is treated as closed territory, beyond the range of outside investigation, and lawyers should not resent entirely proper investigation of this sort as a form of prying into their private concerns.

·THE ROLE OF THE UNIVERSITIES

It is one thing, of course, to say that the law should endeavour increasingly to form links with other disciplines; it is quite another to indicate how this may be effected in practice.

The universities seem to present the most hopeful prospect for cooperation between these different disciplines. The social sciences have enjoyed an established position in the universities in America for some considerable time, and their prestige and importance are beginning to grow and be recognized in England as well as in other European countries. Although in some American universities, such as Yale and Chicago, this type of cross-fertilization has already made considerable headway, there still remains room for a great deal of development on these lines in English universities. Such studies can and already are, in some instances, being aided by the setting up of special institutions for certain particular fields of study such as criminology, where legal and sociological investigations can go hand-in-hand. With increasing emphasis in legal education upon the wider aspects and implications of the legal system, and its impact upon social institutions, it seems not improbable that the idea of law which will prevail among lawyers in the near future will be one which emphasizes not so much the self-contained character of law, but rather its function as an instrument of social cohesion and social progress.

THE ROLE OF LAW IN THE INTERNATIONAL SPHERE

In this nuclear age the idea of law has a crucial contribution to make in the peaceful settlement of disputes and the elimination of war. A distinctive feature of a developed, as compared with a more primitive, form of law is the existence of tribunals charged with the task of deciding matters in dispute, whose jurisdiction is compulsory, and which have at their disposal sufficient organized force to ensure that their decisions are, at least generally speaking, obeyed. Although some advances have undoubtedly been made in the international sphere in the way of providing tribunals with sufficient standing to be able to give authoritative decisions in legal disputes, fundamental problems still remain. These problems relate principally to the question of compulsory jurisdiction, and also to that of enforcement.

International Tribunals

So far as jurisdiction is concerned, the role of international law is still bedevilled by the profound feeling among rulers of states, whose vital interests may be involved in international disputes, that there are certain types of disputes which are not 'justiciable', in the sense that these matters are considered to be political rather than legal, and therefore not an appropriate subject-matter for decision by a court of law. It is in line with this view that the Charter of the United Nations has left to each member the decision whether or not to accept the principle of compulsory jurisdiction. As a result, under the so-called 'Optional Clause', a number of states have bound themselves to commit certain defined categories of legal disputes to the International Court of Justice. Even these limited commitments have been decisively qualified by reservations as, for example, in the case of the United States, which excludes 'disputes with regard to matters which are essentially within the domestic jurisdiction of the United States of America as determined by the United States of America'. This means in effect that the ultimate discretion whether to accept the jurisdiction lies with the signatory state which has attached a reservation of this character to its signature.

It has already been pointed out that the distinction between legal and political, or justiciable and non-justiciable disputes, is not one which lends itself to acceptable analysis.[3] The fact remains that there is here an overriding political consideration which no amount of legal theory in itself can ever hope to overcome, but which can only be eroded by a gradual recognition that national interests will be better served in the long run by the acceptance of independent and impartial adjudication in all disputes, however vital the interests that may be affected, rather than by reserving to states their own ultimate freedom of action to maintain their own viewpoint, by force if necessary. We have seen in other spheres, such as those of labour relations, that this unwillingness to recognize the justiciability of all potential disputes which might arise in the labour sphere has proved an obstacle in some countries to resolving industrial disputes in an impartial and legalistic manner, but that nevertheless it has gradually been recognized that there is nothing sacrosanct about this type of dispute which renders it unsuitable for legal arbitration. Needless to say, in the international sphere, mankind is faced with a much tougher problem, and it must be admitted that, in view of the present unsettled state of world politics, it would involve a considerable act of faith on the part of great states such as the U.S.A., to renounce their ultimate independence by submitting all disputes to an independent court.

The Enforcement of International Judgments

The problem of the enforcement of the judgments of an international tribunal, even if rendered in a matter over which it has compulsory jurisdiction, raises questions of a more far-reaching order, since the problem of enforcement against whole states, as against individuals or private corporations, is one of great complexity. Attention has already been given to the nature of this problem and the fact that international law, in the context of present world history, cannot be approached in the same way as state law, that is to say, as a set of rules which is capable, without provoking effective forcible resistance, of being enforced against any person or body however powerful. In practice there are many instances even in the domestic sphere where the law is unenforceable, either because of the intense resistance of a substantial part of the population, as in the Southern States of America regarding the integration of Negroes, or in the case of overpowerful citizens or corporations, who either by force or corruption are able to subvert the due process of the law. Theoretically, however, there is no unassailable reason why, when a legal system has become fully developed in a well-regulated society, the law should not be enforceable against anyone, however powerful. This is plainly not the situation in the international sphere, for no amount of internationally organized force is likely to be effective against truly powerful militarily organized states. Also quite apart from this, the consequences in the nuclear age of bringing force to bear upon states might well be to launch rather than to avoid a holocaust. In some instances forms of enforcement falling short of ultimate coercion might prove quite effective in the international sphere, for example, bringing various types of economic pressure to bear. But it must always be borne in mind that the aim of the legal régime is to preserve peace and not to take action which might provoke the violent reaction of the state whose conduct is being impugned, with results fraught with peril for the world at large. Moreover a system where enforcement might be workable in relation to small and militarily ineffective states but can be ignored by the more powerful states is so inconsistent with the general considerations of legal justice already discussed[4], that it might be worse than one which lacked any form of coercive enforcement whatever.

Crimes against Humanity and 'Genocide'

This is not the place to try to discuss some of the problems which press so urgently upon mankind in their international relations, but some reference at least must be made to one or two of these. Novel and perplexing enough are many of the questions raised by international air traffic, but the launching of rockets and now man (and woman) into outer space demonstrates the way in which the idea of law will be called upon to develop and adapt itself to realms beyond the imagination of previous generations. But confining ourselves to the limited sphere of international relations on the surface of our own planet, it still remains sufficiently apparent

T–M

that there is an ever-increasing area within which the idea of law will have a major role to play in the world scene. In the sphere of fundamental human rights we have already remarked upon some of the tentative efforts that have so far been made to extend the recognition of such rights among all nations, and even to provide some kind of legal machinery whereby individuals may seek protection against injustices inflicted upon them both by foreign states and by their own national state.

Yet another aspect of human rights is the recognition not only of crimes against individuals but crimes against humanity at large, by measures of race destruction, such as were perpetrated by the Nazis during the last war and which have come to be described as 'genocide'. The proceedings at Nuremberg after the last war against the Nazi war criminals showed the need for some form of international criminal law coupled with an adequate judicial machinery and mode of punishment and enforcement which would prevent those guilty of crimes on this massive scale from evading the arm of legal retribution by virtue of the sheer enormity of their criminal activities. Although doubts have been expressed in some responsible quarters as to the legality of such proceedings, this can surely only be on the footing that law is an essentially static concept which cannot develop to meet new situations.[5]

It must be admitted, however, that some reservation may be felt on the ground that the crime of genocide could arguably be said to have been imposed retrospectively upon those who were accused of it. On the other hand the analogy between law in the international sphere and national state law cannot be exact, and it seems not unreasonable to urge that international law in a civilized world must recognize both the capacity for growth and also that there are some forms of activity which are of so outrageous a character and offend so fundamentally the established norms of civilized society that the law should be capable of recognizing their illegality even though they have not been expressly outlawed hitherto. Some may see in this sort of argument an attempt to resurrect a kind of natural-law principle, and indeed some of the supporters of the Nuremberg proceedings have sought to establish their legality on natural-law foundations. However, the recognition of prevailing moral standards in a particular community, or indeed for some purposes in the world-community, at a particular stage of human development need not rest upon acceptance of immutable natural-law foundations. It may also be mentioned here that in the celebrated *Eichmann* trial in Israel a national state claimed the right to try, and upon conviction to punish, an offender against the law of genocide. The law of that trial was based upon the national law of the State of Israel itself and therefore the legality of the proceedings could be regarded as a deduction from the established principles of national sovereignty. At the same time, as we have already seen, the doctrine of sovereignty is not easily reconcilable with the establishment of fundamental human rights, and it may therefore be said that the validity of the Eichmann trial would be considerably fortified by being shown to be in line with established international legal principles.

Unifying Commercial Law

Lastly may be mentioned, in the international sphere, the many attempts that are being made to introduce some measure of uniformity and rationalization in the commercial law of the various trading countries of the world. Commerce is one of those aspects of man's social life which is very closely tied to the forms of legal regulation, and a chaos of conflicting national laws in this sphere does not ease the task of those who aspire to spread international trade.[6] The aim of a uniform commercial code does not in itself involve the creation of some supra-national organization, but in modern times we have witnessed the creation and development of organizations of this character. Of these perhaps the best known and the most controversial is the European Economic Community, more usually referred to as the 'Common Market'. This form of economic and legal cooperation between a group of European nations is of a permanent character, and has involved the creation of a number of supra-national organs with law-making powers. Groupings of this kind seem likely to become increasingly in evidence in various parts of the world, and to lead to a good deal of new thinking about some of the traditional foundations of Western jurisprudence, such as the doctrine of sovereignty and the relationship of states, both in regard to their own citizens and the citizens of other states, and also *inter se*.

That the idea of law has in the past made an indispensable contribution to human culture seems difficult to deny. The tensions of the modern world make it plain that if civilization is to survive still greater demands are likely to be made upon this fundamental concept. For this reason, if for no other, a creative approach to the idea of law seems more imperative in our present age than ever before.

Notes

1 IS LAW NECESSARY?

1 Consider, for example, the Anabaptist movement, at the beginning of the Reformation: see L. von Ranke, *History of the Reformation in Germany* (translated by Sarah Austin), Book VI, chapter 9. But such movements may still be influential either as a spur to social and legal reform or perhaps more often by provoking a reaction in favour of repression.

2 See Becker and Barnes, *Social Thought from Lore to Science*, 3rd ed. (1961), vol. I, pp. 69–70.

3 ibid., p. 78.

4 *The Prince*, chapter 18.

5 Dryden's translation.

6 From Epistle 2 of Book XIV of Seneca's *Epistulàe Morales*, cited by A. J. Carlyle in *A History of Mediaeval Political Theory in the West*, vol. I, pp. 23–4.

7 The optimistic attitude towards man's social problems which attributes these primarily if not entirely to the result of environmental causes (e.g. juvenile delinquency is traceable to poverty or bad family background and so on) has coloured much of modern sociological thought. But modern sociology has tended to favour more rather than less legal control: cf. below, chapter 9.

8 *Laws*, 890 d.

9 A. Maude, *Life of Tolstoy* (World's Classics edition), vol. II, p. 223.

10 ibid., pp. 226–7.

11 But on the relation of custom to law, see below, chapter 10.

12 A. Maude, op. cit., vol. II, p. 222.

13 Below, chapter 9.

14 Sir Grafton Elliot Smith was Professor of Anatomy at University College, London, from 1919 to 1936.

15 *Human History* (Academy Books edition, 1933), p. 189.
16 See 'The Paradox of Anarchism', reprinted in Sir Herbert Read's *A Coat of Many Colours* (1947), pp. 62–5.
17 H. Read, op. cit., pp. 59–60.

2   LAW AND FORCE

1 See H. and H. A. Frankfort, *Before Philosophy*, p. 156.
2 See Max Weber, *Law in Economy and Society*, ed. Rheinstein (1954), chapters 12 and 13.
3 See H. R. Trevor-Roper, *The Last Days of Hitler* (Pan Books ed.), p. 171. ('Besieged in the shattered capital, cooped up 50 feet below the ground, cut off from ordinary communication, a physical and mental wreck, without power to enforce, or reason to persuade, or machinery to create, Hitler still remained, in the universal chaos he had caused, the sole master, whose orders were implicitly obeyed.')
4 See R. Bendix, *Max Weber: An Intellectual Portrait*, pp. 413–14.
5 op. cit. pp. 379–80.
6 Max Weber in H. S. Hughes, *Consciousness and Society* (1959), p. 13. It should be added that more recent sociology prefers the term 'model' to Weber's term 'ideal type'.
7 *Future of an Illusion*, pp. 4–6.
8 *Civilisation and Its Discontents*, p. 85.
9 H. S. Hughes, *Consciousness and Society*, p. 137.
10 cf. J. A. C. Brown, *Freud and the Post-Freudians* (1961), pp. 13–16. And see A. Storr, *Human Aggression* (1968).
11 D. Macrae, *Ideology and Society*, p. 211.
12 K. Olivecrona, *Law as Fact*, pp. 124–5.
13 For a more exact demarcation between the *primary* rules, which lay down standards of behaviour, and the *secondary* rules, which specify the ways in which the primary rules may be ascertained, introduced, varied, or adjudicated upon, see H. L. A. Hart, *The Concept of Law* (1961), chapter 5.

3   LAW AND MORALS

1 See *The Laws of Plato*, (translated A. E. Taylor), p. 1.
2 Job, xiii, 15.
3 *Crito*, (trans. F. J. Church), pp. 50–51.
4 See chapter 4.
5 This view was of course by no means uniformly held in fifth-

or fourth-century Athens. Thus in Sophocles' *Antigone* there is recognition of a law higher than that of man-made state law. But the conflict remains unresolved save as the symbol of the tragedy of man's fate.

6 The question asked by Lord Parker, C.J., in the recent case concerning the privilege of a journalist to refuse to disclose his sources of information (cf. above, p. 158) seems from this point of view far too absolute. 'How can you say,' asked Lord Parker, 'that there is dishonour on you if you do what is your duty in the ordinary way as a citizen to put the interests of the state above everything?' (see the *Guardian*, 7 March 1963.)

7 cf. below, p. 319.

8 *Report on Homosexuality and Prostitution* (1957), Cmnd 247.

8a See now, Sexual Offences Act, 1967.

8b The Divorce Reform Act, 1969, now bases divorce on the sole ground of irretrievable breakdown of the marriage but the court has to be satisfied either that circumstances have occurred similar to a matrimonial offence under the previous law or that the parties have lived apart by mutual consent for two years, or for five years without such consent.

9 See Sir Patrick Devlin, *The Enforcement of Morals* (1959). For a powerful reply, see H. L. A. Hart, *Law, Liberty and Morals* (1963).

10 *Gollins* v. *Gollins*, [1964], A.C. 644.

11 *Shaw* v. *Director of the Public Prosecutions*, [1962] A.C. 220.

12 See below, p. 352, note 25.

13 See Barbara Wootton, 'Dimished Responsibility', in *Law Quarterly Review*, vol. 76 (1960), p. 224. See also M. Ancel, 'Social Defence', in *Law Quarterly Review*, vol. 78 (1962), p. 491.

14 The Homicide Act, 1957, introduced into England for the first time the defence of 'diminished responsibility', whereby mental abnormality short of insanity may result in conviction for manslaughter instead of murder.

15 *Director of Public Prosecutions* v. *Smith* [1961] A.C. 290. The Criminal Justice Act, 1967, has now reversed this by allowing evidence of the actual intention or foresight of the accused.

16 It may be said to stem partly from a determinist view of human conduct and partly from the view that mental health and mental sickness cannot be defined in objective scientific terms.

17 See H. L. A. Hart, *Punishment and the Elimination of Responsibility* (1962); *The Morality of the Criminal Law* (1965).

18 See *Law Quarterly Review*, vol. 76 (1960), p. 239.
19 See above, p. 203.

4 NATURAL LAW AND NATURAL RIGHTS

1 Joshua, x, 12–13. Of course at this stage of development no clear distinction is made between what is natural and what is supernatural: see Durkheim, *Elementary Forms of the Religious Life* (Collier Books edition), pp. 41–3.
2 See J. Needham, *Science and Civilization in China*, vol. 2 (1956), chapter 18.
3 See, for instance, Marcus Aurelius, *Meditations*, Book iv, §4.
4 *The City of God*. Book iv, chapter 4.
5 See *Bonham's* case (1610), 8 Rep. 114, 118.
6 *The Social Contract*, Book i, chapter 7.
7 See above, p. 202.
8 See above, p. 251.
9 The sociological basis of natural law in such writers as Gény and Duguit tended to consist of abstract rationalizations, rather than being directed to research into the primary facts of psychology and human behaviour, despite Gény's slogan in favour of '*libre recherche scientifique*' and Duguit's emphasis on 'social solidarity' (derived from the French sociologist, Durkheim).
10 On these cases see the discussion between H. L. A. Hart and L. L. Fuller in *Harvard Law Review*, vol. 71 (1958), p. 593; and H. O. Pappe in *Modern Law Review*, vol. 23 (1960), p. 260.
11 The wide currency given to such a work as Spengler's *Decline of the West* provides a characteristic illustration of this tendency.
12 See also chapter 5.
13 See *Bonsor* v. *Musician's Union* [1956] A.C. 104.
14 See e.g. *Macalpine* v. *Macalpine* [1958] P. 58. Foreign nullity decrees have also been refused recognition in circumstances where they have been regarded as offending natural justice: see *Lepre* v. *Lepre* [1963] 2 All E.R. 49.

5 LEGAL POSITIVISM

1 See above, p. 182.
2 E. Halévy, *Growth of Philosophic Radicalism* (trans. M. Morris), p. 27.

2a But he does assert that utility justifies resistance when 'according to the best calculation, the probable mischiefs of resistance appear less than the probable mischiefs of submission'. (*A Fragment on Government*, chapter 4, §21.)

3 See D. V. Cowen, *The Foundations of Freedom* (1961).

4 See above, p. 162.

5 Cited by D. G. Charlton, *Positivist Thought in France during the Second Empire* (1959), p. 28.

6 See Malcolm Cowley, *Literary Situation in America* (1954), pp. 75–6.

7 C. R. Leslie, *Life of Constable* (Phaidon edition), p. 323.

8 Basil Taylor, *The Impressionists and Their World*, p. 7.

9 ibid., p. 11.

10 See chapter 12.

11 cf. above, p. 261.

12 See chapter 11.

13 See above, p. 204.

6 LAW AND JUSTICE

1 This distinction between 'formal' and 'concrete' justice is derived from C. Perelman's *De la justice* (1945), now published in an English version in *The Idea of Justice and the Problem of Argument* (1963).

2 See further as to this C. Perelman, *The Idea of Justice and the Problem of Argument* (1963). cf. also above, p. 267.

3 Most 'private' Acts of Parliament lay down general rules governing a particular institution or body or a special class of institutions.

4 This point will be taken up again when Kelsen's theory of the normal structure of law is examined; see above, p. 193.

5 *Leviathan*, chapter 21.

6 *Institutes*, part 1, §138.

7 It is assumed that such an arrangement is permissible by law. Some legal systems confer on the family a 'legitimate portion' of the inheritance; in English law a court can order a reasonable provision out of a deceased's estate to be made in favour of the surviving spouse and infant children.

8 See chapter 11.

9 e.g. in France.

7 LAW AND FREEDOM

1 See above, p. 33.

2 See above, pp. 89 and 166.

3 Provisions in a written constitution providing for fundamental human rights are not necessarily made 'overriding'. For instance, the recently introduced Canadian Bill of Rights is in the form of an ordinary statute and therefore cannot override subsequent conflicting legislation.

4 The introduction of a free legal-aid scheme or (as in England) of assisted legal aid based on a means test, is of great importance in this connexion.

5 See especially *Brown* v. *Board of Education*, 347 U.S., 483 (1954).

5a See in this connexion the Race Relations Act, 1968.

6 See above, p. 148.

7 See also above, p. 249.

7a Subsequently, a new Labour government has introduced a 'betterment levy' on development values.

7b But cf. note 9a below.

8 See *Faramus* v. *Film Artistes' Association* [1964] 1 All E.R. 25.

9 See *Bonsor* v. *Musicians' Union* [1956] A.C. 104. As to the meaning of 'natural justice' in this context, cf. above, p. 62.

9a This right is protected by the Trades Disputes Act, 1906. The House of Lords has, however, held that where there is a threat to strike in breach of contract those making the threat can be sued for damages (*Rookes* v. *Barnard* [1964] A.C. 1929). This has been reversed by the Trades Disputes Act, 1965.

9b Broadly speaking the Royal Commission Report on Trade Unions (1968) adhered to this view.

10 Modern law admits cases of strict liability, that is, liability without proof of negligence, in certain rather exceptional circumstances, but the general principle remains as stated.

10a As recommended for New Zealand in the Royal Commission on Compensation for Personal Injury in New Zealand (1967).

11 Noteworthy in that Act was the introduction of a new defence based on the scientific or literary value of the work and which may be supported by expert evidence.

11a The recent order of a magistrate for the destruction of copies of Cleland's *Fanny Hill* is arguably not inconsistent with this principle. The most recent decision relates to *Last Exit to Brooklyn*: see *R.* v. *Calder & Boyars* [1968] 3 All E.R. 644.

11b See Theatres Act, 1968.

12 See *Jordan* v. *Burgoyne* [1963] 2 All E.R. 225.

12a The Race Relations Act, 1965, is an attempt to tackle this problem.

13 It remains to be seen whether the recent introduction of an independent chairman and a certain number of independent members of the Council is likely to make a great deal of difference, in view of the fact that these persons are appointed by the Council itself and very inadequate finance is being placed at the disposal of the Council. Also the Council still lacks any actual powers of enforcement.

14 See *A–G.* v. *Mulholland* [1963] 1 All E.R. 767.

15 See above, p. 104.

16 Some legal systems do grant such privileges, e.g. to priests. English law allows it only to lawyers. The reason usually given for this is that the privilege is that of the client, but this is a specious ground of distinction since it could apply equally in other cases. The real basis of this privilege is that without it litigation would be very difficult if not impossible to conduct.

17 See *R.* v. *Brixton Prison (Governor)*, *ex parte Enahoro* [1963] 2 All E.R. 477.

18 *R.* v. *Secretary of State for Home Affairs*, *ex parte Soblen* [1962] 3 All E.R., 373. The Immigration Appeals Act, 1968, now provides for a special appeals procedure.

19 A similar criticism can be made of the ruling in *Chandler* v. *D.P.P.* [1962] 3 All E.R. 142, holding that, under the Official Secrets Act, 1911, it is for the executive to determine in its sole discretion when a purpose is prejudicial to the safety or interests of the state.

20 The International Congress of Jurists at Delhi in 1959 presented a supra-national concept of the Rule of Law which gave a much wider interpretation of this concept, e.g. it laid down the various freedoms which should govern the acts of the legislature, such as freedom of speech, freedom of religious belief, and so on. For the conclusions of this Congress, see the *Journal of the International Commission of Jurists*, vol. 11, (1959), p. 8, and for a commentary see 'The Rule of Law as a Supra-National Concept', by Norman S. Marsh in *Oxford Essays in Jurisprudence* (1961), edited by A. G. Guest.

21 See above, p. 63.

23 A striking illustration is the case of the negligent builder in the Laws of Hammurabi, whose building falls down and kills the owner's son. The penalty is that the builder's son is to be put

to death; see L. T. Hobhouse, *Morals in Evolution*, 7th ed., 82.

24 For instance, in England, where a servant has knowingly supplied liquor to a drunken person the absentee publican can himself be convicted. Such exceptions are based on the idea that the law would in these instances be too easily evaded if responsibility could not be imposed vicariously.

24a A modified form of the Scandinavian Ombudsman was introduced into England by the Parliamentary Commissioner Act 1967.

25 See *Conway* v. *Rimmer* [1968] 1 All E.R. 874.

26 See *Schenck* v. *U.S.* 249 U.S. 47 (1919).

27 See *Palko* v. *Connecticut* 302 U.S. 319 (1937); and *Adamson* v. *California* 322 U.S. 46 (1946).

28 See above, chapter 2.

29 Thus no machinery is provided for enforcement of judgments of the Commission.

8 LAW, SOVEREIGNTY, AND THE STATE

1 From this point of view 'the People' may be identified with 'the state' and so afford a basis of 'popular' sovereignty.

2 See below, note 17.

3 cf. above, p. 32.

4 *The Common Law* (1881), p. 1.

5 For 'undeveloped' law, see above, chapter 10.

6 Austin uses this term to describe 'man-made' morality as opposed to the 'law of God'.

7 *Harris* v. *Dönges* [1952] 1 T.L.R. 1245.

7a Recent events in S. Rhodesia have resulted in totally conflicting decisions on the part of the Rhodesian High Court and the English-based Privy Council (see *Madzimbamuto* v. *Lardner-Burke* [1968] 3 All E.R. 561).

8 See chapter 2.

9 See Transport Act, (1962), s.3 (duty to have due regard to efficiency, economy, and safety of operation).

10 See Electricity Act (1947), s. 1 (duty to maintain an efficient coordinated, and economical system of electricity supply).

11 Crown Proceedings Act (1947), s. 25.

12 cf. above, note 6.

13 See *I.R.C.* v. *Collco* [1961] 1 All E.R. 762.

14 e.g. Holland.

15 See above, p. 40.

16 More familiarly known as 'the Common Market'.
17 Kelsen also rejects the 'command' theory of Austin, as involving the confusion of psychology with law.
18 cf. above, p. 276.

9   LAW AND SOCIETY

 1 See above, p. 98.
 2 cf. above, p. 75.
 3 See above, p. 101.
 4 cf. above, p. 29.
 5 This was the approved doctrine of Nazi law.
 6 See above, p. 112.
 7 See R. H. Tawney, *Religion and the Rise of Capitalism* (1929).
 8 See above, p. 251.
 9 cf. above, p. 105.
10 See chapter 2, above.
11 See chapter 3, above.
12 See above, chapter 11.
13 *The Complexity of Legal and Ethical Experience* (1959), p. 6.
14 But the most balanced of the realists have not overlooked this. See especially K. N. Llewellyn, *Jurisprudence: Realism in Theory and Practice* (1962). In his book *The Common Law Tradition* (1960), Llewellyn endeavours to show that there is in fact a high degree of predictability in American appellate decisions due to the built-in stabilizing factors of legal technique and practice.
15 See above, chapter 11.
16 See especially, Jerome Frank, *Law and the Modern Mind*, 6th ed., (1949).
17 cf. p. 71, above.
18 In England it may well be that the realist approach arouses distaste, if not hostility, as it seems to diminish the dignity of the law.
19 See *Law as Fact* (1939).
20 Above, chapter 2.
21 For a further discussion of the role of concepts in law, see chapter 12.
22 For a striking illustration, consider the attempts of Indian courts to reconcile the power of religious excommunication customarily exercised by the head of a religious community, with the modern notion of religious freedom: see J. D. M.

Derrett in *International and Comparative Law Quarterly* (1963), vol. 12, pp. 693–7.

23 See chapter 8.

24 These are generally referred to as 'civil-law' systems, in contrast to those of the 'common law'.

25 See above, p. 275.

26 See above, p. 37.

27 cf. p. 196, above.

10 LAW AND CUSTOM

1 Or 'embryonic' law: see Becker and Barnes, *Social Thought from Lore to Science*, 3rd ed., (1961), vol. 1, p. 27. See also Salmond, *Jurisprudence*, 11th ed., p. 54.

2 See above, p. 209.

3 The same problem arises in other spheres of man's social life. For instance, the meaning and function of religion can be more fully understood – at least in its sociological implications – if its manifestations at different levels of man's social development are explored and compared.

4 See *Les Lois de l'Imitation* (1890).

5 Cited by E. Durkheim in *Elementary Forms of the Religious Life*, Book 111, chapter 4. (Collier Books edition, p. 415.)

6 See *The Ancient City*, originally published in 1864.

7 See his work referred to in note 5 above. This was first published in 1912.

8 Abridged edition, chapter 3.

9 See Malinowski, *Crime and Custom in Savage Society* (1926).

10 *Quest for Law*, p. 30.

11 See his *Freedom and Civilisation* (1947).

12 See F. Huxley, *Affable Savages* (1956), pp. 106–11.

13 See M. Gluckman, *Judicial Process among the Barotse* (1957).

14 See above, p. 210.

15 See *Law of Primitive Man* (1954).

16 cf. above, p. 196.

17 See above, p. 187.

18 Above, p. 39.

19 cf. above, p. 334.

20 Early judicial procedure also leans heavily on supernatural agency. Generally there is no investigation of disputed fact: where right lies depends on the performance of an allotted task by the parties, e.g. a judicial duel; reliance on the oath;

or the ordeal. The decision thus rests on the 'judgment of God'. The modern English trial, based on the adversary system, which pits the attack against the defence, still retains something of the idea of the old judicial combat.

21 See above, p. 71.

22 See T. F. T. Plucknett, *Legislation of Edward I*.

23 Plucknett, op. cit., p. 6.

24 The description applied by Blackstone to the common law in his *Commentaries*, vol. 1, p. 67.

25 See chapter 9.

26 This date was arrived at on the analogy of a limitation period applied by a statute of 1257 to a particular type of legal proceeding.

27 There are many such conventional practices which are treated as less than binding, e.g. consider the recent controversy regarding the selection of a Prime Minister who is not a member of the House of Commons.

28 *Bechuanaland Exploration Company* v. *London Trading Bank* [1898] 2 Q.B. 658.

29 cf. above, p. 210.

30 All the same, an agreement between associations of builders to press for the use of a standard-form contract of this kind was held to be contrary to the public interest and void under the Restrictive Trade Practices Act, 1956, in *Re Birmingham Association* [1963] 2 All E.R. 361.

31 See above, p. 196.

32 See K. Popper, *The Open Society and Its Enemies*, 4th ed. revised (1962), vol. 11, chapter 12.

33 cf. above, p. 202.

24 *Collected Legal Papers*, p. 187.

35 See above, p. 244.

36 For the meaning of 'equity', see above, p. 124.

11   THE JUDICIAL PROCESS

1 See above, p. 240.

2 See above, p. 245.

3 *Lectures on Jurisprudence* (ed. Campbell), Lecture VI.

4 ibid., p. 219.

5 Above, p. 100.

6 Above, p. 103.

7 Above, p. 56.

8 *Candler* v. *Crane, Christmas & Co.* [1951] 2 K.B. 164.

9 It has since been held by the House of Lords, disapproving the *Candler* case, that there can be liability for negligent statements and for purely financial loss resulting therefrom (see *Hedley Byrne Ltd* v. *Heller* [1964] A.C. 465). It was recognized, however, that there was no exact analogy between 'words' and 'deeds', so that liability for the latter would have to depend upon special considerations as compared, for example, with liability for defective articles. Also, though purely financial loss might be recoverable in such cases, it was not suggested that economic loss was always to receive the same protection as injury to person or property.

10 cf. above, p. 119.

11 English law declines to impose any general duty to rescue or help a person in distress, but many other legal systems do recognize such a duty.

12 See C. Perelman, *The Idea of Justice and the Problem of Argument* (1963), and J. Wisdom, *Philosophy and Psycho-Analysis* (1953), especially pp. 157–8, and 249–52.

13 See above, p. 293.

14 Above, p. 266.

15 See Dennis Lloyd, *Public Policy: A Comparative Study in English and French Law* (1953).

16 Burrough, J., in *Richardson* v. *Mellish* (1824) 2 Bing., p. 252.

17 *Janson* v. *Driefontein Consolidated Mines* [1902] A.C. 484, p. 507, per Lord Lindley.

18 Above, p. 270.

19 In *Donoghue* v. *Stevenson* [1932] A.C. 562.

20 cf. above, p. 214.

21 See *Young* v. *Bristol Aeroplane Co.* [1944] K.B. 718.

22 The contribution of legal writers to the development of the law is much more freely acknowledged in civil-law countries than in those of the common law (with the exception of the U.S.A.). In fact, however, even in England, it has been much more significant than is generally supposed.

23 See, for instance, the treatment accorded to *Elder Dempster and Co.* v. *Paterson, Zochonis and Co.* [1924] A.C. 552, in the later case of *Scruttons Ltd.* v. *Midland Silicones Ltd* [1962] A.C. 446.

24 *Mayor of Bradford* v. *Pickles* [1895] A.C. 587. The doctrine of the abuse of rights establishes that the exercise of a legal right may be treated as wrongful if it is used for an improper purpose.

25 Thus, Lord Justice Denning's admirable, if too candid, state-

ment that, 'We are here to find out the intention of Parliament . . . and we do this better by filling in the gaps and making sense of the enactment than by opening it up to destructive criticism.' was denounced by Lord Simonds as 'a naked usurpation of the legislative function under the thin guise of interpretation'. See *Magor and St Mellons R.D.C.* v. *Newport Corpn* [1952] A.C. 189, p. 191.

26 The new Law Commission, created in 1965, as a permanent full-time body, to advise on law reform, is now considering the codification of various parts of the law, e.g. contract, and is also studying the whole problem of statutory interpretation.

12 CONCEPTUAL THINKING IN LAW

1 The Chinese language is said to be exceptional in this respect in its lack of general concepts: see M. Granet, *La Pensée Chinoise* (1934), p. 31.

2 cf. above, p. 219.

2a Note that the rules of games, unlike law, apply only to voluntary participants.

3 By vesting the club property in trustees continuity can be preserved without the need for incorporation. cf. below, p. 305.

4 See above, p. 109.

5 cf. above, p. 267.

6 See above, p. 208.

7 American law also is much less rigid on this. Thus manufacturers of defective goods have been held liable on an implied warranty to third persons who have suffered injury. This obviates the need to prove negligence.

8 i.e. something of material value done or promised in return for the other promise or undertaking.

9 This doctrine was first formulated in *Central London Property Trust Ltd* v. *High Trees House Ltd* [1947] K.B. 130.

10 See *Combe* v. *Combe* [1951] 2 K.B. 215.

11 See e.g. *Hurst* v. *Picture Theatres Ltd* [1915] 1 K.B. 1; and *Errington* v. *Errington* [1952] 1 K.B. 290. cf. above, p. 315.

12 Copyright Act, 1956, s.19. An exclusive licensee is one who is granted a right to the exclusion of others, e.g. an exclusive right to film a certain work. For the purposes of s. 19 the licence must be in writing.

13 See *Sim* v. *Heinz Ltd* [1959] 1 All E.R. 547.

14 See *Walker* v. *Great Northern Ry of Ireland* (1891) 28 L.R.Ir. 69.
In the American case, *Smith* v. *Brennan* 31 N.J. 353 (1960), on
the other hand, it was held that the infant could sue for pre-
natal injuries.

15 See A. Ross, *On Law and Justice* (1958), chapter 6.

16 See F. C. S. Northrop, *The Complexity of Legal and Ethical Experience* (1959), chapter 3.

13 SOME LEGAL LEADING CONCEPTS

1 Above, p. 297.

2 *Works* (1910 ed.) vol. 11, p. 368.

3 cf. above, p. 202.

4 This 'realist' theory of corporation has nothing to do with the
5 legal realism discussed in chapter 9.
cf. above, pp. 119 and 267.

6 See above, p. 142.

7 In English law, an action against the whole body of individual
members creates considerable procedural difficulties, which
cannot be gone into here, especially where the membership
has changed, as it is liable to do.

7a The Case of *Willis* v. *Association of Universities of British Commonwealth* [1964] 2 All E.R. 39 reveals a tendency to recognize an
unincorporate body as an 'entity' apart from statute.

8 *Bonsor* v. *Musicians' Union* [1956] A.C. 104. For a discussion of
the significance of this difficult case see an article by the present
author on 'Damages for Wrongful Expulsion from a Trade
Union', in *Modern Law Review*, vol. 19 (1956), p. 31.

9 *Taff Vale Ry Co.* v. *A.S.R.S.* [1901] A.C. 426. See also *Knight and
Searle* v. *Dove* [1964] 2 All E.R. 307, relating to an unincorporated Trustee Savings Bank.

10 Trades Disputes Act, 1906, s.4.

11 [1897] A.C. 22.

12 Above, p. 306.

13 From the sociological point of view the members of (say) a large
public industrial or commercial company, whose shares are
owned by a wide section of the public, may be regarded rather
as consisting of the management (including the higher director-
ate), and the staff and workers employed therein. The law,
however, regards the shareholders as the sole members and
legal control is vested in whichever member or members hold
the majority of shares possessing voting rights.

14 Similar problems have arisen in Continental legal systems, See Cohn and Simitis, '"Lifting the Veil" in the Company Laws of the European Continent' in *Int. and Comp. L.Q.*, vol. 12 (1963), p. 189.

15 *Ebbw Vale U.D.C.* v. *S. Wales Licensing Authority* [1951] 2 K.B. 366.

16 *Tunstall* v. *Steigmann* [1962] 2 All E.R. 417.

17 *Daimler Ltd* v. *Continental Tyre Co. Ltd* [1961] 2 A.C. 307.

18 *Bullock* v. *Unit Construction Ltd* [1959] 1 All E.R. 591.

19 *Merchandise Transport Ltd* v. *B.T.C.* [1961] 3 All E.R. 495.

20 *Jones* v. *Lipman* [1962] 1 All E.R. 472.

21 See *Boulting* v. *Association of Cinematograph Technicians* [1963] 1 All E.R. 716.

22 cf. *Davis* v. *Carew-Pole* [1956] 1 W.L.R. 833; and *Byrne* v. *Kinematograph Renters' Society* [1958] 1 W.L.R. 762.

23 See for a discussion of the complicated English case-law on this topic, Salmond, *Torts*, 13th ed. (1961), §59. Cf. above, p. 296.

24 See above, p. 273.

25 cf. above, p. 211.

26 cf. above, p. 211.

27 Thus a so-called 'statutory tenancy', which is protected under the English Rent Restriction Acts, but is non-transferable, is treated as no more than a personal right of the tenant to reside on the premises. This right, however, so far as it goes, entitles the tenant to legal protection of his tenure against the landlord and against persons generally.

28 Some jurists have even maintained that there cannot be such a thing as an 'ownerless' right. This, however, seems no more than an example of the jurisprudence of concepts (cf. above, p. 293). Legal systems in fact commonly treat rights as being temporarily in suspense or in abeyance, as, for instance, in the case of the *hereditas iacens* in Roman Law, which arose at the moment of death until the heir took over the succession of the deceased's property.

29 cf. the French Civil Code, art. 544, which defines ownership as 'the right to enjoy and dispose of things in the most absolute way, provided that no use is made of them forbidden by law or regulations.'

30 See Copyright Act, 1956, s.19, cf. above, p. 246.

31 A 'mercantile agent' is a person who has authority to sell goods in the ordinary course of his business. Such a person may in certain circumstances defined in the Factors Act, 1889, give a

valid title to goods left in his possession by the owner even if he had no authority to sell them.

32 This refers to a sale in a recognized market. Such a sale may convey a good title binding on the true owner even if the goods were stolen.

33 For an attempt to analyse the detailed implications of this approach to ownership, see '*Tu-Tu*' by A. Ross, in *Scandinavian Studies in Law*, vol. 1 (1957), p. 139.

34 Possession may also lead to the acquisition of title by the passage of time (prescription), as well as conferring the right to recover possession by means of a 'possessory' action in which 'title' or ownership is not in issue.

35 For a full discussion, see *Matrimonial Property Law* (1955) ed. W. Friedmann.

36 This is the result of modern English statute law. The older common law conferred upon the husband on marriage either ownership or control of his wife's property.

14 CONCLUSION: SOME PROBLEMS FOR THE FUTURE

1 *Censors*, (1961).

2 cf. above, p. 156.

3 See above, p. 149; and also G. Marshall, 'Justiciability', in *Oxford Essays in Jurisprudence*, ed. A. G. Guest (1961), p. 265.

4 See above, chapter 6.

5 Needless to say, the question of 'genocide' is only one aspect of the whole problem of an international criminal law, a thorny and controversial subject which cannot be explored within the limits of the present work. See G. Schwarzenberger, 'The Problem of an International Criminal Law', in *Current Legal Problems*, vol. 3 (1950), p. 263.

6 Consider also the efforts of O.E.C.D. to secure international agreement to protect foreign enterprises against discriminatory action or expropriation without fair compensation.

Further Reading List

The literature on the subject-matter of this book is very extensive, and it would be inappropriate in a work of this character to provide a detailed bibliography. Some clues as to where material can be found for further reading on particular topics are contained in the Notes at the end of the book. In addition the following is a short list of books which may be useful to a reader who desires to explore in greater depth some of the many topics touched upon in this work. The list is confined to works in the English language which are readily accessible.

C. K. ALLEN, *Law in the Making* (7th edn, 1964)

SIR PATRICK DEVLIN, *The Enforcement of Morals* (1959)

W. FRIEDMANN, *Legal Theory* (5th edn, 1967); *Law in a Changing Society* (1959; Pelican edn, 1964)

M. GINSBERG (ed.), *Law and Opinion in England in the Twentieth Century* (1959)

A. G. GUEST (ed.), *Oxford Essays in Jurisprudence* (1961)

H. L. A. HART, *The Concept of Law* (1961); *Law, Liberty and Morality* (1963)

H. KELSEN, *General Theory of Law and State* (1954)

K. N. LLEWELLYN, *Jurisprudence: Realism in Theory and Practice* (1962)

DENNIS LLOYD, *Introduction to Jurisprudence* (2nd edn, 1965)

G. W. PATON, *A Textbook of Jurisprudence* (3rd edn, 1964)

ROSCOE POUND, *Interpretations of Legal History* (1930); *Philosophy of Law* (revised edn, 1954)

A. ROSS, *On Law and Justice* (1958)

MAX WEBER, *Law in Economy and Society* (ed. Rheinstein, 1954)

Index

Some other books published by Penguins are
described on the following pages.

The Young Offender

D. J. West

Criminal statistics are often quoted to prove that crime is increasing, above all among young people. Actually the picture is more complicated and less dismal.

In a new and balanced study Dr Donald West, of the Cambridge Institute of Criminology, fully examines the extent, nature, causes, and prevention of offences committed by those under twenty-one in England. Most convicted persons, he admits, are young males: but that is nothing new. It remains true that the incidence of conviction declines dramatically after the age of fourteen (which is the peak) and begins to peter out among those in their twenties. Delinquency, in short – and that means, to a large extent, theft in one form or another or very petty crime – is a passing phase of youth.

Donald West devotes his central chapters to the social, hereditary, and psychological factors in delinquency and his final chapters to the penal and remedial measures at present being applied. A special chapter covers the more sensational topics of girls, sex, drugs, and violence, which rate the bold type in the press but feature quite small in the statistics of crime.

Freedom, the Individual and the Law

Harry Street

Civil Liberties are very much in the news. At the heart of every incident that concerns the rights and obligations of the individual lies a conflict, sometimes muted, sometimes violent, between competing interests: freedom of speech *v.* security of the state, freedom of movement *v.* public order, the right to privacy *v.* the demands of a vigilant press. Every day brings fresh reports of 'punch-up' politics banning of controversial posters, curious corners of theatre censorship, abuse of telephone tapping, contempt of Parliament . . . the headlines never stop.

Yet Professor Street's *Freedom, the Individual and the Law* is the first comprehensive survey of the way English law deals with the many sides of Civil Liberty. After an introductory description of the powers of the police, Professor Street addresses himself in detail to the main areas of freedom of expression, freedom of association, and freedom of movement. Protection against private power, the right to work, and other subjects of contemporary importance make up the citizen's first guide to the theory and practice of Civil Liberty.